Teaching Music to Students with Special Needs

Teaching Music to Students with Special Needs

A Label-Free Approach

Alice M. Hammel and Ryan M. Hourigan

OXFORD
UNIVERSITY PRESS

OXFORD
UNIVERSITY PRESS

Oxford University Press, Inc., publishes works that further
Oxford University's objective of excellence
in research, scholarship, and education.

Oxford   New York
Auckland   Cape Town   Dar es Salaam   Hong Kong   Karachi
Kuala Lumpur   Madrid   Melbourne   Mexico City   Nairobi
New Delhi   Shanghai   Taipei   Toronto

With offices in
Argentina   Austria   Brazil   Chile   Czech Republic   France   Greece
Guatemala   Hungary   Italy   Japan   Poland   Portugal   Singapore
South Korea   Switzerland   Thailand   Turkey   Ukraine   Vietnam

Copyright © 2011 by Oxford University Press

Published by Oxford University Press, Inc.
198 Madison Avenue, New York, New York 10016

www.oup.com

Oxford is a registered trademark of Oxford University Press

Library of Congress Cataloging-in-Publication Data
Hammel, Alice.
Teaching music to students with special needs : a label free approach / Alice M. Hammel,
Ryan M. Hourigan.
   p. cm.
Includes bibliographical references and index.
ISBN 978-0-19-539540-2 (cloth)
ISBN 978-0-19-539541-9 (paper)
1. Music—Instruction and study.   2. Children with disabilities—Education.
I. Hourigan, Ryan M.   II. Title.
MT17.H36 2011
780.71—dc22   2010014650

3 5 7 9 8 6 4

Printed in the United States of America
on acid-free paper

Contents

About the Companion Website (http://www.oup.com/us/tmtswsn):

The resource materials included on this website have been developed during a decade of collection and creation by the authors. Materials include information regarding policy, teaching strategies, links, print resource lists, video case studies, and video lesson examples. Full-page word documents of observation protocols and other materials will be available for you to download and adjust to fit your individual needs. This website will be updated regularly by the authors to remain a current reference and information source for music educators. Enjoy!

Foreword

Dr. Colleen Conway
University of Michigan

It is an honor to have this opportunity to present a foreword for *Teaching Music to Students with Special Needs*. This text offers an important resource for music teachers, music education students, and teacher educators. I will begin with a discussion of the key concepts of the book including: (a) a team approach to teaching; (b) label-free learning; and (c) "fair is not always equal." I will then highlight the specific attributes of the book in relation to pre-service and in-service music teacher education and music teacher educator support. The next section of this foreword focuses on three of the current challenges facing music teacher education today and will suggest that this text provides an important resource addressing these challenges. I conclude with an overview of the four sections of the book and revisit important features.

KEY CONCEPTS IN THE TEXT

Although there are many powerful concepts brought forth in this text I have chosen to focus this introduction to the book on just three including: (a) a team approach to teaching, (b) label-free learning, and (c) fair is not always equal. These three important concepts permeate the text and provide a link between the four sections of the book.

Team Approach to Teaching

A common thread throughout this text is a focus on a team approach to teaching music. Almost every chapter in the book provides specific ways for music teachers to work with special education teachers, paraprofessionals who are assisting special education students, therapists, administrators, classroom teachers, parents and other experts.

Chapter 1 highlights the importance of the music teacher as a member of the support "team" for special needs students: "Families need support in many areas for a child with disabilities to have an equal opportunity to learn in public school, and we, as music educators, are an integral part of this support system" (p. 10). In chapter 2 the authors situate the "team" concept within various policies including The Individuals with Disabilities Act (IDEA), Responsiveness to Intervention (RTI) and the Individualized Education Program (IEP). For example:

> ...the Individualized Education Program (IEP) team was expanded to include a general classroom teacher (which may be the music teacher), and further clarification and guidelines for increased funding and early education programs as well as transition programs were put in place (20 U.S.C. 14et.seq.). (p. 26)

In the second part of the book, Hammel and Hourigan make many references to the team approach (i.e., "It is important to implement these ideas and to encourage a dialogue between all members of the team," p. 47; "The most effective approach when working within a school and school system is to become a part of this existing team of professionals," p. 60; and "Working in tandem with the special education team may benefit the child in both language and music," p. 84). The practical examples of teaching strategies, and the stories and vignettes that appear throughout these chapters with the above quotes help the reader to understand how to interact as a key member on a team of professionals who are working together to support a student with special needs.

Label-free Learning

The term "label-free learning" is generally credited to Keefe (1996) who has a complete book on the topic with the title *Label-Free Learning: Supporting Learners with Disabilities.* In a key text regarding teacher education, Banks, Cochran-Smith, Moll, Richert, Zeichner, and LePage (2005) explain that when teaching diverse learners, teachers should move away from focusing on labels and "think pedagogically" about their approach (p. 245). This concept of "label-free" is one of the unique characteristics of *Teaching Music to Students with Special Needs.* Much of the past discussion within music education has focused on the understanding of specific characteristics of various special learners. Students in special needs music methods courses at the college level were sometimes asked to memorize the types of disabilities and their various strategies for music classes. The focus in this text is on learner-centered strategies for music class that can work with all children in large group settings.

As stated in the preface, "A focus of this book is that a student with special needs is an individual who deserves an education free of labels." (p. xxiii).

However, the authors do recognize the need for teachers to make some distinctions regarding labels. Chapter 8 suggests:

> While the philosophy of this text has placed importance on encouraging "label-free learning" for students with special needs, there are times when a distinction is necessary. One of these distinctions is in the cognitive area. Most often, music educators adapt teaching to accommodate students who learn at a slower rate; however, it is important to also consider adapting our teaching for those students who learn at a faster rate than their peers. These students are often identified as being gifted. (p. 165–166)

This chapter goes on to suggest strategies for working with gifted students in music classes. The label-free concept in conjunction with the need to sometimes offer varying strategies for different students supports the notion that in order to support all students, some students may need more teacher support, time, and resources than others. This concept of "fair is not always equal" is addressed next.

Fair Is Not Always Equal

The phrase "fair is not always equal" is mentioned in chapters 4, 5, and 8. The quote here is from chapter 5:

> If we model inclusiveness, acceptance, and kindness, our students will demonstrate these qualities as well. Because we allow all students to participate equally in our classrooms and because we posit a "fair is not always equal" philosophy, we are teaching our students that everyone deserves to be treated fairly within a community. (Stainback & Stainback, 1990)

The concept of honoring what we might call the "personhood" of every learner and providing whatever is necessary to support that person is a key concept throughout the text. Also in chapter 5, Hammel and Hourigan suggest:

> Students who are developmentally able and less affected by their disabilities often appreciate the opportunity to participate in the creation of their own behavior plans, expectations, and consequences. This honors the personhood of each student and creates a partnership between teacher and student that can strengthen the nature of a student-centered classroom and relationships necessary for student success (Wharton-McDonald, Pressley, & Hampston, 1998). Students often are keenly aware of their own limitations and of what strategies will assist them to be more successful during instruction. (p. 99)

The music classroom or ensemble setting can be very exciting as students work together to create music. This type of environment; however, can be overstimulating for some students with special needs. Be alert to the sensory limits of students (see the special education team) and provide a quiet place in the classroom for students who need a break. Use hall passes for students who need to leave the classroom at various intervals to decrease anxiety or sensory overload. This pass can be to another teacher or to a guidance counselor who signs the pass, and the student comes back to class without other classmates being aware of the reason for the brief absence. Strategies that honor the personhood of students with disabilities can benefit the entire school community (SECTQ, 2003) (pp. 102).

These are just two examples from the text to illustrate the practical strategies that are provided in the effort to support a "fair is not always equal" philosophy in *Teaching Music to Students with Special Needs*.

A RESOURCE FOR PRE-SERVICE TEACHERS, IN-SERVICE TEACHERS, AND TEACHER EDUCATORS

Although the needs of teachers may change throughout their career cycle (Conway, 2008), *Teaching Music to Students with Special Needs* provides a resource for teachers in various stages of their careers. This next section highlights the use of this book in pre-service teacher education as well as in-service education (divided into beginning music teachers and experienced music teachers). The final section discusses the role of teacher educators in assisting pre-service and in-service teachers in teaching music to students with special needs.

Pre-service Teachers

One of the most challenging times in the journey to become a teacher occurs early in the undergraduate experience as the music education student grapples with the comparison between what they are learning about teaching and what they think they already know. Feiman-Nemser (2001) suggests:

> The images and beliefs that prospective teachers bring to their preservice preparation serve as filters for making sense of the knowledge and experiences they encounter. They may also function as barriers to change by limiting the ideas that teacher education students are able and willing to entertain....These taken-for-granted beliefs may mislead prospective teachers into thinking that they know more about teaching than they actually do and make it harder for them to form new ideas and new habits of thought and action. (p. 1016)

In the area of working with students with special needs, pre-service teachers may come into teacher education with preconceived notions regarding this population or they may come with no exposure whatsoever to special populations. In either case *Teaching Music to Students with Special Needs* provides important resources. The observation protocols in chapter 1 (focusing on cognitive observation, communication observation, and sensory observation) help young teachers to understand what to look for and "notice" in an observation of a music classroom that includes students with disabilities. The definitions and clarifications regarding policy that are focused on throughout the text will help pre-service students doing observations to know what questions to ask regarding teaching music to special learners.

The chapter on pre-service fieldwork (*Preparing to Teach: Fieldwork and Engagement Opportunities in Special Education for Pre-service and In-service Music Teachers*) will help undergraduate students to picture themselves as teachers in a setting that includes students with special needs and will help them begin to understand what goals teacher educators set for fieldwork experiences. The focus on stories of real P–12 students and the inclusion of discussion questions throughout the text will be of assistance to undergraduate students.

In studying the material in parts II and III of this text, undergraduate students will learn important teaching strategies for working with all students. The strategies for planning and classroom management (chapter 5); curriculum and assessment (chapter 6), and teaching strategies for performers (chapter 7) present "good teaching" regardless of the setting.

Beginning Teachers

I suggest in Conway (2010) that: "All of my work supports the concept that most of learning to teach music occurs in the first years and preservice education can only do so much to prepare music teachers for the realities of schools" (p. 268). Thus, I feel strongly that this text will be an important resource for beginning music teachers who may be working with students with special needs for the first time.

Delorenzo (1992) reported that "adapting lesson material to children with special needs" was one of the top "problems" facing beginning music teachers. Other top concerns included (a) finding time to continue own musical growth, (b) preparing a budget for the music program, (c) finding materials and resources for lessons, (d) classroom management, (e) communicating the value of music education to colleagues and administrators, and (f) motivating students. Part III of this text focuses specifically on "Practical Classroom Adaptations and Modification for Students with Special Needs in the Music Classroom," which directly addresses the concerns reported in the Delorenzo study. In addition other chapters in part III provide some insight regarding the Delorenzo concerns of "classroom management" and "motivating students." In chapter 5, entitled "Developing a Student-centered and Inclusive Classroom," beginning teachers will find many helpful suggestions for classroom management and motivation of all learners.

Experienced Teachers

Based on survey data collected from 108 music teachers Bush (2007) documented that general music teachers seemed more concerned regarding teaching "gifted/special learners" than ensemble teachers. He concludes that: "District administrators and organization officials need to understand that performance ensemble specialists feel less strongly about some types of workshops than general music teachers do. If these areas (student assessment, music education for gifted/special learners, cross-curricular integration, English as a second language) are priorities for districts and organizations, performance area teachers may need to be led to understand their importance" (p. 15). Both the general music teachers who seemed concerned in the Bush study as well as the ensemble directors who may need to be more concerned will be served by the Hammel and Hourigan text. The ensemble teachers who may not be as "individual-student-oriented" as the general music teachers can gain valuable information from chapter 7, which focuses specifically on teaching strategies for performers with special needs in ensembles.

Teacher Educators

Teacher educators are an important link in pre-service and in-service teacher learning. Not only are they responsible for the planning and implementation of the undergraduate curriculum, but many teacher educators are actively involved in graduate programs for in-service teachers as well as teacher in-service workshops and conferences. Many music teacher educators would like to include more preparation for teaching students with special needs within the undergraduate curriculum but find it hard in the face of teacher licensure and National Association of Schools of Music requirements (Colwell & Thompson, 2000). Colwell and Thompson (2000) have documented that many universities do not offer adequate coursework in teaching music to students with special needs.

Hourigan (2007a) suggests:

> The absence of special needs preparation…underscores the need for music teacher educators to find ways to "bridge the gap" somewhere in the curriculum. Fieldwork has been shown to be a powerful tool to assist future teachers in combining theory with practice. Fieldwork could be a way to attempt to fill the void left by lack of curriculum for future music teachers in special education without adding other course requirement. (p. 34)

One of the exciting elements of this text is that co-authors Alice Hammel and Ryan Hourigan have studied various elements of pre-service preparation and fieldwork in special needs and they use findings of that research as a powerful backdrop to this text (Hammel, 1999; 2001, 2003, 2004; Hourigan, 2009, 2007 a/b/c). Chapter 3 ("Preparing to Teach: Fieldwork and Engagement Opportunities in Special Education for Pre-service and In-service Music Teachers") is devoted to planning, implementing, and evaluating pre-service fieldwork in working with children with disabilities in music classes. This chapter is based not just on the practical experience of the authors but on their multiple studies of fieldwork and preparation for teaching students with special needs.

Finally, teacher educators will find the resources in part IV to be especially helpful in their planning for undergraduate and graduate courses as well as teacher in-service workshops.

ISSUES FACING MUSIC TEACHER EDUCATION TODAY

Although there are a myriad of issues facing music teacher education in the 21st century, I focus here on only three: (a) teacher education in the public eye, (b) teacher education versus teacher training, and (c) the need for teacher "adaptive" expertise. For a more comprehensive discussion of issues in music teacher education see "Issues Facing Music Teacher Education in the 21st Century: Developing Leaders in the Field" (Conway, 2010) in Abeles and Custedero (Ed.) *Critical Issues in Music Education: Contemporary Theory and Practice* (Oxford, 2010).

Teacher Education in the Public Eye

In the introduction to a special focus issue of the *Journal of Teacher Education*, devoted to "Teacher Education at the Turn of the Century," journal editor Cochran-Smith (2000) examined some of the political issues surrounding the professionalization of teacher education and suggests that in addition to debates held between academics, there is another debate "...occurring simultaneously, this other debate is played out more in the election rhetoric of politicians than in the discourse of teacher educators, more in the pages of local newspapers than in the journals related to teacher education, and more in the sound bites of television coverage than in the symposia of professional conferences" (pp. 163–164). When I consider this quote in relation to music teachers working with children of disabilities, I am struck that the politics of education and educational issues are often even more controversial in the realm of special education. Belief systems regarding support for all children can often lead to heated debate amongst school boards, tax payers, and communities as well as band, orchestra and choir parents and music teachers.

Darling-Hammond (2000) suggests this public teacher education debate tends to frame teacher education as problematic and teacher educators as the "bad guys." This debate often supports alternative routes to certification and suggests that "content knowledge only" leads to competent teachers. The authors of *Teaching Students with Special Needs* recognize that "content knowledge only" will not prepare teachers to work with special populations and rather than focusing on content knowledge, they focus on attitudes and dispositions for working with all children as well strategies for including all learners in the classroom experience. Many of the teaching suggestions made in the text are useful for all learners in music class, not just those with special needs.

Teacher Education versus Teacher Training

In considering teacher education as "problematic" as discussed above it may be helpful to examine the differing assumptions as one views teacher education versus teacher training (Fredrickson & Conway, 2009). Ur (2000) describes the differences well in a quote attributed to her that I found online:

> The terms "teacher training" and "teacher education" are often used apparently interchangeably in the literature to refer to the same thing: the professional preparation of teachers. Many prefer "teacher education", since "training" can imply unthinking habit formation and an over-emphasis on skills and techniques, while the professional teacher needs to develop theories, awareness of options, and decision-making abilities – a process which seems better defined by the word "education" (see, for example, Richards and Nunan, 1990). Others have made a different distinction: that "education" is a process of learning that develops moral, cultural, social and intellectual aspects of the whole person as an individual and member of society, whereas "training" (though it may entail some "educational" components) has a specific goal: it prepares for a particular function or profession (Peters, 1966: Ch.1). Thus we normally refer to "an educated person," but "a trained scientist/engineer/nurse". (www.phenomenologyonline.com/sean/esl%20tips/training_education.htm)

Teaching Students with Special Needs authors Alice Hammel and Ryan Hourigan approach this text within the realm of what I would consider "teacher education" as they work throughout the book to focus on "theories, awareness of options, and decision-making abilities" (see above) over student labeling, use of low-level skills, and quick-fix teaching strategies.

The Need for Adaptive Expertise

One of the recent concepts in pre-service and in-service teacher education is the idea of teacher "adaptive expertise" (Cochran-Smith, Feiman-Nemser, & McIntyre, 2008). Adaptive expertise refers to the need for teachers to adjust their teaching to various settings and change their approach from class to class, year to year and student to student. It also suggests that teachers will need to change their practices throughout their careers to reflect changes in society. This concept seems relevant for music teachers and in particular music teachers who are working with students with special needs. The key features of this book (team approach, label-free, and fair is not always equal) encourage the level of reflection and teacher thoughtfulness that is required of teachers with adaptive expertise. The cases and vignettes as well as the questions for discussion in each chapter will help both pre-service and in-service teachers consider the contextual teaching issues that lead to the development and/or continuation of adaptive expertise.

BOOK OVERVIEW

Part I (*The Current Landscape of the Special Education System*) includes an extensive discussion of the history of special education legislation and litigation as well as a focus on educational policy (including Individuals with Disabilities Education Act and No Child Left Behind). The authors outline their label-free approach to teaching clearly in these two opening chapters.

Part II (*Preparing to Teach Music to Students with Special Needs)* includes chapters on fieldwork and engagement opportunities (chapter 3); and a resourceful and pedagogical approach to teaching students with special needs (chapter 4);. The key concepts of a team approach to teaching as well as the idea that "fair is not always equal" is made apparent in these chapters. All three chapters provide useful strategies not only for special learners but for all learners in a music classroom.

Part III (Practical Classroom Adaptations, Modifications, and Assessment Techniques for Teaching Students with Special Needs in the Music Classroom) includes: developing a student-centered and inclusive classroom (chapter 5), curriculum and assessment (chapter 6), teaching strategies for performers with special needs (chapter 7), and teaching music to students who are intellectually gifted (chapter 8).

Part IV (*Resources for Music Educators*) of the text provides an extensive list of research, textbooks, practitioner articles, and websites drawn from music therapy as well as music education. It should be noted that one of the primary strengths of this section as well as the book overall is a clear understanding of the differences in goals between music education and music therapy. The authors do an excellent job of keeping the focus in the book on music education.

CONCLUSION

I intend to recommend *Teaching Music to Students with Special Needs* to my undergraduate students, graduate students, in-service teachers and to my teacher education colleagues as I firmly believe that it will be a helpful resource for each of those populations. It provides research-based strategies and the voice of music teachers in an effort to push the profession forward toward a more inclusive pedagogy of music education.

REFERENCES

Abeles, H. F., & Custodero, L. (Eds.), (2010). *Critical issues in music education: Contemporary theory and practice*. New York: Oxford University Press.

Banks, J., Cochran-Smith, M., Moll, L., Richert, A., Zeichner, K., & LePage, P. (2005). Teaching diverse learners. In L. Darling Hammond & J. Bransford (Eds.), *Preparing teachers for a changing world* (pp. 232-274). San Francisco: Jossey-Bass.

Bush, J. E. (2007). Importance of various professional development opportunities and workshop topics as determined by in-service music teachers. *Journal of Music Teacher Education, 16*(2), 10-18.

Cochran-Smith, M. (2000). Teacher education at the turn of the century. *Journal of Teacher Education, 5*(3), 163-165. *Education, 51*(3), 166-173.

Cochran-Smith, M., Feiman-Nemser, S., & McIntyre, J. (Eds.). (2008). *Handbook of research on teacher education* (3rd ed.). New York: Routledge.

Colwell, C. M., & Thompson, L. K. (2000). "Inclusion" of information on mainstreaming in undergraduate music education curricula. *Journal of Music Therapy, 37*(3), 205-221.

Conway, C. M. (2008). Experienced music teacher perceptions of professional development throughout their careers. *Bulletin of the Council for Research in Music Education, 176,* 7-18.

Conway, C. M. (2010). Issues facing music teacher education in the 21st century: Developing leaders in the field. In H. Abeles & L. Custodero (Eds.), *Critical issues in music education: Contemporary theory and practice* (pp. 259-275). New York: Oxford University Press.

Darling-Hammond, L. (2000). How teacher education matters. *Journal of Teacher Education, 51*(3), 166-173.

DeLorenzo, L. (1992). Perceived problems of beginning music teachers. Bulletin of the Council for Research in Music Education, *113,* 9-25.

Feiman-Nemser. S. (2001). From preparation to practice: designing a continuum to strengthen and sustain teaching. *Teachers College Record, 103(6),* 1013-1055.

Fredrickson, W., & Conway, C. M. (2009). Teacher education in music: to train or not to train. *Journal of Music Teacher Education, 19*(1), 4-8.

Hammel, A. M. (1999). *A study of teacher competencies necessary when including special learners in elementary music classrooms: The development of a unit of study for use with undergraduate music education students*. DMA Dissertation, Shenandoah University (AAT 9926079).

Hammel, A. M. (2001). Preparation for teaching special learners: Twenty years of practice. *Journal of Music Teacher Education, 11*(1), 5-11.

Hammel, A. M. (2003). Preparation for teaching special learners: Twenty years of practice. In *Readings on diversity, inclusion, and music for all*. Reston, VA: MENC-The National Association for Music Education.

Hammel, A. M. (2004). Inclusion strategies that work. *Music Educators Journal, 90*(5) 33-37.

Hourigan, R. M. (2007a) Teaching Music to Students with Special Needs: A Phenomenological Examination of Participants in a Fieldwork Experience. Doctoral Dissertation, The University of Michigan (ISBN# 9780549174868/VDM Verlag (2008) ISBN#: 978-3-8364-7663-8).

Hourigan, R. M. (2007b). Music majors as paraprofessionals: A study in special needs field experience for preservice music educators. *Contributions to Music Education, 34*, 19–34.

Hourigan, R. M. (2007c). Preparing music teachers to teach students with special needs. *Update: Applications of Research in Music Education, 26(1)*, 5–14.

Hourigan, R. M. (2009). Preservice music teachers' perceptions of a fieldwork experience in a special needs classroom. *Journal of Research in Music Education, 57(2)*, 152–168.

Keefe, C. H. (1996). *Label-free learning: Supporting learners with disabilities.* York, ME: Stenhouse Publishers.

Peters, R. S. (1966), *Ethics and education.* London: Alan and Unwin.

Richards, J. C., & Nunan, D. (Eds.). (1990). *Second language teacher education,* Cambridge: Cambridge University Press.

Stainback, W., & Stainback, S. (1990). Facilitating peer supports and friendships. In W. Stainback & S. Stainback (Eds.), *Support networks for inclusive schooling* (pp. 51–63). Baltimore: Paul Brookes.

Ur, P. (2000). *A course in language teaching.* Cambridge: Cambridge University Press.

Wharton-McDonald, R., Pressley, M., & Hampston, J. M. (1998). Outstanding literacy instruction in first grade: Teacher practices and student achievement. *Elementary School Journal, 99*, 101–128.

Preface

The concept of *Teaching Music to Students with Special Needs: A Label-free Approach* was developed from our travels teaching and presenting seminars, in-services, and clinics at the national, regional, and local level as well as our communications with music educators about their challenges in the classroom. In addition, we both currently teach students with special needs. We have found that many music teachers find themselves teaching either in classrooms that include students with disabilities or in dedicated self-contained classrooms without the support they need. There is a large gap that exists in our methods content in the area of research-grounded best practice approaches to teaching students with special needs.

Teaching Music to Students with Special Needs: A Label-free Approach is designed for faculty, in-service music administrators, in-service music teachers, and pre-service music teachers. It is designed as a comprehensive manual and reference guide that introduces those in the field of music education to best practices when teaching music to students with special needs. It includes research-based strategies for methods courses, and professional development. In addition, this text will address curricular strategies for methods teachers as well as in-service music educators. This information is grounded in research, special education law, and best practice.

A LABEL-FREE APPROACH

A focus of this book is that a student with special needs is an individual who deserves a music education that is free of labels. The philosophical premise of a label-free approach is centered in the preservation of the individual personhood of each student. Through this approach, music educators will be able to gain and advocate for support, understand their rights and responsibilities, and offer an affective and effective music education for students with and without special needs. This includes learning strategies for effective collaboration with special educators, teacher educators, and classroom teachers. We also include curriculum development ideas, lesson plan strategies, observation strategies (methods classroom), and fieldwork ideas (methods classroom).

In our experience we have found that "quick fix" strategies learned by applying a technique based on the specific disability label of a student often lasts for a short time until a music educator can find the next new trick to assist a student with disabilities. By applying a label-free approach, educators can create a theoretical and philosophical underpinning that will serve as an effective base of knowledge for use in each individual situation.

A further consideration when choosing this approach is that the Individuals with Disabilities Education Act (IDEA) does not specify that each teacher is to be told of the specific disability of every student. It is possible that music educators may teach students with special needs and not have access to the label listed in the paperwork for that student. Teachers are given the list of strengths and areas of challenge for the student and are also notified of specific adaptations and accommodations that are to be used for the student. By approaching the education of students with special needs from a label-free perspective, teachers are not stymied by the possible lack of access to further information. While we recognize that educators may be able to glean valuable information through the disability categories, it is also "good teaching" to look at each student as an individual and to design instruction based on the areas of need as seen in the music classroom.

These resources are all offered within the context of learning to navigate the special education system within the framework of developing culturally responsive classrooms that are free of labels. The focus of this book is to effectively approach various learning domains when developing pedagogy for both the music classroom and the music methods classroom.

HOW TO USE THIS BOOK

Teaching Music to Students with Special Needs: A Label-free Approach will be of most interest to in-service music teachers and music teacher educators who are seeking research and practical information regarding the inclusion of students with special needs in their classrooms. In addition, undergraduate and graduate students in music education programs will find this book to be useful in their future careers as music educators. Our goal was to provide a book that meets the needs of music educators at all levels of instruction.

This book is organized into four parts. *Part I* is focused on the current landscape of teacher preparation within the context of the special education system. Chapter 1 is intended for all music educators and music teacher educators to increase the knowledge and understandings of music educators as they plan, implement, and advocate for the appropriate instruction of students with special needs. This advocacy is a natural outcome for music educators who are aware of special education policy within the special education structure of our public schools. This chapter includes strategies used to engage and observe in special education settings to assist with a complete understanding of the ways students learn in other environments.

The label-free approach to music teaching and learning transfers focus from a student's disability to examination of how he receives music information, processes this information, and expresses himself musically. We introduce five teaching and learning domains in this chapter: cognition, communication, behavioral/emotional, sensory, and physical. It is hoped that as a result of this shift in concentration, music educators will center their attention on music teaching and learning rather than merely labels that are attached to students with special needs.

Part II introduces effective methods utilized in preparation to teach students with special needs both in pre-service and in-service music education settings. Chapter 3 is specifically designed for engagement and fieldwork within the structure of special education. This includes observation protocols for self-contained classrooms, resource rooms, summer enrichment programs and therapy sessions (e.g., speech or arts therapy) and how observations in these settings may enhance the understandings music teachers have regarding learning needs of students with special needs.

Chapter 4 uses the learning domains that are introduced in chapter 1 and provides specific music education strategies for use in the music classroom. This chapter includes a complete introduction to Individualized Education Programs (IEP) and 504 Plans as well as music-specific strategies and transfers of accommodations that will enhance the ability of music educators to deliver instruction to students with special needs.

Part III provides practical applications of theory and policy from the previous chapters for use in the music classroom (e.g., behavioral strategies, curricular strategies, etc.). Chapter 5 is intended for teacher educators, pre-service music teachers (methods classes), and in-service music teachers and provides many practical and effective classroom management strategies for music teachers in a variety of settings.

Chapter 6 is designed to provide specific curriculum understandings and demonstrate how these approaches affect students with disabilities. Specifically, how the fundamentals of curriculum design (e.g., materials-centered, constructivism) can be used to enhance the music teaching and learning environment. Chapter 6 also provides assessment accommodations that have been seen as successful for students with special needs.

Chapter 7 offers specific ideas for conductors in instrumental and vocal music ensemble settings. Both co-authors have extensive training in these areas and provide not only rehearsal techniques but also challenge band, orchestra, and choir conductors to review and reflect on their current philosophy of teaching considering the vast changes put in place to assist the inclusion of students with special needs in all aspects of school life. The use of technology to assist in practice techniques as well as classroom-tested adaptations and accommodations are presented to enhance the ensemble experience for students with special needs.

The decision to discuss students who are gifted as part of this text was intentional and purposeful. The challenges mentioned in this chapter are often not included in discussions of students with special needs. This is the topic of chapter 8. While the premise and philosophy of the text is to encourage a label-free environment for students with special needs, the specific cognitive needs of students who are gifted necessitate a discussion that includes information about their unique differences.

This chapter includes the historical, philosophical, and practical issues involved in teaching students who are gifted. These include, the history of intelligence testing, varied models for educational placement options, and common characteristics of students with this type of special need. Practical information for successful inclusion of students who are gifted in the music classroom is presented. Finally, research-derived characteristics of teachers who are successful when teaching students who are gifted are also included.

Part IV is intended to provide the most up-to-date resources and technology information for music educators at all levels. Current research articles, best practice articles, and books and Internet websites are listed for music educators to use as they seek information regarding specific disabilities. This information reinforces the overall philosophy of the text as it challenges music educators to be resourceful in their approach to teaching students with special needs. In addition, this text includes many vignettes for thoughtful and reflective discussion among in-service teachers and by pre-service music educators in methods classes. These vignettes are actual stories that have occurred in public school situations within the last few years.

For music teacher educators this book provides strategies that are research-based and provide best practice for teaching all students regardless of the challenges they face. Chapters can be used to not only address this topic, but to embed other subjects within the context of teaching students with disabilities (e.g., assessment, classroom management, etc.). Many methods instructors are inundated with the amount of materials necessary to adequately address each topic within a given methods class. It is our firm belief that good teaching is good teaching. Therefore, this text allows you the option of covering multiple topics simultaneously.

This text was designed purposefully to chart a new direction in the preparation of music educators, music teacher educators, and in-service music educators as they design, present, and assess their practices when teaching students with special needs. The focus on creating meaningful and support-ive relationships with the faculty, staff, and administration partners in the schools, the importance of a label-free environment to create truly inclusive and welcoming school experiences for students with special needs, and the extraordinary value in approaching the classroom with a "fair is not equal" philosophy are the rationale for this new direction. By preparing to create an inclusive, team-oriented environment that ensures every student receives what he or she needs, we will perhaps begin to create true equity and "fair-ness" for all students in our public school systems.

ACKNOWLEDGMENTS

We would like to thank the wonderful students we have taught over the years both in K–12 and in higher education. You have given us the insight and moti-vation to write this book. We would also like to thank Christa Hensley, James Byrn, Nancy Muncey, and Allison Wright for their vignette contributions. Thanks to Chad West at Ithaca College and Scott Hippensteel at Ball State University for their assistance in gathering resources for chapter 9. Thank you to Amy Hourigan MT-BC for her contribution to this text from the music therapy perspective and Bruce Hammel at Virginia Commonwealth Univer-sity for his editorial support. Moreover, we thank Jacob McCarthy for being an inspiration and a student who influenced an entire career.

Thank you to Colleen Conway at the University of Michigan, for review-ing the text and for writing the Foreword for us. We would also like to thank Norm Hirschy for his guidance and support during this process.

Finally, we would like to thank our children—Hannah, Hollie, Andrew, and Joshua—who remind us each day of the uniqueness of every child. They are the true inspiration for this book.

PART I

THE CURRENT LANDSCAPE OF THE SPECIAL EDUCATION SYSTEM IN THE UNITED STATES

Chapter 1

Public School Education within a Democracy

An Equal Opportunity for All Students

Vignette 1.1 Mrs. Johnson

It is the first day of school. Mrs. Johnson's bulletin boards are complete, and her chairs and music stands are ready. Her class lists are prepared and the lesson plan is set. She stands at the door awaiting her first class of the day. The students begin walking down the hall and she wonders which ones will stop at her door. Her first class walks in and takes their seats. However, two of her students were escorted to her music room with paraprofessionals. The paraprofessionals then proceeded to take their scheduled break.

During class there were multiple outbursts from each of these students. Mrs. Johnson spent the entire 30-minute class pacifying these outbursts and little was accomplished. The other students seemed frustrated and bored.

After class Mrs. Johnson realized that she needed to make drastic changes to how she teaches music in this particular class. She began to ask herself: I have no idea how to help these kids, what do I do? Who do I talk to? This cannot happen tomorrow.

Discussion:

1. Have you heard of a similar story?
2. What should Mrs. Johnson do first?

The beginning of the school year is a time when situations similar to Mrs. Johnson's first day occur. It is when these first lessons go awry that some music teachers first begin to think of their individual students, rather than the collective group. Who is the girl who moves slower than the rest and uses a walker? Who are the students in the small group who come late each day with a teacher to assist them? Who is the boy who bounds down the hall and begins to take down one of the brand new bulletin boards that have just been finished?

The answer to the questions above is that they are *all* our students. They all have a place in our schools and they all deserve to have an education that includes music. As music teachers, we have both the right and responsibility to educate *all* the students in our schools. We are charged with studying each student who enters our classroom and with providing all students the music education they deserve. To do this, however, we must begin to plan for the inclusive education of all students before that first group heads down our hall on the first day of school.

Unfortunately, until recently this was not the educational philosophy of public schools within the United States. This chapter will introduce the process we as a nation have experienced as we have come to the understanding of what an education for all students in the United States entails, including: challenges within families; the real-world realities of inclusion in practice; and a label-free approach to teaching music in the public school setting. This book is designed to facilitate the planning, implementation, and assessment of music education for students with special needs. It is written from a paradigm that advocates thoughtful inclusion and honors the teaching and learning relationship between music teachers and their students. It is hoped that this text will present a philosophy and a set of guiding principles for teaching students with special needs in a helpful and pragmatic manner. We believe this is possible for all music educators and celebrate the progress made in recent years to provide a truly appropriate music education for each student we teach.

UNEQUAL OPPORTUNITY

Unfortunately, not all students within our current public education system have an equal opportunity to learn. John Dewey regarded public education as a crucial pillar to upholding a democracy: He stated:

> In order to have a large number of values in common, all members of the group must have equable opportunity to receive and take from others. There must be a large variety of shared undertakings and experiences. Otherwise the influences which educate some into masters, educate others into slaves.
>
> (John Dewey, *Democracy and Education*, 1916/1944)

The school experience for some students is vastly different from those of others and, in some situations; students have more opportunities than others. Even when one considers the recent acts of legislation as well as the history of litigation, our public school education system is far from equal for many demographic groups. According to Banks, Cochran-Smith, Moll, Richert, Zeichner, Lepage, Darling Hammond, Duffy, and McDonald (2005): "There are marked discrepancies in the educational outcomes and learning conditions for students in a variety of learning categories, including students with disabilities" (p. 237). Laws, protections, and procedures for students with learning differences have entered our system of public education during the past 40 years, and educators are now challenged to expect achievement from all students, regardless of their background or relative strengths and areas of challenge.

The basis for some of the continued differences can, in part, be traced to opportunity. It is clear that an equity gap remains in the public education system. This disparity affects children in poverty, certain ethnic and racial groups, *and* students with disabilities. It is important to look at all aspects of public special education to understand the context a student with special needs experiences as she enters the music classroom. In addition, it is important to understand the current framework of the modern special education system. This chapter offers a fundamental look at the current practice of teaching students with special needs. At the end of this chapter we will discuss our view of a label-free approach to teaching music to students with disabilities, and will begin to offer suggestions regarding the implementation of this approach.

A Brief Look at Special Education in the 21st Century

Special education is defined as "specially designed instruction, which meets the unique needs of an exceptional child" (Hallahan and Kauffman, 1978, p. 4). The practice of special education has evolved from segregated schools and institutions in the early 19th century to an integration model in the latter half of the 20th century (Winzer, 1993). Recently, our public schools have moved toward the full inclusion of students with disabilities into the regular classroom. Advocates for full inclusion insist "the general education classroom is the most appropriate full-time placement for all students with disabilities" (Lewis and Doorlag, 2006, p. 4).

The specifics of these policies and their implications for music educators will be discussed in chapter 2. However, for now, it is important to look at inclusion as a concept within the larger context of special education. It is also important to understand that the number of students needing assistance from public school programs for students with disabilities is continuing to increase. This is due to many factors including: the increasing ability of service providers to identify students with special needs as well as improved diagnoses of childhood illnesses, injuries, and an increase in the number of babies born with low birth weight (Pamuk, E., Makuc, D., Heck, K., Rueben, C., & Lochner, K., 1998).

In practice, teachers that work in full inclusion environments sometimes struggle with large class sizes, a perceived lack of support (either instructional or for specific skill sets), and very busy schedules (sound familiar?). In addition, pressures from a continuing standardized test-driven school culture have made full inclusion difficult to implement. Furthermore, like other federally mandated programs (e.g., NCLB or RTTT), special education programs are expensive (with most of the burden placed on the local school district) and are typically underfunded. These mandates require many teachers to advocate even more effectively for their special education programs as limits are increasingly placed on time, talents, and finances. In addition, the special education profession has been going through an identity crisis as a result of the implementation of mainstreaming, and more recently, inclusion. According to Kauffman (1999): "...the profession of special education is viewed as apologetic for its existence, over concerned with image, proceeding without direction, unrealistic in its expectations for children with disabilities, focused on issues other than teaching and learning, oblivious to sociopolitical changes in society, and immobilized by sweeping reforms in the American public education system" (p. 244). Vignette 1.2 was written by a special educator in an urban public school. This vignette shows the challenges of special education in practice.

Vignette 1.2 A Day in the Life of a Special Educator

I am a kindergarten through third grade, moderate disabilities, special education teacher. I currently have 12 students in a self-contained classroom. The teacher day runs from 8:00 a.m. to 3:30 p.m. The student day runs from 8:30 a.m. to 2:30 p.m. However, my students arrive at 8:05 a.m. This means that I have to have everything ready for the next day before I leave each afternoon. My students require an extremely structured environment from the moment they walk in the door until the moment they leave. There is no room for being ill prepared, or planning on the fly during the day. Part of my daily planning even requires a plan for unexpected events. And, all of this planning is done without any teacher guides or textbooks from which to get my lessons/activities.

Each of my students has their own picture schedule that shows them what they will be doing each moment of the day. I develop a master schedule that has each student's activities for each moment of the day as well as the duties of each of my two instructional assistants for every moment of the day.

One of my instructional assistants must go out and get each student off the bus and make sure that each child makes it into the correct classroom safely. My other instructional assistant waits for each child at the door, greets them and assists them with getting their personal belongings put away, taking care of morning restroom needs, brushing teeth, checking their schedule, and going to their first activity of the morning, which is designed to be an independent recreation activity. I spend this part of the morning going through backpacks, reading communications from home, and writing in each student's notebook what their individual activities are for the day. This may seem a little excessive, but most of my students are unable to communicate messages from home or events/messages from the school day. As I am sitting at the table trying to fill out student notebooks, Sam is hitting Tommy with the blocks, Karl is pulling out every puzzle in the cabinet rather than playing with the one set out for him, and Robbie has wet his pants. So, I must get up and take care of these issues before I can finish the communication notebooks. Once all of the students are in the classroom, one of my instructional assistants takes the five kids who eat breakfast at school over to the cafeteria while the other instructional assistant continues to man the restroom/grooming activities. By 8:30 a.m. our daily goal is to have every student to the restroom, teeth brushed, hair brushed and face/hands washed. At this point, morning announcements are given over the intercom.

The volume of the intercom bothers Mary's ears, so she begins screaming and pinching Amanda. While my instructional assistants are trying to get Mary calmed down, headphones put on, and Amanda's consequences given for pushing Mary, Will sees this as a prime opportunity to bolt from the classroom. As I chase Will down the hallway, the notebooks are still sitting on the table waiting to be completed. After announcements, we start morning circle time. We work on counting, the alphabet, name recognition and spelling, colors, shapes, days of the week, months of the year, weather, seasons, sitting in chairs, raising hands, speaking clearly, and keeping our hands to ourselves. During this process, Robbie yells out every answer, someone has to sit next to Will to keep him in his chair, Mariah and Arryanna are playing hair salon rather than listening. And I have six other students that need constant verbal prompting in order to participate.

After calendar, each student checks his individual picture schedule and proceeds to the scheduled activity. Some of the five students need physical assistance to do this task. The other students are able to check

(continued)

Vignette 1.2 (continued)

their schedule independently, but then are required to wait while the teachers try to get the other students transitioned. Will never likes to do what is on his schedule because he would rather do puzzles, so we must redirect him once or twice to math group and remind him that after he does his math work, he can play with the puzzles. Luke does not like Arryanna, so he has punched her while waiting for reading group to begin. Consequences must be given for this behavior. Mariah is waiting patiently at the door for someone to take her to her general education classroom. Once everyone is settled, Mrs. D takes Mariah to her general education classroom for reading time. I am teaching four students at reading group. Mrs. F has three students for math group. Two students are listening to books on tape, one student is at the computer, and one student is folding laundry. Everything is very calm and orderly for a few brief moments. Then, it is time to turn the tape over, so Robbie screams as if in pain and begins crying because the tape has stopped. This prompts Mary to throw all of the laundry she has just folded onto the floor. I have to get up to help Robbie and Mary, so Luke takes this as opportunity to pick on the other students in the group. Mrs. F gets up from her group to deal with Luke, so Will leaves math group and grabs the puzzles. After I get Robbie and Mary settled, I redirect Will back to math group and settle back in to try to teach reading. This is a very typical activity session in the room.

During the parts of the day when all of the teachers are in the classroom, there is always someone working one-on-one at a workstation with a child. For each life skills activity such as laundry, brushing teeth, using the telephone, etc., one of the teachers is also recording data as they are instructing the student on how to complete the activity. We also have community-based experiences in which one of the staff takes one to two students into the community to go shopping, get a haircut, go to the library, go to the YMCA, etc. At any given point in the day, there are parents calling me, other teachers needing assistance, paperwork that needs to be completed for case conferences, progress reports, behavior plans, eligibility determination surveys, and other typical school paperwork.

At lunchtime, two teachers must be in the cafeteria with the students in order to take data on cafeteria skills as well as monitor behavior and help the students who are unable to independently feed themselves. Two teachers must go to recess with the students in order to facilitate social interactions, appropriate play skills and monitor behavior as well as assist any students with mobility issues on safe use of the playground equipment. During specials classes, when most teachers have prep time, I am typically in the specials class to assist. After school, each student must be escorted all the way onto the bus to ensure safety. After all of the students are gone, picture schedule cards must be collected, sorted, and put back up for the next day's activities as well as all lesson plans and materials set our for the following day.

There are always six or seven activities happening at once in the classroom. None of the children do any activities completely independently. With only three teachers in the room, this requires us to constantly be on our toes. People say that teachers have eyes in the back of their heads. Special education teachers must have eyes all the way around their entire heads. The job of a special education teacher is extremely exhausting, stressful, and unappreciated by most but made completely gratifying and fulfilling by all of the smiles and hugs received from the students throughout the day.

As you can see, special educators are on the difficult front line of two reform initiatives: general special education and inclusion. These challenges are often causal to drastic turnover in the field of special education and sometimes, to a lack of coordination or communication between special and regular (music included) education teachers. There is always a demand for special educators because of the stresses involved with special education.

Funding of Special Education: A Demographic Snapshot of Support

It is no surprise to hear that students with special needs in wealthy areas tend to have better services and therefore better opportunity to learn from higher-paid special educators and better-equipped (and staffed) classrooms. This is especially true in urban areas. Urban school systems are typically underfunded and understaffed. In addition, there is a disproportionate representation of students from minority groups who receive special education services (Patton, 1998; Gottlieb, 1994). In addition, special educators in these areas are in a constant struggle to meet the requirements for continued federally mandated initiatives (e.g., NCLB) that have compounded these challenges (Simpson, LaCava, & Graner, 2004).

Rural school systems undergo support challenges similar to those found in urban school systems. However, support for persons with disabilities in rural areas can be more often linked to access to appropriate services. Families may find themselves traveling long distances to get the health care and school support they need. This may come at a considerable expense to the family (Lishner, Richardson, Levine, & Patrick, 1996). Rural school systems face major funding shortfalls similar to those in urban settings (Arnold,

Newman, Gaddy, and Dean, 2005). If public education continues to be primarily funded by a real estate tax-based system, rural and urban schools will continue to face these challenges.

Family Challenges and Children with Disabilities

Families may face enormous financial burdens in an effort to provide care to their children with disabilities. Whether it is therapy (i.e., speech therapy, occupational therapy, physical therapy, behavioral therapy), equipment and transportation, or legal and administrative expenses, services for children with special needs can be very expensive. Because of all these challenges, an inordinate amount of stress may be placed on parents and adult family members. Because of these obstacles, family structures may disintegrate and, as a result, many children with disabilities will be raised in single-parent households or by grandparents. It is important for music educators to be aware of this as they seek to be part of the team that provides school-based family support services to the families of students with special needs (Fiedler, Simpson, and Clark, 2007). Families need support in many areas for a child with disabilities to have an equal opportunity to learn in public school, and we, as music educators, are an integral part of this support system.

Music educators should take into account these challenges when teaching music to students with special needs. For example, if a child wants to start an instrument, the expense of that instrument (added to the speech therapy bill) can be insurmountable. If a student is encouraged to attend an event or participate in a trip with a music group, the challenges associated with that experience may be more than a family of a student with special needs (or any student who is part of a family experiencing financial, emotional, or health stressors) can navigate. All of these issues are important considerations when including students with special needs in school music programs. Two parents of children who are profoundly affected by autism wrote vignette 1.3 (below). This vignette shows the basic challenges and stresses that families encounter while raising children with special needs.

Vignette 1.3 Parents of Children with Special Needs

My name is Ron. My wife Ann and I are raising two children with autism. Our mornings can start out rough. Our children are all about schedule. On this particular day we have had a two-hour delay because of snow. Adam, who is nonverbal, does not understand and is becoming violent.

He thinks it is a Saturday because of the school delay. When he figures out that he needs to go to school, he begins a "meltdown." He kicks, bites, hits, and tears anything in his path. He scratches his brother Jonathan in the eye.

This all happened after a sleepless night with Adam. Children with autism typically do not sleep well. Adam takes a "cocktail" of medications to calm him down and help him sleep. This puts enormous strain on everyone else in the household because none of us function well on little to no sleep.

Adam's teachers and other staff members (bus drivers and paraprofessionals) have a difficult time keeping him from hurting his classmates, especially on a day like this. He does not hurt others because he is mean. He is trying to communicate his frustration.

Jonathan is off to school after witnessing this event and having his parents spend all of their time focused on his brother Adam (which happens to a lot of kids who have siblings with disabilities). He also has autism. He has a one-on-one aide and is doing rather well in school. The only issue is the lack of lasting relationships he has with his peers. His best friends are his parents. His classmates are nice to him. However, he has only been invited to a few birthday parties. Other than that, he is at home. No friends to run over and play with him after school.

After both children are home (and we find out about the damage done), we sift through the notes that come home from school for both kids. There is information about Cub Scouts, Little League, and basketball. Unfortunately, none of these activities are possible for our children. Our children then go outside to play. However, one of us needs to always be alert and outside watching their every move. Both of them got away from us when they were younger. We had an alarm system installed to let us know when doors open and close.

It is time for dinner and then bed. Once they finally sleep we are beyond tired and know that our rest is short lived. Inevitably one of them will be up. Potentially with a meltdown.

As parents we are exhausted. We love our children. However, it is a constant fight either at an IEP meeting or with an insurance company. We consider of all of this in the midst of thinking about the future. Every day we think about what life will be like for them as adults. Will they be self-sufficient? If not, how will we pay for a lifetime of care? Many of our friends talk of college tuition. College is a temporary expense. A disability like autism lasts a lifetime.

As mentioned above, success in music may not be on the minds of families who have children in special education. Music teachers must take into consideration that, in the beginning, parents maybe more concerned with the challenges faced with inclusion and/or learning goals in other areas. However, since music has many access points, it may be a place where families can find interest, participation, social learning, and most of all success.

Teaching Music in the 21st Century: A Label-free Approach to Teaching Music to Students with Special Needs

Music teachers share many of the same advocacy and funding challenges experienced by other teachers in the current educational environment. Because of equal access provisions within the law, music teachers are under increased pressure to deliver instruction, often without preparation or support. In addition, in-service music teachers are not always prepared to work with students with disabilities (Culton, 1999; Frisque, Niebur, & Humphreys, 1994; Hammel, 2001). There is a considerable lack of coursework within our current undergraduate and graduate music education programs to prepare students for teaching diverse student populations, including students with disabilities (Colwell & Thompson, 2000). If programs do exist, they are often in tandem with an existing music therapy program. Often, music teacher educators themselves lack the preparation and therefore do not always include the subject of teaching students with disabilities in their undergraduate methods courses.

Considering the challenges presented in this chapter, how do we as music teachers and music teacher educators deliver quality instruction to students of all learning differences? How do we as music educators deliver quality instruction and design effective curricula for students with special needs considering the challenges we face? To enhance achievement in education students must have an equal opportunity to learn. For students with learning challenges, this opportunity coexists with various support systems within the framework of special education. Banks et al. concludes that "to support a democracy, educators must seek to eliminate disparities in education opportunities for all students" (p. 233). John Dewey reminds us that in a democracy, all students must have access to similar experiences in education. This requires that music educators not only learn to be advocates for equity but also that we construct "learner adaptive pedagogy, curriculum, and assessment" (Banks et al., 2005, p. 234).

Research and best practice in special education is moving toward a focus on disability domains, rather than specific disabilities as listed in IDEA, in exploring the teaching and learning relationship in the classroom. This does not mean that a music teacher should not explore the nuances and obstacles associated with a single disability or diagnosis. Music teachers should use all resources available to understand the challenges, and areas of strength a student brings to the classroom as a part of his or her disability. Moreover, music teachers should, as they do with all students, focus on the teaching and learning relationship and what obstacles may hinder that student from learning in the classroom. Focusing on these challenges may allow music teachers to simplify their instructional strategies and deliver higher quality instruction to students. In addition, this approach will allow music teachers to focus on the whole person instead of the disability that challenges the student. Music teachers will feel less overwhelmed with acronyms and terms and will be able to focus on the music education of students with and without special needs.

The next section of this chapter will focus on five disability categories (cognitive, communication, behavioral and emotional, physical, and sensory). We introduce these in the first chapter to begin the exploration of the music teaching and learning relationship and to set the foundation for discussing specific teaching strategies later in this book. It is important to remember that these categories may overlap. A student may have challenges associated with multiple categories. It is hoped that these strategies will make an impact on the music classroom by focusing on music teaching and learning rather than the sometimes-overwhelming litany of disability citations and descriptions. Observation protocols have been developed in this chapter to assist you in obtaining an initial understanding of these areas and how they may impact your teaching and learning relationship with a student with special needs. Specific modifications, adaptations, and accommodations will be discussed as we progress through this text.

Cognition

"Cognition" or "cognitive function" are the generally accepted terms used to describe the ability of a student to receive, process, and commit information to memory (Davis, Gfeller, and Thaut, 1999; Lipscomb, 1996). In order for cognition to occur, a person must convert sensory energy into neural information. After this occurs, our perception utilizes sensory information to make further sense of the world (including our musical world). Finally, our cognition "involves the acquisition, storage, retrieval, and use of knowledge obtained by the sensory and perception systems" (Lipscomb, 1996).

In assessing the teaching and learning relationship, music teachers must gather and examine information regarding how students hear or receive music, remember musical concepts and understandings, and express themselves musically. In accomplishing this task, music teachers should begin by observing the student in question either in music class or in other classes to begin to understand the cognitive challenges that she brings to music class. Specific adaptations and accommodations in the area of cognition will be discussed in chapter 4. In all five of the suggested domains, an observation protocol has been provided. Figure 1.1 is designed to assist music educators as they observe potential challenges in the area of cognition. This will assist you as you define areas of concern and establish a baseline of understanding regarding the needs of a student. In addition, within this protocol is a section designed to remind music teachers to discuss the learning needs with the student's primary teacher. This may include a classroom teacher or a special educator. These discussions may also include a paraprofessional or aide who works with a student during the school day.

Student Name:_____

Primary Teacher(s):_____

Notes from discussion with Primary Teacher in the area of Cognitive Needs and Learning Strategies **(after reading the IEP document*)**:

Class Observed:

Strategies used in the area of input (e.g. repetition, visual icons, etc.):
- Are there any sensory challenges that may contribute to cognitive challenges (i.e. vision or hearing)
- Potential input strategies in music (including strategies to enhance sensation and perception):

Strategies used in the area of retention (multiple modes of delivery, review outside of class, etc.):
- Potential retention strategies in music (including strategies to enhance sensation and perception):

Strategies used in the area of output:
- Potential output or expression strategies in music (e.g. write instead of speak, point instead of tell, etc.):

General observations and ideas for music class:

* Please note that student or pre-clinical teachers will not have access to IEP without permission

---

Figure 1.1 Cognitive Observation Protocol (for Music Educators)

Communication

Let's face it, if a teacher and a student cannot communicate, there probably is a learning obstacle. There are many reasons to explain why a student may struggle with communication. He may be developmentally delayed; English might not be his primary language; or he may have other neurological or cognitive challenges that affect processing in the brain. In any event, it is important to understand the function of communication (both the preferred output as well as the current level) in a student's life and how that might affect his ability to participate and demonstrate understanding in music class. There are four areas of concern when assessing a student's ability to communicate: receptive language, expressive language, cognitive function/processing, and cultural use of language. There also may be extraneous circumstances that may hinder assessment in these areas such as common language cues that a student may or may not understand. Music itself is a form of communication. Students who struggle to communicate may express themselves to you as their music teacher in ways they may not express in any other class they attend. This is why it is important for music teachers to assess these areas in a formative manner, prior to the inclusion of the student in the classroom if at all possible, to understand potential challenges that a teacher and student may face in the music teaching and learning relationship. A communication observation protocol (Figure 1.2) has been created for use in identifying areas of strength and weakness in a student with challenges in the area of communication.

Receptive and Expressive Language

Because of a multitude of challenges, students may have the inability or be limited in their ability to receive and express language. Receptive language refers to the ability of a student to receive and process information. There are a number of reasons why this process may be interrupted. These reasons could include sensory obstacles (vision or hearing), cognitive processing interruptions, or other challenges that may impede a student's ability to understand a teacher. A student may also have delays in cognitive function or processing. Expressive language
thoughts (Lewis & Doorl;
has a delay in receptive a
challenges in her ability to

Language and Culture

Over the past decade, there has been an increasing number of English Language Learners (ELL) in general education classrooms (Banks et al., 2005).

In addition, there have been an increasing number of ELL students in music classrooms. It is important to understand the cultural influences of language, and the different experiences students bring to your music classroom. Communication and language are of primary importance when allowing access to students from different cultures and language origins. Banks et al. explains that when teachers use knowledge about the social, cultural, and language

---

Student Name:_____

Primary Teacher(s):_____

Notes from discussion with Primary Teacher in the area of Communication Needs and Language Learning Strategies **(after reading the IEP document*)**:

Class Observed:

Receptive Communication Strategies observed (e.g. simplified language, picture icons, etc.):

  • Potential strategies in music class:

Expressive Communication Strategies observed (e.g. pointing to a picture icon, small one or two word phrases, assistive technology, signing etc):

  • Potential strategies in music class:

Does the student have cultural language differences (i.e. Is English his/ her first language)?

  • Potential strategies in music class:

Notes:

* Please note that student or pre-clinical teachers will not have access to IEP without permission

---

Figure 1.2 Communication Observation Protocol (for Music Educators)

backgrounds of their students as they plan and implement instruction, the academic achievement of students can increase dramatically (p. 233). Therefore, the inclusion of ELL students and the way language affects our teaching and learning sequences in the music classroom are important considerations when preparing to teach students with special needs. Figure 1.2 has been provided to assist music teachers in understanding strategies used in other classrooms for an English Language Learner. Further adaptations will be discussed later in this text.

Behavioral or Emotional Challenges

The Individuals with Disabilities Education Act (IDEA) defines emotional disturbance as a condition that affects students in one or more of the following ways: a) an inability to learn that cannot be explained by intellectual, sensory, or health factors; b) an inability to develop and maintain interpersonal relationships with peers or teachers; c) inappropriate types of behavior or fears in normal circumstances; d) a general pervasive mood of unhappiness or depression; and e) a tendency to develop physical symptoms related to fears associated with personal or school problems (Turnbull, Heurta, & Stowe, 2004).

Because of many challenges associated with disabilities, students may struggle in the area of behavior. Research suggests that emotional and behavioral disabilities occur more often in boys than girls and these disabilities have a tendency to become more evident in secondary education (middle or high school) (U.S. Department of Education, 2002). Every student exhibits behavior at times that is considered inappropriate. It is important to consider the following when making modifications to instruction for a student: a) is there an antecedent to the behavior? b) is the behavior considered inappropriate for a student's sex or age? c) is the behavior interrupting his learning (e.g., attention, impulsivity, hyperactivity)? d) is the behavior external (e.g., aggression) or internal (e.g., withdrawal)? e) is the behavior interrupting the learning of other students in your classroom? If the answer to the above questions is yes, then it is time to consult a special education professional and create a plan that will assist you in your teaching.

When a music teacher first experiences the behaviors mentioned above, it is important to visit other classes to see if similar behaviors are occurring in a variety of settings and what might encourage positive and negative behaviors within the music classroom setting. In addition, it is important to reach out to parents and other teachers with similar goals to share your ideas about promoting positive behaviors in your classroom. An observation protocol has been developed to assist you in this area (see figure 1.3).

Student Name:_____

Primary Teacher(s):_____

Notes from discussion with Primary Teacher in the area of Behavioral Strategies **(after reading the IEP document*)**:

Class Observed:

Positive and appropriate behaviors observed (internal and external):
- Are there any noticeable triggers that cause negative behaviors
- Strategies to promote these behaviors in music class:

Negative or inappropriate behaviors observed (internal and external):

- Strategies to discourage these behaviors in music class:

Notes:

* Please note that student or pre-clinical teachers will not have access to IEP without permission

Figure 1.3 Behavioral Observation Protocol (for Music Educators)

Sensory Challenges

Many students have obstacles to overcome in the area of sensory needs. Sensory needs are often associated with students who have an impairment that involves their vision or hearing. However, while these students do have sensory challenges, there are other types of special needs that include challenges to sensory input and/or output. Students may demonstrate a hypo (less than) or hyper (more than) reaction to sound, sight, touch, smell, and/or taste. For many students with special needs, there are accompanying sensory challenges. An excellent first step is for music teachers to observe the student in other settings and to talk with special educators and parents. By being aware of how a student is challenged, extreme reactions to classroom activities can be predicted, and sometimes alleviated. Many students who struggle with sensory challenges engage in sensory integration therapy as part of their overall services through the school system. Some will have sensory items listed in

Student Name:_____

Primary Teacher(s):_____

Notes from discussion with Primary Teacher in the area of Behavioral Strategies **(after reading the IEP document*)**:

Class Observed:

Sensory Challenges (Visual or hearing impairment or hypo/hyper reactions to sound, sight, touch, taste or smell):

Communication Tools Used

Mobility Needs and Strategies

Orientation Needs and Strategies

Notes:

* Please note that student or pre-clinical teachers will not have access to IEP without permission

Figure 1.4 Sensory Observation Protocol (for Music Educators)

their IEP or 504 Plan and will bring those with them to the music classroom. An observation protocol has been developed that includes questions you may ask to understand the communication, orientation, and mobility needs of a student (see figure 1.4). This will guide you as you begin to make appropriate modifications, adaptations, or accommodations in your music classroom. Specific adaptations will be discussed in chapter 4.

Physical and Medical Conditions

A student's physical condition may or may not affect his academic performance in school. A student may have full cognitive function yet have a debilitating disorder that requires accommodation. Students with physical disabilities sometimes have difficulty achieving the skills necessary to be independent (Lewis & Doorlag, p. 313). If a student has a physical disability, it is important to create a learning environment that not only allows opportunity for achievement but also the skills necessary to achieve independence.

Student Name:_____

Primary Teacher(s):_____

Notes from discussion with Primary Teacher in the area of Behavioral Strategies **(after reading the IEP or 504 document*)**:

Class Observed:

Overview of physical or medical challenges:

Specific healthcare needs:

Gross motor needs:

Fine motor needs

Notes:

* Please note that student or pre-clinical teachers will not have access to IEP without permission

Figure 1.5 Physical or Medical Condition Observation Protocol (for Music Educators)

Increasing numbers of students with extensive health challenges are currently enrolled in public schools. This, in part, is due to advances in medicine that enable students to manage their chronic (long-term) or acute (short-term) illness while still attending public school (Lewis & Doorlag, p. 315). When teaching students with health challenges there are many issues. These students may be in pain or discomfort. They also may appear fine on one day and have great difficulty the next day. Students may require medication that, depending on the time of day administered, may affect their performance in the music classroom. It is important for teachers to learn about the specific medical condition to effectively plan for the student and to offer her the best possible opportunity to learn in the music classroom. Figure 1.5 was designed to assist music educators in attempting to identify these concerns in an attempt to provide the most comfortable learning environment possible.

It is also important to state that physical disabilities and health conditions can be temporary. If this is the case, a temporary Section 504 Plan may be designed for that child for the duration of the challenge at hand. Section 504 Plans can be temporary or long-term and may be very useful for a student with a short-term physical or health condition. Section 504 Plans will be discussed in-depth in chapter 2. These documents can be very beneficial as you plan to include a student with a health condition or physical disability in your classroom.

CONCLUSION

It is hoped that this chapter will set the scene for a label-free approach to teaching music to students with special needs. The rest of this text is designed to assist music teachers and music teacher educators as they define and implement adaptations and accommodations within an inclusive philosophy, in the music classroom. In addition, it is our goal to provide a clear understanding of policy and procedures within the public school special education system. The vignettes and discussion questions included in each chapter are designed for use in methods classes or for in-depth reflection by the practicing music educator to focus on the music teaching and learning relationship within music education.

DISCUSSION QUESTIONS

1. How should public education function within a democracy?
2. Discuss the inequities within our current public school education system.
3. What is special education?
4. What are the continued challenges with inclusion in the 21st century?
5. Describe how public school programs are funded.
6. How does question five affect students in urban and rural settings?
7. How can raising a child with a disability affect a family?
8. Describe the five categories of disabilities and the label-free approach.

REFERENCES

Arnold, M. L., Newman, J. H., Gaddy, B. B., & Dean, C. B. (2005). A look at the condition of rural education research: Setting a direction for future research. *Journal of Research in Rural Education, 20*(6), 1-25.

Banks, J., Cochran-Smith, M., Moll, L., Richert, A., Zeichner, K., & LePage, P., Darling-Hammond, L., Duffy, H., and M. McDonald (2005).Teaching diverse learners. In L. Darling Hammond & J. Bransford (Eds.), *Preparing teachers for a changing world* (pp. 232–274). San Francisco: Jossey-Bass.

Colwell, C. M., & Thompson, L. K. (2000). "Inclusion" of information on mainstreaming in undergraduate music education curricula. *Journal of Music Therapy, 37*(3), 205–221.

Culton, C. L. (1999). *The extent to which elementary music education textbooks reflect teachers' needs regarding instruction of students with special needs: A content analysis.* Unpublished doctoral dissertation, The University of Iowa.

Davis, W. B., Gfeller, K. E., & Thaut, M. H. (1999). *An introduction to music therapy.* Boston: McGraw-Hill.

Dewey, J. (1916/1944). *Democracy and education.* New York: Macmillan.

Fiedler, C. R., Simpson, R. L., & Clark, D. M. (2007). *Parents and families of children with disabilities: Effective school-based support services.* Upper Saddle River, NJ: Pearson, Merrill, Prentice-Hall.

Frisque, J., Niebur, L., & Humphreys, T. (1994). Music mainstreaming practices in Arizona. *Journal of Research in Music Education, 42,* 94–104.

Gottlieb, B. W. (1994). Special education in urban America. *Journal of Special Education, 27*(4), 453–465.

Hammel, A. M. (2001). Preparation for teaching special learners: Twenty years of practice. *Journal of Music Teacher Education, 11*(1), 5–11.

Hallahan, D. P., & Kauffman, J. M. (1978). *Exceptional children: Introduction to special education.* Englewood Cliffs, NJ: Prentice-Hall.

Kauffman, J. M. (1999). Commentary: Today's special education and its messages for tomorrow. *Journal of Special Education, 32*(4), 244–254.

Lewis, R. B., & Doorlag, D. H. (2006). *Teaching special students in general education classrooms.* Upper Saddle River, NJ: Prentice Hall.

Lipscomb, S. D. (1996). The cognitive organization of musical sound. In D. A. Hodges (Ed.), *Handbook of music psychology* (pp. 133–177). San Antonio, TX: IMR Press.

Lishner, D. M., Richardson, M., Levine, P., & Patrick, D. (1996). Access to primary health care among persons with disabilities in rural areas: A summary of the literature. *Journal of Rural Health,* Winter, 45–53.

Pamuk, E., Makuc, D., Heck, K., Rueben, C., & Lochner, K. (1998). *Socioeconomic status and health chartbook.* Hyattsville, MD: National Center for Health Statistics.

Patton, J. M. (1998). The disproportionate representation of African Americans in special education. *Journal of Special Education, 32*(1), 25–31.

Simpson, R. L., LaCava, P. G., & Sampson Graner, P. (2004). The no child left behind act: Challenges and implications for educators. *Intervention in School and Clinic, 40*(2), 67–75.

Turnbull, R., Huerta, N., Stowe, M. (2004). *The individuals with disabilities education act as amended in 2004.* Upper Saddle River, NJ: Pearson Merrill Prentice Hall.

U.S. Department of Education (2002). *The facts about adequate yearly progress.* Retrieved on April 9th, 2009 at www.NoChildLeftBehind.gov.

Winzer, M. A. (1993). *The history of special education: From isolation to integration.* Washington, DC: Gallaudet University Press.

Chapter 2

The Current Structure of Special Education in Our Schools

A Brief History of Legislation and Litigation in the United States

---

Vignette 2.1 Linda

Linda was six years old and was very excited at the thought that she may be allowed to attend school down the street from her house. She had played with her friends in the neighborhood and almost all of them went to the Sumner School, their local elementary school. One day, Linda and her Dad walked the few blocks to the Sumner School together. Linda remembers how big the school looked. School buildings and steps can look very large when you are a very small child. She walked up the steps with her Dad and entered the school office. Her Dad then went into the principal's office while Linda stayed in the waiting area. Before long, Linda began to hear raised voices and she could tell her Dad was not happy with whatever the school principal was telling him. Then, her Dad walked out of the office, took her small hand in his, and the two of them walked home. Linda would not be attending Sumner School with her friends. Instead, Linda must attend another school built for students like her that was farther away from her neighborhood and farther away from the friends she played with each day. What possible reason could exist for Linda to be considered unacceptable to a local elementary school? What disability must she have had to not be admitted? In reality, Linda did not have a disability. The answer is that Linda and her family were African-American and the year was 1951. Linda's last name was Brown and her family became part of the class action lawsuit that eventually included over 200 students in several states by the time the case was heard by the United States Supreme Court in 1954.

KEYSTONE LEGISLATION AND EDUCATING STUDENTS
WITH SPECIAL NEEDS

Legal wrangling, court decisions, and the timeline of a bill as it becomes law are not always met with public scrutiny or interest. However, there are many seminal moments that have shaped policies, legislation, and litigation in the areas of civil rights and the education of students with special needs. The keystone legislation examined in this chapter has continued to define us as a country and shape our public policy. Influenced by the civil rights movement, parents and advocates of students with special needs learned that true progress for their causes is steeped in the court houses and lawmaking bodies of our states, districts, and in Washington, DC. It is through legislation and litigation that change becomes reality. It was through this paradigm shift that the lives of students with special needs and their families improved. In addition, advocates learned that it is also possible to improve the quality of life for all students. It is through inclusion and an increasingly widened lens when viewing differences and diversity that *all* students (those with and without special needs) in our schools have the opportunity to learn and grow with those who are different. The path for all, then, is expanded and enriched for the experiences shared through an inclusive and diverse environment.

While Linda Brown, and all other students who are African-American are now eligible to attend their neighborhood schools, students with special needs are often bused far from their neighborhoods to be educated with other students because the school system has decided to segregate them according to ability and disability. If Linda had autism today, she might have to ride a bus for an hour and a half (each way) to school every day when her local elementary school is no farther from her home than the Sumner School was in 1951. We clearly still have a long way to go in delineating the rights of all citizens to equal access under the law.

The *Brown v. Board of Education* (1954) case was very important to the cause of those seeking to have students with special needs included in the public schools. The Supreme Court ruled, in *Brown v. Board of Education*, that it is unlawful to discriminate against a student for reasons that are not justified (Cartwright, 1995). The *Brown v. Board* case challenged an earlier Supreme Court case that held that "separate but equal" facilities for transportation were acceptable. This earlier case was heard in 1896 and was titled *Plessy v. Ferguson*. While we know Linda as the face of the *Brown* case, this case was actually a class action lawsuit that combined several lawsuits from five states that were all sent to the Supreme Court at the same time, and all were challenging the idea of "separate but equal" and discrimination without cause.

Much of the legislation and litigation in the area of education over the past fifty-five years has a foundation in this very important court ruling. Moreover, this decision is a symbol of the beginning of the advocacy movement as well as an ongoing discussion in our country regarding students with special needs and their place in American society (Paul & Warnock, 1980). The *Brown* case challenged the educational placement of students who were African-American, yet, the decision resonated throughout the special needs community as well.

Parents and supporters of children with special needs continued to organize within schools and communities throughout the 1960s as advocacy groups worked on their behalf and utilized techniques from the civil rights movement to further their cause. Because much of the overall discussion in education during that time had a focus on the improvement of educational opportunities for all students, those working on behalf of students with special needs were timely and justified in adding their voices and opinions (Melcher, 1976).

An important piece of legislation during this time was the Elementary and Secondary Act of 1965. This act focused on education for the "disadvantaged." The specific goal was to "strengthen and improve educational quality and educational opportunities in the Nation's elementary and secondary schools" (Congressional Record, 1965, p. 1340). The Elementary and Secondary Act was amended to include specific financial support for school systems that included students who lived in poverty (Senate Report, 1965, p. 1).

The Elementary and Secondary Act was part of a general legislative focus on the protection of students who were economically disadvantaged. This created a stir within the movement for those with disabilities. These advocates began asserting that if education was to be provided to create equity for students who were economically disadvantaged, then students with disabilities were also to be provided with equity as they were disadvantaged as a result of their particular need as well. As a result of this advocacy, funds were allocated for services to students who were considered at risk because of educational as well as economic needs (Senate Report, 1965). Soon, federal courts rendered decisions in Pennsylvania (1971) and the District of Columbia (1972) to establish, "a free and suitable publicly supported education despite the degree of a child's mental, physical, or emotional disability or impairment" (Atterbury, 1990, p. 6).

In 1973, the Health and Rehabilitation Act was passed by Congress (Public Law 93-112). This piece of legislation helped increase equal access to facilities, services and treatment for students with disabilities. Sections 503 and 504 of the act included antidiscrimination language reminiscent of the civil rights movement that had been adapted to prohibit discrimination against persons with disabilities (Congressional Information Service, 1972). Section 504 states that, students with disabilities will be provided with a "free appropriate public education" (Student Access, 1992, p. 1). We will discuss Section 504 later in the chapter as it applies specifically to students with special needs.

PUBLIC LAW 94–142

Public Law 94-142 (1975) was the first legislation that specifically mandated a free and appropriate public education for all students with special needs. This law, the most comprehensive ever passed by Congress regarding education, has a direct effect on music teachers in schools today (Heller, 1994). Public Law 94-142 requires that:

> (a) all children ages 5-21, regardless of the nature or severity of their handicaps, are provided a free and appropriate public education; (b) handicapped children will be educated to the maximum extent possible with non-handicapped peers; (c) special classes, separate schooling, or removal of a handicapped child will occur only if the severity of the handicap impedes the education of a child within the general education classroom with the use of supplementary aids and services; (d) each child identified as having a handicap will have an Individualized Education Program (IEP) to match their educational needs and; (e) all children and their families will be offered the right to due process under the Constitution of the United States. (20 USC 1412 Section 612 89 Stat. 780)

P.L. 94-142 was, and still is, a very controversial piece of legislation. It was signed into law in December of 1975 (C.I.S., 1975, p. 1021). Music is specifically mentioned in the language of P.L. 94-142 as being an integral part of the education of students:

> The use of the arts as a teaching tool for the handicapped has long been recognized as a viable, effective way not only of teaching special skills, but also of reaching youngsters who had otherwise been unteachable. The committee envisions that programs under this bill could well include an arts component and, indeed, urges that local educational agencies include arts in programs for the handicapped funded under this act. Such a program could cover both appreciation of the arts by the handicapped youngsters and the utilization of the arts as a teaching tool per se." (Senate Report, 1977, p. 324)

LEGISLATIVE HISTORY ON BEHALF OF STUDENTS
WHO ARE INTELLECTUALLY GIFTED

As legislation and litigation began to shape the education of students with special needs, the special needs of students who are intellectually gifted was also an important consideration. In 1972, the U.S. commissioner of education was tasked with determining the quality and quantity of programs in public schools for students who are considered gifted and talented. The report was termed the Marland Report.

The Marland Report noted the lack of services and programs for students who are gifted. At that time, 96% of students identified as gifted were not being served through their school systems. As a result of the Marland Report, $2.56 million were allocated for gifted education in 1974 (approximately $1.00 for each student who was gifted in the United States) (Marland, 1972).

Further studies, reports, and legislation have been proposed subsequent to the initial acts; however, gifted education is still sparsely funded (approximately 2 cents for every $100 spent on education) (Winner, 1996).

As part of the report, the U.S. Office of Education stated in 1972:

> Gifted and talented students are those identified by professionally qualified persons who by virtue of outstanding abilities are capable of high performance. These are students who require differentiated educational programs and/or services beyond those normally provided by the regular school program in order to realize areas of their contribution to self and society. (Walker, 1991, p.16)

Areas included in their definition of giftedness were: general intellectual ability, specific academic aptitude, creative and productive thinking, leadership ability, visual and performing arts, and psychomotor ability.

THE JACOB K. JAVITS GIFTED AND TALENTED STUDENTS EDUCATION ACT

The Jacob K. Javits Gifted and Talented Students Education Act was passed by congress in 1988 (Winner, 1996). As part of this act, funding was made available for programs that serve students who are gifted (Walker, 1991). One primary purpose of the Javits Act was to increase the accurate identification of and provision of services to students from diverse backgrounds (VanTassel-Baska, 1998). In the 20 years since passage of the Javits Act, little has been accomplished in this area that can be directly attributed to it as the act has been historically and critically underfunded. Testing and other methods of identification for students who are gifted have increasingly been refined to increase the identification of students from diverse backgrounds, and cultural sensitivity has also been raised to address this issue as well.

MORE RECENT LEGISLATION AND LITIGATION REGARDING STUDENTS WITH SPECIAL NEEDS

Through subsequent decades, litigation has continued to refine legislation, and the path to full inclusion has been delineated with more clarity. The Supreme Court decided a groundbreaking case, *Hudson v. Rowley* (1982), stating that while a student has a guarantee to an appropriate education, she is not automatically guaranteed "maximum possible achievement" in an educational setting. By deciding the case this way, the question of whether a school system is required to ensure maximum possible achievement was answered. Maximum possible inclusion in the least restrictive environment is a right of all children (Cartwright, 1995); however, maximum achievement is not the responsibility of the school system.

In 1986, P.L. 94-142 was clarified with the passage of P.L. 99-457. The scope of this law includes early intervention and early childhood education. This law expanded the range of age of services for students with disabilities to include every child aged 3-21. Students are guaranteed these services without regard to the type or severity of their disabilities. States were also offered funding through the federal Department of Education to provide early intervention programs to young children with disabilities (C.I.S., 1986).

P.L. 94-142 was amended and renamed the Individuals with Disabilities Education Act in 1990. The law quickly became known as IDEA (C.I.S., 1990). IDEA significantly altered P.L. 94-142 in four ways: (a) children were re-termed individuals, (b) the term handicapped was changed to persons with disabilities, (c) transition plans were put into place for students preparing to enter the workforce or education beyond secondary school and, (d) autism and traumatic brain injury were added to the list of identified disabilities (Cartwright, 1995; Hallahan, 1997). The addition of transition services opportunities increased the options students with disabilities had when transitioning from school to work or higher education. The term "handicapped" was eliminated from the special education language and "person first" language was introduced as an alternative. Additionally, related services were redefined "to include therapeutic recreation, social work services, and rehabilitation counseling" (C.I.S., 1989, p. 5). Through this legislation, the secretary of health, education, and welfare is required to "give priority to programs that increase the likelihood that severely handicapped children and youth will be educated with their non-disabled peers" (C.I.S., 1989, p. 7). Figure 2.1 represents a list of disabilities identified in this important piece of legislation.

An important IDEA amendment became law in 1997. This legislation (P.L. 105-17) reorganized IDEA into four parts: (a) general provisions for students with disabilities, (b) assistance for education of all children with disabilities, (c) the inclusion of infants and toddlers with disabilities, and (d) national activities to improve education of children with disabilities. In addition to these modifications, the Individualized Education Program (IEP) team was expanded to include a general classroom teacher (which may be the music teacher), and further clarification and guidelines for increased funding and early education programs as well as transition programs were put in place (20 U.S.C. 14et.seq.).

Disabilities Included in the Individuals with Disabilities Education Act

Autism
Deaf Blindness
Deafness
Emotional Disturbance
Hearing Impairment
Mental Retardation
Multiple Disabilities
Orthopedic Impairment
Other Health Impairment
Specific Learning Disability
Speech or Language Impairment
Traumatic Brain Injury
Visual Impairment Including Blindness

Figure 2.1 Disabilities included in the Individuals with Disabilities Education Act

A controversial point of this legislation is the alteration of the policy regarding disciplinary actions taken against students with special needs. The act "allows application to children with disabilities of the same relevant disciplinary procedures applicable to children without disabilities, if the behavior is determined to be not a manifestation of the disability" (C.I.S., 1997, p. 4). According to IDEA 1997, students with special needs cannot be denied educational services, regardless of the behavior of the student (IDEA 1997: Let's Make It Work, 1998). This means that if a student with a disability commits an infraction of a school rule and that behavior takes place as a manifestation of the disability, the student may be disciplined differently than if the behavior was not related to the disability. The law protects students with disabilities from being repeatedly suspended, or expelled: thus denying them equal access to education.

Further reauthorizations to IDEA took place in 2002 and 2004. During this process, new procedural safeguards, highly qualified teacher provisions, a focus on reduction of overrepresentation of some ethnicities, genders, and students from specific socioeconomic levels were added. Other new considerations included a reduction in IEP paperwork, closer monitoring and enforcement of compliance, No Child Left Behind, assessment issues, discipline, and the identification of students who have specific learning disabilities. Of these changes, No Child Left Behind (NCLB), the IEP team composition, and the identification of and provision of services to students with specific learning disabilities have become the most important new considerations for music educators who teach students with disabilities in their classrooms.

No Child Left Behind affects music educators in a profound way. Because of the demands placed on schools to achieve Adequate Yearly Progress (AYP), music educators are routinely asked to assist in classroom reading and mathematics goals, and students are sometimes denied access to music because they are instead receiving remediation to prepare them for this testing. Because the music educator is considered a member of the team, it is empowering and practical for them to know and act upon their full membership in the process. Finally, the new process for identification of students with learning disabilities involves a school-wide initiative as students are assessed and receive remediation in a more holistic setting. This setting may include the music classroom.

The most recent changes to IDEA came in December 2008. An amendment to a 2006 directive now says a school system must cease provision of services to a student with special needs upon written notification from the parents requesting an end to all special education measures (34 C.F.R. § 300.300(b) (4)). Action upon this request is to be immediate and no services are to be provided unless the parents ask that the special education process begin again (Zirkel, 2008b). As a music educator, and therefore a member of the special education team for a student with special needs, you should be made aware if this situation occurs in your school.

THE AMERICANS WITH DISABILITIES ACT

The Americans with Disabilities Act (ADA) (P.L. 101–336) was passed in 1990. A highlight of this legislation is the guarantee of nondiscrimination to all persons with disabilities in employment, transportation, public accommodations, state and local government, and telecommunications situations. Students with special needs are not specifically addressed in the ADA; however, the practices utilized by employers and those in higher education when interacting with students with special needs are an important component of this legislation. Nondiscriminatory practices and accessibility to all public buildings are the largest legacies of this act (C.I.S., 1990). A significant amount of litigation has refined this legislation, and the ADA has been a prominent feature in lawsuits involving discriminatory practice and lack of access to public buildings and spaces.

The ADA was amended in late 2008 as the Americans with Disabilities Act Amendments (ADAA). These new regulations took effect in January 2009. The most important portion of this amendment connects the ADAA with Section 504 Plans by expanding the options for eligibility and monitoring the enforcement of provision of services for students who have both IEP and 504 Plans (Zirkel, 2008a). The expansion of the "major life activity" category includes the addition of reading, thinking, concentrating, sleeping, bowel functions, bladder functions, digestive functions, and eating (see figure 2.2, © Zirkel, 2008). As music educators, it will become increasingly important for us to be very aware of the students in our classrooms who have special needs. With the implementation of new ADAA measures, it is likely that more students will be eligible for Section 504 Plans.

Section 504/ADA Student Eligibility Form
(Shaded Areas Denote Changes Due to ADAA, Effective 1/1/09)

Child's Name: _____ Date of Birth: _____

Eligibility Team Members: Fill in names, and check areas of knowledge for each team member:

Names:	about the child	about the meaning of evaluation data	about accommodations/ placement options

Note: Make sure there is at least one check in each column.

Sources of evaluation information (check each one used):
    ____ aptitude and/or achievement tests   ____ teacher recommendations
    ____ adaptive behavior   ____ others(specify):_____

1. Specify the mental or physical *impairment* _____
    (as recognized in *DSM-IV* or other respected source if not excluded under 504/ADA, e.g., illegal drug use)

2. Check the *major life activity*:

____ seeing	____ hearing	____ walking	____ learning
____ performing manual tasks		____ breathing	
____ reading	____ thinking	____ concentrating	____ sleeping
____ bowel functions	____ bladder functions	____ digestive functions	____ eating

Or specify alternative of equivalent scope and importance: _____

3. Place an "X" on the following scale to indicate the specific degree that the impairment (in #1) limits the major life activity (in #2).

- Make an educated estim **without** the effects of mitigating measures, such as medication; low-vision devices (except eyeglasses or contact lenses); hearing aids and cochlear implants; mobility devices, prosthetics, assistive technology; learned behavioral or adaptive neurological modifications; and reasonable accommodations or auxiliary aids/services.
- Similarly, for impairments that are episodic or in remission, make the determination for the time they are active.
- Use the average student in the general (i.e., national) population as the frame of reference.
- Interpret close calls in favor of broadcoverage (i.e., construing items 1-3 to the maximum extent that they permit). Thus, for an "X" at 4.0 or below, fill in specific information evaluated by the team that justifies the rating.

5 ———— Extremely ————————————————
4 ———— Substantially ————————————————
3 ———— Moderately ————————————————
2 ———— Mildly ————————————————
1 ———— Negligibly ————————————————

4. If the team's determination for Item #3 was less than "4," provide notice to the parents of their procedural rights, including for an impartial hearing. If the team's determination was a "4" or above, the team also should determine and document the reasonable accommodations necessary for the child to have an "appropriate education" in accordance with Section 504 and the ADA.

Figure 2.2 Section 504/ADA Student Eligibility Form

With the expanding eligibility criteria for Section 504 Plans and the increasing common characteristics of 504 Plans and IEPs, it is necessary for music educators to be vigilant regarding the needs of all students with identified special needs. As seen in the Student Eligibility Form created by Zirkel (2009), students with physical challenges that substantially affect their ability to learn in the music classroom will have specific needs that we must acknowledge and meet. When traveling with music students, these relatively new student needs, as stated on their 504 Plans, may be very important and may change a well-planned itinerary or number of stops a group must make en route. In general, as a music educator, the awareness of the physical, emotional, academic, and social needs of our students is both our right and responsibility.

THE SIX PRINCIPLES OF IDEA: IMPLICATIONS FOR MUSIC EDUCATORS

There are six overarching principles that have been a part of IDEA since it's inception in 1975. These principles are: (a) "Zero Reject," (b) "Non-discriminatory Evaluations," (c) free appropriate public education, (d) least restrictive environment (LRE), (e) procedural due process, and (f) parental involvement (Lewis & Doorlag, 2006). These principles also create an important framework for music educators as we continue to improve our abilities to include and educate students with special needs in our classrooms. Turnbull, Huerta, and Stowe (2006) state: "So many people fail to understand IDEA wholly and conceptually because they lack a framework" (p. 17). Our goal in this next section is to frame the basic underlying elements of IDEA in a way that is useful for music educators.

ZERO REJECT

Perhaps the most important principle is that of "Zero Reject." This means that a student cannot be excluded from a classroom or educational setting merely because he or she has a disability. Even if a student has committed disciplinary actions that cause the system to change the specific setting for that student, he still has the right to an education. This includes students who may have been expelled from a traditional school situation (Turnbull et al., 2006). The most important aspect of this principle is that *all* means *all*. The equal access discussed earlier applies to music educators as well as general classroom teachers (Turnbull et al., 2006). As a result of the application of "Zero Reject" for a considerable period of time, the attitudes of children toward their peers with disabilities have changed. As we know, education is not purely "book knowledge." We have also learned a great deal about society and the place we hold, as well as the places our peers hold, as we work together in inclusive classrooms (Colwell, 1998; Darrow, 1999; Johnson & Darrow, 1997; Wilson & McCrary, 1996).

NONDISCRIMINATORY EVALUATION

Once a school system has admitted a student with special needs, under the provision of "Zero Reject," the next principle is that of a "Nondiscriminatory Evaluation." This process, sometimes referred to as a "Child Study," includes several professionals within the school system. A student is evaluated and observed by the professionals who are assigned to the team. This team then meets to discuss the most appropriate educational setting, provisions, accommodations, and related services (speech therapy, occupational therapy, music therapy, physical therapy) that may be utilized to provide the student with equal access and support within the educational environment (Adamek & Darrow, 2005). The team will also include administrators, classroom teachers (sometimes the music teacher), as well as the professionals who assisted in the evaluation and observation procedures. In addition, the parents are also an integral part of this team (Turnbull et al., 2006).

If you, as the music educator, think a student in your classroom may have a disability, the first and most appropriate step is to discuss your concerns and observations with the classroom teacher or a colleague who works within the special education structure of your school (Turnbull et al., 2006). As music educators, we are not specifically qualified to presuppose disability categories or cite specific labels we think are appropriate for students. It is our responsibility to seek assistance, as a part of the total school team, from those professionals who are qualified and charged with the responsibility of conducting assessments of students who may have special needs (Adamek & Darrow, 2005).

FREE AND APPROPRIATE EDUCATION (FAPE)

Once a student has been identified as having a special educational need, the next principle of IDEA, the provision of a Free Appropriate Public Education" (FAPE), becomes important. This is the part of the process where the specific educational placement of a student with special needs is determined. As part of the application of a FAPE, an Individualized Education Program (IEP) is created. The first step when creating an IEP is to determine the most appropriate placement. This step includes a statement of the present level of functioning of the student, noting their areas of strength and challenge (Lewis & Doorlag, 2006). It also states how the student is particularly affected by the specific school setting.

The second set of statements in an IEP, under FAPE, is a list of the specific level of academic functioning of the student. These statements describe specific goals for the forthcoming academic period as well as any particular benchmark periods used to evaluate progress throughout the school year. These benchmark goals are important for music educators as we include students with special needs in our classrooms. It is highly recommended that we consider the goals included in a student's IEP as we plan modifications and adaptations to our lesson plans and classroom environments. In fact, it is our legal responsibility to be aware of, and to provide, accommodations for all students who have been identified as having special educational needs (Hammel, 2004).

One of the first "items of business" as a music educator begins a school year, or begins to teach at a new school, is to identify and study all students with special needs who will be a part of music classes and ensembles. While this may seem a daunting task, it is enormously helpful when creating a curriculum, a scope and sequence for teaching, and when writing individual lesson plans for classes. Remember, it is also our responsibility according to the law (IDEA). Once we have begun to study and apply adaptations and modifications, the process becomes more streamlined and we are much better informed through having participated in these preparation guidelines (Hammel, 2001; Hammel & Gerrity, In Review).

LEAST RESTRICTIVE ENVIRONMENT (LRE)

Education in the "Least Restrictive Environment" is a principle that has been somewhat confusing for music educators in the past (Hammel, 2004). This part of IDEA states: "to the maximum extent appropriate, students with disabilities will be educated with students who are not disabled" (Turnbull et al., 2006, p. 67). It also states that the "Least Restrictive Environment" (LRE) is the environment where a student learns best. This includes the application of appropriate and supplementary aides and services (Burkett & Hammel, 2007). Many students learn best in a general classroom environment with heterogeneous grouping. Some students, however, learn best in an environment that is homogenous, has a smaller student to teacher ratio, or is at a different time of day. We would never deny a child access to a music education. There are times, however, when changes to the classroom setting may greatly increase the educational appropriateness for a student with special needs (Zigmond, 1997).

The fundamental assumption of an inclusive philosophy is to start with a student in a general classroom setting. As a team studies the level of functioning, adaptations necessary, and addition of personnel and services, they may determine that a student with special needs may need to participate in a classroom other than the traditional setting (Turnbull et al., 2006). This can also be an issue when the behavior of a student is such that it is inappropriate for the student with special needs, as well as the other students in the class, to participate in an inclusion setting. Webber (1997) states: "The practice is especially controversial when applied to students with emotional and behavioral disorders who have the potential to become aggressive and/ or noncompliant" (p. 27). The educational setting agreed upon by the team after all options have been discussed is then considered to be the "Least Restrictive Environment" for that student (Lewis & Doorlag, 2006).

PROCEDURAL DUE PROCESS AND PARENT INVOLVEMENT

The final principles of IDEA are "Procedural Due Process" and "Parental Involvement." If the parents of a student with special needs consider the placement of their child to be inappropriate, they may request a review of placement, services, and personnel. If the process continues to a formal review, it is known as "Procedural Due Process" (Turnbull et al., 2006). Each state has separate procedural laws that govern due process. Parents are encouraged to participate throughout the process to advocate for their child. These reviews conducted by the team, as well as the continued encouragement of parents to participate, are important elements of the system of checks and balances within the special education framework (Turnbull et al., 2006).

THE EFFECT OF THE NO CHILD LEFT BEHIND ACT
ON SPECIAL EDUCATION

In 2001, Congress passed the No Child Left Behind Act (NCLB). This legislation significantly altered the way schools and students are assessed (Simpson, Lacava, Sampson, & Graner, 2004). A controversial portion of NCLB is that each school must make "Adequate Yearly Progress" (AYP) toward closing the achievement gap in reading and mathematics. The deadline for AYP to have been met is the 2013–2014 school year. This mandate includes every student in every school district (including students with special needs) (http://www2.ed.gov/nclb/landing.jhtml). Schools were and still are under tremendous pressure to meet AYP and standardized test scores, graduation rates, and attendance records are evaluated yearly. In addition, students are grouped for sub-evaluation. These groups include race, socioeconomic status, and disability. Students with disabilities fail to meet AYP at a greater rate than other students, and they contribute to failing school scores more than other subgroupings (Simpson et al., 2004). This failure creates an even more palpable sense of stress in schools as they struggle to meet AYP while attempting to meet the needs of all students in their school. Moreover, federal funding is tied to successful AYP under NCLB (NCLB, 2001).

Students within a school who are struggling to meet the standards of NCLB may be temporarily denied access to music if they are required to attend remediation and tutoring sessions prior to testing days (Simpson et. al., 2004). Music educators who advocate for music education and the importance of music for all students may be more effective when demonstrating the ways participation in music instruction benefits students in both musical and nonmusical academic studies. With the advent of school-wide intervention strategies that emphasize a partnership and sense of teamwork from the entire school staff, this may become increasingly important.

RACE TO THE TOP (RTTT)

The Obama administration has promised to move away from the emphasis on testing for children enrolled in special education. In his speech on November 4, 2009, he stated:

> This Bush administration policy placed heavy emphasis on the development of standardized tests, which created a rigid set of guidelines for education performance and provided little room for creativity in curriculum. States had every incentive to set the bar low in order to avoid having large numbers of their schools labeled as "failing" under NCLB. Thus not only were special education and English as a second language (ESL) students being left behind by schools that did not wish to lower their performance grade, the system also failed in its most important objective: encouraging higher educational standards across the board (http://www.whitehouse.gov/the-press-office/remarks-president-strengthening-americas-education-system).

It is yet to be seen how Race to the Top will affect students in special education.

RESPONSIVENESS TO INTERVENTION

While the six principles of IDEA have been in place for more than 30 years, new legislation has refined our approach to including students with special needs in music classrooms and continues to improve our approach and practices (Fletcher et al., 2002; Winzer, 1993). Much of the more recent legislation and litigation have focused on the role of general classroom educators in teaching students with special needs. Music educators are considered "general classroom educators" according to the law (§614(d)(3)(C); Fairbanks et al., 2007) and have an obligation to participate in all school-wide efforts to increase the effectiveness of delivery of a "Free Appropriate Public Education" for all students. With the recent passage of legislation, including NCLB and IDEA 2004, a new initiative has been introduced that combines the need for accountability, as detailed in NCLB, and the improvement of education for students with special needs, as noted in the continued reauthorizations of IDEA (Cummings, Atkins, Allison, & Cole, 2008). This new initiative is termed "Responsiveness to Intervention" (Kame'enui, 2007).

"Responsiveness to Intervention" began as a response to the long-standing tradition of identifying students who have learning disabilities primarily revealed by a discrepancy between their ability (IQ score) and their achievement as demonstrated by standardized tests. Students who showed a significant difference between these, generally by two or more standard deviations (according to the universal bell curve), were often labeled as having a specific learning disability (Fuchs & Young, 2006). Unfortunately, students were often either mislabeled or undiagnosed, as these markers were not always accurate. Students also sometimes experienced significant failure in school prior to being tested and identified as needing special education services.

When IDEA was amended in 2004, one modification implemented, as a result of the changes in identification of students with learning disabilities, was the use of "Responsiveness to Intervention" (RTI) strategies to more accurately identify these students (Fuchs & Young, 2006). This approach is more global and problem solving in nature. RTI was also welcomed by many teachers because it gave them the opportunity to provide additional services to students before they began to experience failure in school (Chidsey, 2007; Kame'enui, 2007).

The basic philosophy of RTI is that all students should be given the opportunity to receive research-based instructional interventions provided by highly qualified teachers to determine if the underlying issue is a disability or the lack of access to best practice teaching (Fuchs & Young, 2006). Instruction is the focus of RTI and assessment is considered secondary. While students are receiving RTI, instruction-based assessment data is continuously taken and studied by teachers, to measure change over time (Peck & Scarpati, 2007). All models of RTI include research-based reading screenings, universal screenings (all students in the school) to determine who may be at risk, continuous screenings, and problem-solving strategies for students who show a need for RTI strategies (Bradley et al., 2007). Through RTI implementation, students benefit from earlier intervention (Fairbanks et al., 2007), a strong emphasis on prevention, and clear, classroom based, assessments to assist teachers in creating curriculum modification (Fuchs & Fuchs, 2007).

Music educators are considered part of the total school team and some schools follow an RTI model school-wide (Fairbanks et al., 2007). It is also possible that music educators may be asked to provide evidence of research-based instruction in their classrooms as part of compliance with RTI initiatives. Our ability to present, describe, and confirm our research-based and best practice teaching in the music classroom is important as part of the school-wide effort to apply RTI for the benefit of all students in our schools (Bradley et al., 2007; Chidsey, 2007).

RTI is often applied through a tiered system. There are usually two or three tiers to the system, and students are placed in increasingly specialized situations with faculty members who have expertise in the particular area of struggle for the student (Fuchs & Fuchs, 2007). Small group and individual intervention strategies are applied over a period of weeks. During this time, data is taken as students experience various high quality research-based strategies. The school then measures the "slope of improvement" (rate of amelioration demonstrated during data collection) as well as the final status (percentile rank on standardized test) (Hammel & Hourigan, In Press p. 13) to determine improvement shown as a result of RTI. These two measures are considered to be of primary importance when evaluating responsiveness to intervention (Fuchs & Fuchs, 2007).

APPLICATIONS AND CONSIDERATIONS FOR MUSIC EDUCATORS

Legislation, litigation, and public policy continue to refine our educational approaches, and the procedures we follow to include students with special needs in our classrooms will change as a result. An awareness of these regulations and policies is part of our responsibility as music educators. Moreover, the careful application of guidelines as presented through contact with our school administrators, special education teams, and through professional development opportunities will lead to an improvement of our ability to provide the most appropriate education for our students with special needs.

While the specifics of legal details may sometimes be confusing, and the field of special education continues to define itself, the most important caveat to remember is that each student with special needs is an individual child. When we consider the seemingly cavernous world of acronyms and definitions, we sometimes forget that we are considering the present and future possibilities for a child. Taking a moment to remember the individual child and the lifetime ramifications of decisions we make often brings into focus the true importance of the education of students with special needs.

DISCUSSION QUESTIONS

1. Discuss how the advocacy efforts employed during the civil rights movement was mirrored by those advocating for persons with special needs (and students with special needs).
2. How did P.L. 94-142, and later IDEA, expand during the 35-year history?
3. What are the six principles of IDEA and how does each apply in the music classroom?
4. Describe "least restrictive environment" and state how this may be achieved in the music classroom (at least three examples).
5. How would you respond to a teacher who wants to keep a student from attending your class to take part in remediation to meet AYP under NCLB? What data demonstrating the effectiveness and applicability of your instruction would you be able to cite?
6. What are some ways you, as the music teacher, could participate as part of the RTI system at your school?

REFERENCES

Adamek, M. S., & Darrow, A. A. (2005). *Music in special education.* Silver Spring, MD: The American Music Therapy Association.

Atterbury, B. W. (1990). *Mainstreaming exceptional learners in music.* Englewood Cliffs, NJ: Prentice Hall.

Bradley, R., Danielson, L., & Doolittle, J. (2007). Responsiveness to intervention: 1997 to 2007. *Teaching Exceptional Children, 39*(5), 8-12.

Burkett, E. I., & Hammel, A. M. (2007). *On Music for Special Learners.* Reston, VA: Connect for Education.

Cartwright, G. P. (1995). *Educating special learners.* Albany, NY: Wadsworth Publishing Co.

Chidsey, R. B. (2007). No more waiting to fail. *Educational Leadership, 65*(2), 40-46.

Colwell, C. M. (1998). Effects of information on elementary band students' attitudes towards individuals with special needs. *Journal of Music Therapy, 35*(1), 19-33.

Congressional Information Service (1972). Abstracts of congressional publications and legislative histories. Washington, DC: U.S. Government Printing Office.

Congressional Information Service. (1986). Abstracts of congressional publications and legislative histories. Washington, DC: U.S. Government Printing Office.

Congressional Information Service. (1989). Abstracts of congressional publications and legislative histories. Washington, DC: U.S. Government Printing Office.

Congressional Information Service (1990). Abstracts of congressional publications and legislative histories. Washington, DC: U.S. Government Printing Office.

Congressional Information Service (1997). Abstracts of congressional publications and legislative histories. Washington, DC: U.S. Government Printing Office.

Congressional Record (1965). 89th congress first session volume III. Washington, DC: U.S. Government Printing Office.

Cummings, K. D., Atkins, T., Allison, R., & Cole, C. (2008). Response to intervention. *Teaching Exceptional Children, 40*(4), 24–31.

Darrow, A. A. (1999). Music educators' perceptions regarding the inclusion of students with severe disabilities in music classrooms. *Journal of Music Therapy, 36*(4), 254–273.

Fairbanks, S., Sugai, G., Guardino, D., & Lathrop, M. (2007). Response to intervention: Examining classroom behavior support in second grade. *Exceptional Children, 73*(3), 288–310.

Fletcher, M. J., Lyon, G. R., Barnes, M., Stuebing, K. K., Francis, D. J., & Olson, R. K. et al. (2002). Classification of learning disabilities: An evidence-based evaluation. In R. Bradley, L. Danielson, & D. P. Hallahan (Eds.), *Identification of learning disabilities: Research to practice* (pp. 185–250). Mahwah, NJ: Erlbaum.

Fuchs, D., & Young, C. (2006). On the irrelevance of intelligence in predicting responsiveness to reading instruction. *Exceptional Children, 73*(1), 8–30.

Fuchs, L. S., & Fuchs, D., (2007). A model for implementing responsiveness to intervention. *Teaching Exceptional Children, 39*(5), 14–20.

Hallahan, D. (1997). *Exceptional learners.* Boston, MA: Allyn & Bacon.

Hammel, A. M. (2001). Preparation for teaching special learners: Twenty years of practice. *Journal of Music Teacher Education, 11*(1), 5–11.

Hammel, A. M. (2004). Inclusion strategies that work. *Music Educators Journal, 90*(5) 33–37.

Hammel, A.M., & Gerrity, K.W. (In review). The Effect of Instruction on Teacher Perceptions of Competence When Including Students with Special needs in music Classrooms.

Heller, L. (1994). *Undergraduate music teacher preparation for mainstreaming: A survey of music education teacher training institutions in the Great Lakes region of the United States* (Doctoral dissertation, Michigan State University, 1994). Dissertation Abstracts International, 56–03A, 858.

IDEA 1997: Let's make it work. (1998). Reston, VA: The Council for Exceptional Children.

Johnson, C. M., & Darrow, A. A. (1997). The effect of positive models of inclusion on band students' attitudinal statements regarding the integration of students with disabilities. *Journal of Research in Music Education, 45*(2), 173–184.

Kame'enui, E. J. (2007) A new paradigm: Responsiveness to intervention. *Teaching Exceptional Children, 39*(5), 6–7.

Lewis, R. B., & Doorlag, D. H. (2006). Teaching special students in general education classrooms. Upper Saddle River, NJ: Prentice Hall.

Marland, S.P. (1972). *Education of the gifted and talented: Report to the Congress of the United States by the Commissioner of Education.* Washington, DC: U.S. Government Printing Office.

Melcher, J. W. 1976. Law, litigation, and handicapped children. *Exceptional Children, 43*, 26–130.

No Child Left Behind (2001). Retrieved March 9, 2009, from . http://www2.ed.gov/nclb/landing.jhtml

Paul, J. L., & Warnock, N.J. 1980. Special Education: A changing field. *Exceptional Child, 27*, 3–28.

Peck, A., & Scarpati, S. (2007). Responsiveness to intervention. *Teaching Exceptional Children, 39*(5), 4.

Senate committee on labor and public welfare. (1965). Elementary and Secondary Act of 1965 (45-779 0-65-1). Washington, DC: U.S. Government Printing Office.

Senate committee on labor and public welfare. (1977). The Education of All Handicapped Children Act (121a320). Washington, DC: U.S. Government Printing Office.

The Individuals with Disabilities Education Act: Public Law 105-17 - 20 U.S.C. 14et. seq. (1997).

Simpson, R. L., LaCava, P. G., Sampson, P., & Graner, P. (2004). The no child left behind act: Challenges and implications for educators. *Intervention in School and Clinic, 40*(2), 67-75.

Student access: A resource guide for educators. Section 504 of the Rehabilitation Act of 1973. (1992). Albuquerque, NM: Council of Administrators of Special Education, Inc.

Turnbull, R., Huerta, N., & Stowe, M. (2006). *The individuals with disabilities education act as amended in 2004.* Upper Saddle River, NJ: Prentice Hall.

VanTassel-Baska, J. (1998). *Excellence in educating gifted and talented learners.* Denver, CO: Love Publishing Company.

Walker, S. Y. (1991). *The survival guide for parents of gifted kids.* Minneapolis, MN: Free Spirit Publishing.

Webber, J. (1997). Responsible inclusion: Key components for success. In P. Zionts (Ed.), *Inclusion strategies for students with learning and behavioral problems* (pp. 27-56). Austin TX: Pro-ed, Inc.

Wilson, B., & McCrary, J. (1996). The effect of instruction on music educators' attitudes toward students with disabilities. *Journal of Research in Music Education, 44*(1), 26-33.

Winner, E. (1996). *Gifted children: Myths and realities.* New York: Perseus Books Group.

Winzer, M. A. (1993). The history of special education: From isolation to integration. Washington DC: Gallaudet University Press.

Zigmond, N. (1997). Educating students with disabilities: The future of special education. In J. W. Lloyd, E. J. Kameenui, & D. Chard (Eds.), *Issues in educating students with disabilities* (pp. 377-390). Mahwah, NJ: Lawrence Erlbaum Associates Publishers.

Zirkel, P. (2008a). What does the law say? New Section 504 and student eligibility standards. *Teaching Exceptional Children, 41*(4), 68-71.

Zirkel, P. (2008b). What does the law say? *Teaching Exceptional children, 41*(5), 73-75.

Zirkel, P. (2009). Section 504/ADA Student Eligibility form. *Teaching Exceptional Children, 41*(4), 70.

PART II

PREPARING TO TEACH MUSIC TO STUDENTS WITH SPECIAL NEEDS

Chapter 3

Preparing to Teach

Fieldwork and Engagement Opportunities in Special Education for Pre-service and In-service Music Educators

There are varying degrees of undergraduate and graduate preparation for students with special needs. Music educators may have had a general special education class or the opportunity to study topics regarding students with special needs embedded within a music methods course. The topic of students with special needs may have been included in an educational psychology course, or a teaching music to students with special needs course that was part of the curriculum (Heller, 1994, York & Reynolds, 1996). More often than not, music educators have little or no background or instruction in this area (Wilson & McCrary, 1996). Therefore, music educators must be resourceful in gaining insight into the skills, strategies, and understandings that accompany the experience of teaching a student with special needs.

Music teacher educators often have little or no preparation as to how to educate future music educators regarding the inclusion of music students with disabilities or how to plan, implement, and assess lessons in self-contained and inclusive music classrooms. Oftentimes, this lack of understanding results in either glossing over the topic or ignoring it altogether. Licensure requirements can leave little room for "special" topics in the methods classroom.

Fieldwork and engagement with special education faculty and staff in a variety of environments can assist music educators in finding ways to reach students with special needs. This chapter may appear to be designed for the music teacher educator. However, practicing music educators are encouraged to utilize the observation protocols and other strategies to obtain on-the-job and authentic experience through self-imposed fieldwork, observation, and discussion within the special education framework. This may be beneficial to music educators in understanding the subculture of students, parents, educators, and administrators that surround a student with special needs. This fieldwork may need to be conducted during preparation/planning time or through permission from an administrator.

For music teacher educators, this chapter is designed as a guide to develop fieldwork opportunities for pre-service music educators. Included in this chapter will be strategies for engagement in self-contained classrooms, resource rooms, inclusive settings, and summer enrichment programs. This chapter is designed to offer insights into this process and to provide strategies for optimizing fieldwork experience for the music teacher educator, the pre-service music teacher, and the cooperating teacher.

As mentioned in earlier chapters, the goal of the current special education system is to offer an appropriate education within the least restrictive environment. Students who are in need of special education attend classes in public school in a variety of settings to meet their specific needs. Parents of music students with special needs are becoming more active in advocating for equal access to curricula. Therefore, music educators, particularly those who work in elementary general music settings, often find themselves teaching at least part of their day within one or more different types of special education classes (described in this chapter). Music teacher educators can establish an outstanding fieldwork experience for methods students in this instance. Before these experiences are described in detail, this section will review the types of special education settings, and will provide an initial observation protocol to give music educators and music teacher educators ideas regarding the instructional goals in these learning environments.

BECOMING ACQUAINTED THROUGH OBSERVATION, ASSISTING, DISCUSSION, AND PLANNING

Many of the fieldwork and observation sites mentioned in this chapter may be different from other teaching and learning settings. Depending on the setting, it may be difficult initially to ascertain the curricular goals and objectives of these classrooms. Through research (Hammel, 1999; Hourigan, 2007a; Hourigan, 2007b), and personal experience teaching practicing music educators, the co-authors have found that music educators learn to teach students with special needs in a sometimes unique way. The following components are crucial for a successful fieldwork experience for both pre-service and in-service music teachers (observation; serving as a one-on-one assistant; discussion and coaching; reflection; and planning) to gain as much as possible through observation and participation in field experiences.

Observation has been mentioned (and protocols added) in previous chapters. Observation should happen at two levels. First, as discussed in chapter 1, music educators should observe with the intent to understand the student's needs in regard to the teaching and learning relationships that must develop between teacher and student. In the next section of this chapter we focus on the second level of observation, centered within the student's primary placement. These placements may have an impact on how music educators design, deliver, and assess instruction within the music classroom.

Serving as a one-on-one assistant allows music educators a small window into what a classroom and learning environment is like for a student with special needs. It will become clear how a student communicates, processes information, uses successful adaptations, as well as how his unique personality traits affect him in the learning environment. Often our in-service and pre-service students form bonds with students with special needs that are powerful and add to a rich learning environment for both student and teacher. This opportunity may also allow music educators to learn techniques from the current paraprofessional working with the student with special needs that may be useful in the music classroom.

Whether you are an experienced music educator or an aspiring in-service music educator, it is important to receive some coaching from experienced special educators or therapists when teaching students with special needs. There are nuances that music educators may not be accustomed to including as part of a typical music lesson (e.g., self-care, hand-over-hand assistance), and music educators will need strategies regarding how to include these adaptations appropriately. In addition, an experienced special educator may not know music content; however, they do know the challenges students face in the areas of language (e.g., speak too fast or use too many words), physical needs, and cognitive and sensory limitations. It is important to implement these ideas and to encourage a dialogue between all members of the team.

Reflection can occur in a number of ways. There are, however, important considerations when reflecting upon the improvement of music teaching with students who have learning differences. First, write strategies and thoughts down as soon as you finish teaching. Find time to sit and reflect on what just happened and how it may impact future lessons with students or the overall environment in the music classroom. Second, when finishing a long-term field placement (i.e., pre-service practicums or graduate-level fieldwork) take the time to reflect on the overall experience and how this influences your philosophy of music teaching. Students with special needs overcome obstacles that we often would never attempt and their experiences in music will impact them for a lifetime. Our ability to reflect on their goals and achievements will result in stronger teaching practices.

After reading the IEP or 504 Plan, attending an IEP or 504 Plan meeting, observing and assisting students or a specific student in their primary classroom setting, and reflecting on these experiences, music educators will be able to provide the foundation for planning future lessons with students with special needs. As part of this planning process, it is also important to be resourceful. Chapter 9 is devoted to providing current research and practitioner-oriented materials in music education, websites, and online tools.

In the area of music teacher education (i.e., practicum settings), we have found that peer-planned lessons (undergraduate students planning lessons together) in small groups work well for initial experiences in teaching music to students with special needs (Hourigan, 2007a). This has also worked well with other studies involving fieldwork (VanWeelden & Whipple, 2005). This allows for a step between observations and "solo" delivered lessons that can increase the confidence of new teachers who are attempting to teach for the first time. More of how this is implemented will be discussed later in this text.

TYPES OF FIELDWORK OPPORTUNITIES IN SPECIAL EDUCATION FOR PRE-SERVICE AND IN-SERVICE MUSIC EDUCATORS

Fieldwork in Self-contained Classrooms

Self-contained classrooms exist in public schools for a variety of educational reasons. The most common use of the self-contained setting is for students who would not be successful in an inclusive or integrated classroom. However, many self-contained classrooms are used to group students together who have similar needs (i.e., students who are intellectually gifted). More often, a self-contained classroom contains students who have a variety of learning needs. Typically a self-contained classroom has one lead teacher who is a certified special educator, and multiple paraprofessionals to assist that lead teacher. Within these classes it is important to observe the variety of instruction taking place. Typically there will be several different methods of instruction occurring together or in tandem (see figure 3.1).

There are many advantages to establishing a fieldwork setting in a self-contained classroom. First, there will obviously be a number of different students with special needs in this classroom with a wide range of learning styles. Second, many self-contained classrooms are grouped by disability. Therefore, in-service and pre-service music educators can gain strategies and understandings about how to teach students within a specific learning category. We have provided a fieldwork observation protocol (figure 3.2) for use in gaining insight into the goals of a self-contained classroom. The form provided is a framework regarding the type of questions used for effective reflection. However, they should not replace asking questions of the music teacher (who teaches in this setting) and the special educator when given the opportunity.

Skill-specific Grouping: Students are grouped together based on shared skills or abilities.

Heterogeneous Grouping: Students with mixed levels of understandings or skills are grouped together to learn from their peers.

Flexible Grouping: Using several types of groups at the same time.

Learning Centers: Organized self-instruction areas of a classroom used to promote independent learning.

Figure 3.1 Types of Instruction for Self-Contained Classrooms

Name: _____

Type of classroom setting (e.g., self-contained moderate disabilities): _____

Grade range:_____

Special Educator(s): _____

Music Educator: _____

Physical arrangement of classroom (e.g., centers; desks in rows):

Instructional goals articulated by the music educator (if visited by a music education student):

   • How these techniques might be used in the music classroom:

Instructional adaptations articulated by the special educator:

Types of learning groups observed (e.g., skill-specific or heterogeneous):

Specific music teaching and learning ideas for future use in self-contained music classrooms:

Assessment strategies used by the music educator/special educator:

Figure 3.2 Fieldwork Observation Protocols for Self-Contained or Resource Classrooms

Fieldwork Resource Rooms

A resource room is a type of self-contained classroom. It is designed for students who are partly or completely included in regular education classrooms. Students can attend these classrooms for a variety of reasons. Typically students attend resource rooms for assistance in specific subject areas or more detailed accommodations including intensified one-on-one instruction.

In-service and pre-service music educators may use an observation in a resource room to gain understanding of the instruction most beneficial when working with a specific student or small group of students. These strategies may also be used to teach music. For example, if a child attends a resource room for help in language or reading, similar learning goals could be applied to music class (e.g., visual vs. aural learning tools).

Fieldwork in Inclusive Classrooms

An inclusive classroom, as a philosophy of teaching, was discussed at length in previous chapters. There are, however, important factors to consider when observing and assisting a student within an inclusive setting to gain the appropriate understanding of how and why a student is included within that specific setting. A student may be included for a variety of reasons. These aims may include academic, social, and experiential goals.

The first consideration is whether or not a student is truly being included or is merely being mainstreamed into a classroom. Inclusion is a newer concept based on the idea that when initial placement decisions are made for a student (for Least Restrictive Environment purposes) the regular education classroom must be considered first before other settings and services are considered as additional assistance is needed. Mainstreaming is an older understanding based on the idea that a student may be mainstreamed into a subject (Lewis & Doorlag, 2006) from a special education setting. Often, mainstreaming was based on the premise that the student would be mainstreamed into the general classroom if his behavior and/or academic needs did not interrupt the learning of others in the classroom. We have found that the inclusion philosophy is far more beneficial for students with and without special needs, and that mainstreaming, while seemingly well intended at the time, does not reflect a true inclusive philosophy or provide the appropriate and Least Restrictive Environment for all students. However, not all students function well in either an inclusive or a mainstreamed schedule. There are instances where students need to start in an exclusively self-contained classroom. For these students, the self-contained classroom is the Least Restrictive Environment and will remain so until they are able to function best in a more inclusive environment.

In inclusive settings, the special education team is concerned with the whole school experience and the peer relationships that may develop as a result (Lewis & Doorlag, 2006). The idea is that if students are isolated from their peers, they will make assumptions about each other. In inclusive schools, all students are encouraged to attend and participate as a community of learners. The overall goal of inclusive schooling is to assist all students as they develop an increasing social awareness, understanding, and appreciation for differences within their community.

It is important that students who are included within regular education classrooms are placed correctly and are well supported (Lewis & Doorlag, 2006). In addition, it is critical that teachers who have a lack of experience in teaching students with special needs are also well supported in their efforts to provide the best education for all of their students. If a student participates in music class and is part of an inclusive environment, it is important to visit him or her in a class other than yours. A fieldwork protocol has been developed for use when visiting a student in an inclusive environment (see figure 3.3).

Fieldwork in Summer Enrichment Programs

Many students with special needs or who are at risk continue with some sort of school program (if available) during the summer. Proponents of such programs advocate that students with special needs need continuing education in the summer to maintain skills. Often schools with summer programs spend less time reviewing during the fall semester.

We (the co-authors) often send in-service music educators to these types of settings when teaching our summer graduate courses in teaching music to students with special needs. Summer enrichment programs are often easily accessible for teachers and provide a wealth of information, including getting to know special educators, teaching and classrooms management techniques, and a knowledge of the individual students you may be teaching in the fall semester. Oftentimes, these programs group students into self-contained classrooms based on ability (use the fieldwork protocol above, see figure 3.2).

Fieldwork in Specific Therapy Environments

Many students in special education receive related services provided by the school district. These services often include speech, occupational, and physical therapy. Other adjunct therapies are utilized when deemed necessary by the IEP Team. In addition, some school districts have music therapy or other arts-related therapy programs. In certain instances, it is important to visit

Student's name: _____

Grade range:_____

Special Educator(s) (including paraprofessionals and contact information):

Music Educator: _____ (If visited by a music education student)

Does the child have a full-time paraprofessional with him at all times?

- How does the paraprofessional assist with instruction?
- How might these strategies work in music?

Do the other students in the classroom appear to assist the teacher with this student?

Does the student appear to have a social group or a friend?

Instructional adaptations, accommodations, or modifications used either in music or other classes and settings:

How might these adaptations, accommodations, or modifications be used or changed in the future?

Notes:

Figure 3.3 Fieldwork and Observation Protocols for Inclusive Classroom Settings

students or observe them in these specific therapy settings. Music educators will gain insight into specific learning challenges such as language or physical obstacles that may be obstructing the ability of a student to learn in the music classroom. For example, if a child has speech challenges, it may be beneficial to observe the student in speech therapy. Consulting with the speech therapist after the session may provide insight into communication within the music classroom. Understanding how to make specific accommodations in these areas can be critical to a successful music classroom experience. A fieldwork protocol has been developed to give music educators (both pre-service and in-service) suggestions regarding what to look for in these settings (see figure 3.4).

Music Therapy and Music Education

A true text on teaching students with special needs is not complete without a discussion of music therapy, including how music therapists address the needs of their clients and how this can directly relate to the music educator. The American Music Therapy Association defines music therapy as an established health care profession that uses music to address the individual needs (nonmusical) of its clientele. In this context, think of the clientele as music students in your classroom. The needs of the students in the music education classroom are the following: cognitive, communication, behavioral or emotional, physical, and sensory.

These needs are similar to those discussed in this text; however, music therapists are concerned with developing goals for their clients based on their individual needs. For example, when developing goals for a child who is nonverbal, one must think of the needs of that specific child. With just the knowledge of a child being nonverbal, what needs would be evident? It is possible that this child will have difficulty interacting with his peers; therefore, a social goal might be appropriate. Also, the child has to be able to communicate with his peers whether he is verbal or not. Therefore a communication goal may be indicated. While these are not the only goals this child would need to work toward, this is the context in which goals are created.

Music therapists are more concerned with how music can assist in the development of nonmusical goals rather than skill sets. It is important for music educators and music therapists to collaborate and share knowledge of techniques used in each profession. It is also important for music teachers, whenever possible, to attend music therapy sessions in order to learn how to integrate individual developmental goals into a music lesson.

Student's name: _____

Age:_____

Therapist's name and contact information:

Type of Therapy (i.e., Speech, Occupational, Physical, Music, Other):

Therapy goals (articulated by the therapist):

How often does the child attend therapy?

Types of activities observed during therapy (including goals addressed):

Challenges observed:

Successes observed:

Potential uses in music education classrooms:

Figure 3.4 Fieldwork Protocols for Therapy Sessions

Creating Fieldwork Experiences with Students with Special Needs for Pre-service Music Educators

Integrating topics such as teaching students with disabilities is a common theme in the teacher education literature (York & Reynolds, 1996; Banks et al., 2005). Often, other program areas across campus are struggling with the same topics, and they may be open to collaborating on providing fieldwork for pre-service teachers. Vignette 3.1 is an example of how this can be achieved at the university level. This vignette will encourage ideas for further development of fieldwork in music teacher education.

Vignette 3.1 An Example of a Collaborative Special Needs Field Experience at the University Level

The Ball State University Prism Project: An Immersive Learning Fieldwork Opportunity for Music, Theatre, Dance, and Special Education Majors

It is well known throughout the special education community that many students with special needs struggle in developing and maintaining social relationships with peers. Oftentimes, because of their disabilities, students with disabilities become isolated from society and have higher incidence of depression as well as other mental health challenges. Due to changing legislation, increasing diagnosis rates, and a continued focus on inclusion within many teaching and learning environments (including the public school system), schools and partner programs such as arts are seeing an increased population of students with special needs.

The Ball State Prism Project is a Saturday afternoon program using the performing arts as a medium to explore and develop social skills for children ages 6-14 who are challenged with special needs. Annually, in the spring semester, the Prism Project presents a capstone performance of the music, theatre, and dance scenes that were created during the semester by Ball State students and the students with special needs who are enrolled in the project. The Prism Project is a partnership between the School of Music, the Department of Theatre and Dance, Interlock: The East Central Indiana Autism Society of America, and Sibshops (a program for siblings of children with special needs). A music therapist is also on staff to provide assistance in integrating all of the disciplines and to provide insight into appropriate techniques for the performers.

Ball State University students are directly involved in the creation, implementation, organization, administration, and production of this project within an authentic teaching and learning environment. This project gives each Ball State student a unique opportunity to test his or her skills as a teaching artist within an authentic setting serving as one-on-one assistants, coordinating programming and planning, and administrating this program. On a pragmatic level, each student is required to

(continued)

Vignette 3.1 (continued)

attend collaborative plenary meetings that will be chaired by the student leadership. At this time, lesson plans are developed, scenes are created, and music is composed based on the needs of the students who are enrolled in the project. This is an authentic environment that allows Ball State students to improve their skills. Ball State students receive a variety of academic credits while being involved in the program (e.g., fieldwork hours, and observation hours).

Many music education, music performance, theatre education, and theatre performance majors have had little or no experience in teaching students with special needs. Increased curricular and licensure requirements have left little time for training arts educators to teach students with special needs. This lack of experience may deter them from including students with disabilities in their own future programs.

The Prism Project serves to enhance the lifelong learning for three groups of people who will be involved in this project. First, the students with special needs that enroll in the project are, through engagement with the arts, developing enhanced potential for lifelong learning. The Ball State students have more experience with children with disabilities and therefore possess tools necessary to include them within their future programs. Finally, the parents not only get a few hours of much-needed respite but they have an opportunity to see their children perform.

Visit us on the web at: http://prismproject.iweb.bsu.edu. This website includes show clips, interviews of participants, and interviews with performers.

CONCLUSION

Fieldwork experiences are the cornerstone for provision of near authentic practice teaching to inexperienced educators as well as for educators seeking to increase their effectiveness when working with students with special needs. Research has shown that fieldwork with students in diverse learning environments increases confidence, understanding, and reflective thinking ability among pre-service and in-service educators (Barry, 1996; Emmanuel, 2002; Fant, 1996; Hourigan, 2007a; Hourigan, 2007b; VanWeelden and Whipple, 2005). Current in-service music educators, music teacher educators, and pre-service music educators will benefit from opportunities to incorporate understandings and materials provided in this chapter. In addition, music educators may find their overall goals and philosophy change as a result of working with students who overcome challenges to learn music. Music has many access points for all students. A team approach that encourages dialogue and the sharing of strategies and information through engagement will enhance music teaching and learning in music classrooms.

DISCUSSION QUESTIONS

1. What are the advantages or disadvantages of fieldwork in a special needs setting?
2. Discuss the steps mentioned in this chapter and how you plan to implement each step in your future fieldwork.
3. Discuss your experiences (if you have had them) in each type of special education environment.
4. Discuss your experiences (if you have had them) serving as a one-on-one assistant to a student with special needs.

REFERENCES

Banks, J., Cochran-Smith, M., Moll, L., Richert, A., Zeichner, K., & LePage, P. (2005). Teaching diverse learners. In L. Darling Hammond & J. Bransford (Eds.), *Preparing teachers for a changing world* (pp. 232–274). San Francisco: Jossey-Bass.

Barry, N. H. (1996). *The effects of special training and field experiences upon preservice teachers' level of comfort with multicultural teaching situations.* Paper presented at the annual meeting of the American Educational Research Association, New York.

Emmanuel, D. (2002). *A music education immersion internship: Pre-service teachers' beliefs concerning teaching music in a culturally diverse setting.* Unpublished doctoral dissertation, Michigan State University, East Lansing.

Fant, G. R. (1996). *An investigation of the relationships between undergraduate music education students' early field experience and student teaching performance.* Unpublished Doctoral Dissertation, The University of Arizona, Tucson.

Hammel, A. M. (1999). *A study of teacher competencies necessary when including special learners in elementary music classrooms: The development of a unit of study for use with undergraduate music education students* (Doctoral dissertation, Shenandoah University, 1999) *Dissertation Abstracts International,* 40–10A, 5299.

Heller, L. (1994). *Undergraduate music teacher preparation for mainstreaming: A survey of music education teacher training institutions in the Great Lakes region of the United States.* Unpublished doctoral dissertation, Michigan State University, East Lansing.

Hourigan, R. M. (2007a) *Teaching Music to Students with Special Needs: A Phenomenological Examination of Participants in a Fieldwork Experience.* Doctoral Dissertation, The University of Michigan. (ISBN # 9780549174868/VDM Verlag (2008) ISBN#: 978-3-8364-7663-8).

Hourigan, R. M. (2007b). Music majors as paraprofessionals: A study in special needs field experience for preservice music educators. *Contributions to Music Education, 34,* 19–34.

Lewis, R. B., & Doorlag, D. H. (2006). *Teaching special students in general education classrooms*. Upper Saddle River, NJ: Prentice Hall.

VanWeelden, K., & Whipple, J. (2005). The effects of field experience on music education majors' perceptions of music instruction for secondary students with special needs. *Journal of Music Teacher Education, 14*(2), 62–68.

Wilson, B., & McCrary, J. (1996). The effect of instruction on music educators' attitudes toward students with disabilities. *Journal of Research in Music Education, 44*(1), 26–33.

York, J. L., & Reynolds, M. C. (1996). Special education and inclusion. In J. Sikula (Ed.), *Handbook of Research on Teacher Education* (2nd ed., pp. 820–836). New York: Simon & Schuster Macmillan.

Chapter 4

A Resourceful and Pedagogical Approach to Teaching Students with Special Needs

---

Vignette 4.1 Gregory

Gregory Smith is a second grader, age eight. Gregory attended Head Start at age four. He adjusted well to school and liked it. Gregory loved the gross motor activities both in and outside like swings climbers, and big blocks. He enjoyed water play, the sand table, and listening to music. He showed age-appropriate social development. Gregory's health screening revealed he suffered from frequent ear infections and colds. His speech screening showed mispronunciations of w, s, th, and l in all positions. The speech teacher also noted that Gregory did not focus visually on her during assessment. He did not seem to pick up on subtleties in language such as plurals and possessives. His teachers reported that he had difficulty following directions, attending to stories, and answering questions. He also had trouble with tool control and generally did not choose centers that involved fine motor control.

Gregory's kindergarten teacher reported that Gregory was a sociable youngster who enjoyed school. He was good at singing and seemed to learn the alphabet and other things through music. His math skills were age-appropriate. He exhibited great difficulty with concentration on rhyming activities and associating sounds with alphabet letters. In oral language, Gregory often used incorrect noun-verb agreement and he often had trouble selecting the correct word when speaking. His lack of progress in pre-reading and writing prompted his teacher to refer him to the Child Study Team.

Music is Gregory's favorite class. He looks forward to seeing Mrs. Fletcher each week. He waits for Thursdays all week long! He seems to veer away from Orff Instruments when given a choice in the classroom. He has trouble focusing on Mrs. Fletcher during group instruction. He

(continued)

Vignette 4.1 (continued)

can, at times, be a distraction to other students. Gregory also has difficulty waiting his turn because he is so excited about being in his favorite class. He wants to answer all the questions and pick his instrument first—perhaps to avoid instruments requiring fine motor skills. Mrs. Fletcher finds this lack of attention confusing because he likes music class so much. Gregory has difficulty relating to peers who often tease him because of his differences.

Now, consider the following questions:

- What is the dilemma? Briefly outline the issues to be addressed.
- Who are the stakeholders in this scenario? Who will be most affected by the actions to be taken?
- Draft a brief solution. Are there alternate solutions available?

PARTICIPATION IN THE PROCESS/GATHERING SUPPORT

The vignette regarding Gregory introduces an approach to teaching students with special needs that may be new for many music educators (and music education students). Collegiate students are not always given the opportunity to think critically and constructively about adaptations and accommodations for students with special needs prior to graduation from undergraduate school (Hammel, 1999; Nocera, 1979). Skills developed while brainstorming ideas for students via vignettes may assist music educators as they derive strategies for students with special needs in music classrooms. This skill preparation also introduces the idea of a "team approach" when interacting with faculty, administration, students, and families (Ansuini, 1979; Atterbury, 1993). For these reasons, vignettes are included within the text to encourage this process when preparing to teach students with special needs.

The most effective approach when working within a school and school system is to become a part of the existing team of professionals (Dalrymple, 1993). Teachers often become compartmentalized when teaching music in another part of the building or when traveling from building to building. Successful child-centered schools function as teams, and active participation is important for each individual teacher as well as for the overall success of the school (Gfeller, Darrow, & Hedden, 1990; Gilbert & Asmus, 1981; Heller, 1994; Williams, 1988). Being proactive and positive can assist teachers as they become involved as integral "team members" within a school. Maintaining a positive and inclusive attitude will increase the view that the music program is an important and necessary component of school life for all students (Ozonoff, Rogers, & Hendren, 2003; Pierce & Schreibman, 1997; Wagner, 1999).

Being aware of the students in the music classroom, as well as their academic and behavioral needs, is a critical initial strategy in developing an inclusive scope and sequence for classrooms and ensembles (Hart & Risley, 1975; Prizant & Wetherby, 1998). Knowing that we teach students, with music as a catalyst, and that students come to the music classroom with a variety of independent and individualized needs is important to inclusive-oriented music educators.

Another important initial technique in this process is to review class lists with a guidance counselor, special education teacher/staff member, or administrator to determine the students in music classes who have special needs (McGee, Almeida, & Sulzer-Azaroff, 1992; Thorp, Stahmer, & Schreibman, 1995). Many of these students will have an IEP or 504 Plan on file at the school. These documents are critical as strategies, accommodations, and adaptations are developed to include all students in the music classroom (Coe, Matson, & Fee, 1990). More strategies concerning these documents will be discussed later in this chapter.

SPEAKING WITH SPECIAL EDUCATION PROFESSIONALS AND STAFF

Special education faculty members will be able to provide a great deal of information about effective inclusion practices for a particular student (Stronge, 2007). Welcoming them into the music classroom and asking for assistance is a way to begin this process. When other faculty members know that you are actively seeking strategies, it increases the sense of teamwork in your school (Wang, Haertel, & Walberg, 1993/1994; Weiss & Pasley, 2004). Individual special education teachers have areas of strength, just as we all do, and it is appropriate to ask for their input regarding behavior strategies, adaptive equipment, understanding special education paperwork, and other issues that may arise as inclusion strategies are designed. Each of us brings a unique skill set to the educational environment, and we all appreciate being recognized for our contributions (Shellard & Protheroe, 2000). Reaching out to colleagues and being gracious in accepting assistance are powerful pieces to the team building process (Rowan, Chiang, & Miller, 1997).

A very important, and sometimes overlooked, member of the team is the paraprofessional (or aide). These professionals are employed by the school system to work with a specific student, or small group of students, during the school day. They sometimes travel with a student on the bus to school, and may stay with the student for the entire day as well as the trip home. Paraprofessionals assist the student with daily tasks, mobility within the school, and behavior management. According to Adamek and Darrow (2005): "Paraprofessionals can be an enormous help assisting the student, the music specialists, and the other students" (p. 62). They know the student very well and, unfortunately, they are sometimes not included and considered as full members of the school team. It is critical that music educators develop relationships with paraprofessionals. This advocacy skill is imperative when requesting that paraprofessionals work with students in music classrooms, particularly when music educators perceive this will increase the appropriateness of an educational setting for a student with special needs (Pressley, Raphael, Gallagher, & DiBella, 2004).

You, as the music teacher, are a part of the "Child Study," or IEP, team, and your input is important in the process. Once music educators are aware of the needs of students in the music classroom through studying student documents and speaking with classroom teachers and special education teachers, the true preparation of instruction that will reach all students can begin. While teaching, take data (notes, charts, brief notations) regarding academic and behavioral struggles and successes of students with special needs. This preparation will be very beneficial as it enhances the sense of teamwork with other members of the IEP team (see observation protocols in chapter 1).

PARENT PARTNERSHIPS

A recurring theme in this text is the goal of creating a channel of communication with parents of students with disabilities. It is important for music teachers to understand that this may be difficult. Parents may be under financial hardship or even in denial about their child's disability. Attempt to keep these conversations about music teaching and learning. The following questions are examples of how you may choose to approach a parent: (a) How might I assist Jennifer in my class? (b) Jennifer is having trouble sitting in her seat during class. What strategies do you use at home in this situation? (c) Jennifer sometimes becomes anxious and upset when we do movement activities in music class. Is there a way I can make this experience more comfortable for her?

It is often helpful to not mention knowledge regarding a special need. Let the parent begin this discussion (unless both persons involved in the discussion have been in the same IEP or 504 meeting). Once the parent does begin to discuss the special need, the music educator may then acknowledge an awareness of the need. This recommendation is made because, in many ways, students with special needs are just like students without special needs. There are times when their behaviors and academic challenges are the result of being a child who is learning rather than a student with a disability. Remember, students with special needs have often experienced failure in many areas. The last thing a parent wants to hear is that music class is next on the list of things his child cannot do. Keep conversations positive and maintain a problem-solving attitude when communicating with parents.

It is also important to begin and end conversations by relating successes and areas of strength noticed during music instruction.

INDIVIDUALIZED EDUCATION PROGRAMS (IEP) AND 504 PLANS

All IEPs and/or 504 Plans follow a similar structure; however, different states, and school systems, are given the latitude to create their own template for these plans based on general guidelines presented in the law. All IEPs contain: (a) a statement of the child's present levels of academic achievement and functional performance; (b) measurable goals statements (academic and functional); (c) benchmarks and short-term objectives for students who take alternate assessments; (d) how progress will be measured and when reports will be provided (reports must be provided at least as often as reports for students without disabilities are provided); (e) for students participating in alternate assessments, a statement as to why and which assessment will be included; (f) an initial evaluation that is conducted within 60 days of parental consent for evaluation (or within the timeframe chosen by a state); (g) transition services for children 16 years of age or older; (h) a stipulation that the child must be present when post-secondary goals and transitions are considered—or the child's interests must be considered.

Figure 4.1 is a portion of an actual IEP. The section represented below is Joshua's present level of academic achievement narrative that was written by his primary teacher of record. This particular statement was completed at the end of his kindergarten year.

Figure 4.2 represents a goals page in an actual IEP for the same student, Joshua. The challenges a student encounters, basic needs, and goals are clearly represented in the present level of academic functioning narrative. As is apparent when viewing this IEP, music educators can get a great deal of information about students prior to having a student with special needs in music class. There are clear, measurable goals set forth by the members of the team. Goals can be set in each academic area as well as each therapy domain (e.g., speech, physical, occupational, etc.). The team evaluates each goal annually.

An imperative consideration to note from this specific page (figure 4.2) is Joshua's unique language skills. He can receive much more than he can express. This may require a music educator to observe Joshua in other classes to see how teachers communicate with him. In addition, it is clear in figure 4.2 that Joshua has difficulty with peer relationships. This might mean careful consideration for turn taking, group interaction, partner songs, and other such interactive lessons in the music classroom. Finding a student to place next to him that will model good peer relationships would benefit Joshua.

Notice the key at the bottom of the page. This details how, when, and what criterion will be used to determine whether a student has reached a

Present Level of Academic Achievement and Functional Performance (PLAAFP)

Specify the Student Needs for Learning: What is the student's level of functioning and how does the disability affect his or her involvement in and progress in the general education curriculum?

    Josh is finishing up his kindergarten year at Abbot Elementary School. Josh was in school for a full day, spending the first half of his day in a general education kindergarten class with a one-on-one teaching assistant. The second half of his day was spent in a special education, self-contained classroom (without the additional one-on-one teaching assistant). The ratio in his special education classroom averaged 3 teachers to 3-4 students. Josh has improved greatly with his independence in transitioning to and from classes and with taking care of his personal belongings. He continues to need prompting to follow through with transition and routine tasks and to stay in the designated area. Wandering and gazing are very reinforcing for Josh, and he frequently gets side-tracked during transitions and direction following. Josh is able to comprehend simple verbal directions, he does best with visual/written directions. Josh's initial reaction when given an assignment is to oppose. He needs adult prompting to start, follow through with and complete and assignment. He has difficulty engaging in unfamiliar tasks. Once the tasks become familiar, he shows less resistance. Josh does not like loud areas, he wears headphones when attending an assembly. He also has a difficult time remaining in his seat. These 2 behaviors make it difficult for Josh to eat in the cafeteria with his peers. Josh wears underwear to school. He does not initiate using the toilet and he often protests when asked to use the toilet. Josh is able to manipulate his clothing and he needs prompting as to where he is in completing the bathroom process. Josh has had approximately 10 toileting accidents at school or during his transition to/from school. Joshua is in progress with all of his independence goals (see attached goal pages). He is working on moving with his class form one area to the next with a whole group routine direction, completing arrival and departure routines with a whole group directive and visual supports, sequencing daily activities, gathering needed materials, working independently and following a schedule for using the bathroom.

    Josh is a very adorable and social guy. He loves being in school and likes to watch and take interest in his peers from a distance. Josh loves music, however, he is quite the perfectionist when it comes to music and the musical abilities of others. At the beginning of the school year Josh had difficulty going into the music room and listening to people sing aloud! Josh is very engaging and loves sharing various pieces of information (typically in a stereotypical, rote manner) with the adults in his environment. He likes to watch his peers and report their actions to an adult. Josh has recently started to initiate physical interactions with his peers when he wants an item from them. He has also demonstrated the ability to initiate a comment to a peer when the peer is engaged in something that Josh enjoys. When a peer initiates an interaction with Josh, Josh typically ignores the peer's comment or request. Josh is in progress with both of his social/emotional/behavioral goals (see attached goal page). He is working on requesting his peers to perform actions and responding to his peers for multiple exchanges.

    Josh's ability to decode is far above his ability to comprehend what he reads. He is ahead of target and comprehending at a level E (roughly a beginning first grade level). Josh has difficulty and little interest in focusing on the teacher, attending to tasks and remaining seated for group times (approximate 5 minutes or less). His self-stimulatory behaviors interfere with group instruction (vocalizations, stimming on materials, wandering, gazing). Josh is in progress with all of his reading comprehension goals (see attached goal page). He is working on verbally retelling a story with a beginning/middle and end, answering WH questions and making personal comments/connections to a story.

    Josh is right handed and holds a regular pencil either with a painter's grasp or a static/arm off the table tripod. He is able to hold a short pencil with a static tripod 4:5x without prompting and his forearm is more likely to be resting on the table. Josh is able to copy short words with legible letters 4:5 x but attention is typically inconsistent and letters are unlikely to be on or close to the line. When copying a sentence that he is able to read, Josh will slant down from one line to the next without recognition of his error. Josh sometime protests loudly when asked to complete a writing activity. He responds well to first this/ then this, and adult start prompt with the adult then walking away which seems to help Josh remember what he is suppose to be doing. He is able to fill in to complete a prestarted picture.

    Josh is in progress with all of his math goals (see attached goal page). He is working on identifying and forming groups of 0-5, using abstract language associated with math concepts and using 1:1 correspondence to count, compare and order sets of objects to 10. Joshua is able to rote count to 100+, and he is able to count by 10's to 100 with adult demonstartion. He knows basic concpets such as big/little/medium, heavy/light, sorting, and simple patterning. He is understands basic measuring and weight concpets. Josh has difficulty counting by 2's and 5's, graphing objects and is not able to add or subtract numbers.

The Clinical Evaluation of Language Fundamentals Preschool-2 was administered to determined Josh's current language strengths and weaknesses. Josh scored 2-3 standard deviations below the mean in receptive/expressive language skills. While he demonstrated skill in following one-step auditory directions involving size relationships as 'point to the big_____', he experienced difficulty recognizing likenesses among objects in order to form categories and identify things that were the same/match. Spatial and sequential markers as next to and before/after also proved difficult for Josh.

Figure 4.1 IEP Present Level of Academic Functioning Statement

particular goal. This particular goal area is speech. Many speech and language goals can be addressed in music and often students experience similar challenges in music. In Joshua's case, simplified language in music class with visual reinforcement would be excellent accommodations to add after viewing this page of his IEP. Music educators should also consider that Joshua has a reduced vocabulary. Using a simplified vocabulary that includes fewer words in music class will help Joshua succeed.

    The next section of the IEP (figure 4.3) represents how a school district fulfills the Least Restrictive Environment (LRE) of IDEA. Notice that this

Data Used to Determine Present Level of Academic Achievement and Functional Performance

Present Level of Performance Data: Josh's expressive language was characterized by reduced vocabulary, pronoun confussion and deletion of verb markers.

Annual Goal:

To improve expressive language

Short-Term Objectives (at least two per goal)	Evaluation	Criterion	Schedule
1. J. will name pictures within categories describing their similarities as "fruits, clothes"	S	On 4 out of 5 trials	G
2. J. will a. appropriately use personal pronouns (he, she, you, I) b. produce a noun-verb-object sentence incorporating the auxillary verb "is" when shown a picture stimulus	S	On 4 out of 5 trials	G
3. J. will produce pronoun-verb-object sentences when shown a picture stimulus	S	On 4 out of 5 trials	G

Date	Status Obj. 1	Status Obj. 2	Status Obj. 3	Comments/Data On Progress
3/17/06	4	2	4	
6/16/06	2	2	2	

Evaluation	Criterion	Schedule	Status of Progress on Objectives
S Student's Daily Work	%	W Weekly	1 Achieve/Maintained
D Documented Observation	Accuracy of Rate	D Daily	2 Progressing at a rate sufficient to meet the annual goal for this objectives
R Rating Scale		M Monthly	3 Progressing below a rate sufficient to meet the annual goal for this objective (explain above)
T Standardized Test	Achievement Level	G Grading Period	4 Not applicable during this reporting period
O Other (specify above)	Other (specify above)	O Other (specify above)	5 Other (specify above)

Reporting Progress

The parents will be regularly informed in writing of progress on goals objectives of this IEP at the regular reporting periods applicable to general education students. Additional reporting:

How:		When:	

Figure 4.2 Academic Goals Page (from an IEP)

page is distinctly concerned with placing Joshua in a learning environment that is best for him, his teacher, and the other students. This includes the number of hours Joshua will attend regular education and special education classes per week, extra-curricular activities, and support services.

Music educators looking at figure 4.3 should consider how these accommodations will enhance Joshua's experience in music class. It is clear that a picture schedule (see later in this chapter) would assist with his anxiety about transitions. Based on figure 4.3, music educators should modify tests and assignments. Also, it is clear from this page that Joshua needs one-on-one support during music class. Joshua also needs very frequent repetition and simplification of directions. Therefore, simple classroom routines in music class need reinforcement (e.g., redirect or repetition from aide).

The present level of academic functioning statement, along with goals pages in other areas are important pieces of information for music educators.

Least Restrictive Environment

This student will:

Fully participate with students who are nondisabled in the general education setting except for the time spent in separate special education programs/services provided outside of the general education classroom as specified in this IEP.

☒ Yes ☐ No (Expalin):

Be fully involved in and make progress in the general education curriculum.

☐ Yes ☒ No (Expalin): student participates with accomodations, some of his day is spent in special education classroom.

Have the same opportunity as general education students to participate in nonacademic and extracurricular activities.
☒ Yes ☐ No (Expalin):

Programs ans Services

Supplementary Aids/Services/Personnel Support

Supplementary Aids/Services/Support	Time/Frequency/Conditions	Beginning Mo/Day/Yr.	*Ending Mo/Day/Yr.	Setting
1. Visual schedules / supports 2. ASD coordinator	1. daily 2. daily	6-14-06 First day of school 06-07 year	6-17-06 6-14-07	Elementary School
3. Pre-teaching of material / concepts	3. daily	6-14-06 First day of school 06-07 year	6-17-06 6-14-07	Elementary School
4. general education setting 5. Modified assignments / tests (multiple choice, paraphrasing questions)	4. 27.85-29.85 hours/week 5. daily	6-14-06 First day of school 06-07 year	6-17-06 6-14-07	Elementary School
6. additional adult support during general education setting for safety, social interactions, academics, personal care	6. daily	6-14-06 First day of school 06-07 year	6-17-06 6-14-07	Elementary School
7. Repetition of directions / check for comprehension of directions given 8. Priority seating	7. daily 8. daily	6-14-06 First day of school 06-07 year	6-17-06 6-14-07	Elementary School

All supplementary aids, services, and supports listed above will begin on the initiation date of the IEP as indicated on the signature page, following the approved school district calendar. ☒ Yes or ☐ No. If no. comment: _____

Special Education Programs/Related Services
Is there a need for a teacher with a particular endorsement? ☒ No ☐ Yes, specify:
Resources Program Only:
Is a Teacher Consultant with endorsement matching the student's disability needed? ☒ No ☐ Yes
Departmentalized Program (R 340.1749c) ☒ No ☐ Yes

Figure 4.3 Least Restrictive Environment Page (from an IEP)

It would be ideal for the music educator to gain access and review the IEP prior to instruction. Typically, IEPs are on file in the school or district office. Members of the special education team (and the music educator is part of the team) are required to have access to these files.

504 PLANS

Students who have a disability that is included in IDEA, yet, the severity of their disability does not require them to have the level of services of an IEP, or students who have a disability not included in IDEA, may participate in instruction under a 504 Plan rather than an IEP. 504 Plans are derived from

Section 504 of the 1973 Health and Rehabilitation Act. A 504 Plan is put in place to "level the playing field" for a student so that she receives equal access to educational opportunities. A 504 Plan includes adaptations to the general classroom environment for a student with special needs. These plans do not require staff members to monitor progress and do not include supplementary aides and services (personnel) to achieve equal access to education. Some common 504 accommodations include: an extra set of books at home, extra time on classroom assignments and assessments, separate or quiet areas when participating in assessments, preferential seating, frequent progress reports, use of a calculator or spell checker, use of a computer or keyboard for written assignments, reduction in amount of assignments or homework, and behavior plans. These plans are legal documents, as are IEPs, and it is both the right and responsibility of all music educators to follow all accommodations and adaptations listed on 504 Plans (CASE, 1999).

An example of a 504 Plan for a middle school student is listed below. The template for the document varies by school district and state. The information included in a 504 Plan, however, is fairly consistent throughout the United States. The 504 Plan will list the strengths and challenges a student experiences, the accommodations required for state level testing procedures, classroom accommodations and modifications, and any other specific information necessary to the equal inclusion of that student in the classroom. These accommodations will not be music specific, and it is the responsibility of the music educator to transfer these strategies to the music classroom.

Listed below are the accommodations listed in the example 504 Plan for a middle school student.

Underneath the general accommodations list of the 504 Plan for Jane Doe, we have created a list of strategies for the music classroom based on the 504 Accommodations for Jane Doe. These are included in italics. Almost every accommodation listed on a 504 Plan can be implemented in the music classroom. The following are examples of accommodations and music specific accommodations:

1. Copies of notes from teachers

This student will need notes from the teacher of anything written on the chalk, white, or Smart Board. She may be unable to take adequate notes while attending to instruction in a music class or ensemble situation. Anything stated during class should be written or copied for the student to include in her materials for music class.

2. Extended time to complete all classroom assignments

This student may have great difficulty completing assignments in the standard amount of time. This may include composition or improvisation assignments,

Jane Doe
Student ID:
FTE Number:
Date of Birth:

Somerset Public Schools
111 Elm St.
Somerset VA 11111
111-111-1111

Accommodations/Modifications	
	Date:
Student's Name: Jane Doe Student ID Number: 111111	

This student will be provided access to the general education, special education, other school services and activities including non-academic activities and extracurricular activities, and education related settings:

    with no accommodations/modifications
    X with the following accommodations/modifications

Accommodations/modifications provided as part of the instructional and testing/assessment process will allow the student equal opportunity to access the curriculum and demonstrate achievement. Accommodations/modifications will provide access to non-academic and extracurricular activities and educationally related settings. Accommodations/modifications based solely on the potential to enhance performance beyond providing equal access are inappropriate.

Accommodations may be in, but not limited to, the areas of time, scheduling, setting, presentation, and response. The impact of any modifications listed should be discussed. This includes the earning of credits for graduation.

Figure 4.4 (Continued)

Accommodations/Modifications   (please list, as appropriate):

Accommodation(s)/Modification(s)	Frequency	Location	Duration m/d/y to m/d/y
Content Area Copies of notes from teachers.	As needed.	SPS	01/01/0000 - 01/01/0000
Extended time to complete all classroom assignments.	Always	SPS	
Use of classroom computer when lengthy assignments are given	As needed	SPS	
Environmental Preferential seating near teacher	As needed	SPS	
General Extra set of books at home for all subjects.	During school year	SPS	
Organization Study guides should be provided.	Prior to testing	SPS	
Testing Accommodation Extended time to take test.	As needed	SPS	
Use of calculator/multiplication chart.	During math class when related to instruction	SPS	
Write answers in test booklet for all test including SOL test	As Needed	SPS	

504 Plan   Somerset Public Schools Exceptional Education Dept.   Page

Figure 4.4 ((Continued)

Jane Doe
Student ID:
FTE Number:
Date of Birth:

Somerset Public Schools
111 Elm St.
Somerset VA 11111
111-111-1111

Accommodations/Modifications	

State and District-Wide Assessments

This student's participation in state or district-wide assessments must be considered and discussed. During the duration of this 504 Plan:

Will the student be at an age or a grade level for which the student is eligible to participate in state or district-wide assessment?	☐ No ■ Yes
Will the student be enrolled in a course for which there is a SOL End-of-Course test or district-wide-assessment?	☐ No ■ Yes
Will the student be participating in a SOL remediation recovery program?	■ No ☐ Yes
Will the student need to take a state assessment as a requirement to earn a Modified Standard Diploma, Standard Diploma, or Advanced Studies Diploma?	☐ No ■ Yes

Figure 4.4 (Continued)

70

If Yes to an of the above, check the assessment(s) considered and attach the assessment page(s), which will document the assessments and decisions made about participation and any needed accommodations and/or modifications.

■ State Assessments
- ■ SOL Assessments and retake (SOL)
- ☐ Virginia Grade Level Alternative (VGLA)*
- ☐ Virginia Substitute Evaluation Program (VSEP)*
- ☐ Other State Approved Substitute(s)
- ■ District Wide Assessments (list)
  - ■ Benchmark Test- Science, Math, History, English. All state wide and school given test.

* Refer to Procedures for Determining Participation in the Assessment Component of Virginia's Accountability System and the Procedural Manuals for VGLA and VSEP.

504 Plan

Page

Somerset Public Schools Exceptional Education Dept.

Figure 4.4 (Continued)

Jane Doe
Student ID:
FTE Number:
Date of Birth:

Somerset Public Schools
111 Elm St.
Somerset VA 11111
111-111-1111

Virginia's Standards of Learning Assessments	
Student's Name: Jane Doe	Date:
Student ID Number: 1111111	

Participation In The SOL Assessments

For the student who will be (1) in a grade level for which the student is eligible to participate in the SOL Assessment; (2) enrolled in a course for which there is an SOL end-of-course test; (3) participating in a remediation recovery program or (4) needs to take a SOL Assessment as a requirement to earn a Modified Standard Diploma, Standard Diploma, or Advanced Studies Diploma, list each test below. Next determine if the student will participate in the SOL test and then list the accommodation(s) and/or modification(s) that will be made based upon those the student generally uses during classroom instruction and assessment. For the accommodations and/or modifications that may be considered, refer to "Accommodations/Modifications" page of the 504 Plan and the Virginia Board of Education's guidelines.

Figure 4.4 (Continued)

72

- State Assessments
  - ■ SOL Assessments and retake (SOL)
  - □ Virginia Grade Level Alternative (VGLA)*
  - □ Virginia Substitute Evaluation Program (VSEP)*
  - □ Other State Approved Substitute(s)

* Refer to Procedures for Determining Participation in the Assessment Component of Virginia's Accountability System and the Procedural Manuals for VGLA and VSEP.

SOL Tests	Participation	Accommodations Modifications	If YES, List Accommodation(s) and/or Modification(s) by Test
SOL ALGEBRA I	■ Yes □ No	■ Yes □ No	Extended time to take test. Use of calculator/multiplication chart. Write answers in test booklet for all tests including SOL test.
SOL EARTH SCIENCE	■ Yes □ No	■ Yes □ No	Extended time to take test. Write answers in test booklet for all test s including SOL test.
SOL GRADE 8 CIVICS & ECONOMICS	■ Yes □ No	■ Yes □ No	Extended time to take test. Write answers in test booklet for all test including SOL test.
SOL GRADE 8 READING	■ Yes □ No	■ Yes □ No	Extended time to take test. Write answers in test booklet for all tests including SOL test.

Figure 4.4 (Continued)

73

Mark any nonstandard administration with an asterisk*. These test scores will be reported as scores that result from a nonstandard administration. A student with a disability who has passed an SOL assessment utilizing any accommodation including a nonstandard accommodation has passed for all purposes.

Explanation For Non-Participation And How The Student Will Be Assessed:

If no is checked for any test, explain in the space below why the student will not participate in this test, the impact relative to promotion or graduation, and how the student will be assessed in these areas.

504 Plan   Page

Somerset Public Schools Exceptional Education Dept.

Figure 4.4 [IEP]

timed playing or scales testing, writing in phrases, breath marks, or noting dynamic markings, numbering measures, learning drill for marching band, memorizing music, creating rhythms or melody patterns in elementary music, or studying sight-reading material prior to singing or playing.

3. Use of classroom computer when lengthy assignments are given

This student may need accommodations when asked to write papers about composers or other music topics. She may not be able to adequately express herself during short answer, description, or essay responses (in writing) and may need to respond orally instead. She may need to use a keyboard to organize her thoughts prior to speaking. This may affect a music classroom that includes music theory, history, or extensive long-form responses regarding performance practice or compositional styles. This accommodation sometimes indicates a challenge in the area of fine motor control that can also lead to difficulties in using mallets, rhythm percussion instruments, and the fine motor control necessary to play an instrument.

4. Preferential seating by teacher

Transferring this accommodation to the music classroom or ensemble can be difficult. In elementary music, this can be accomplished by seating a student near instruction (the instruments being played, the book shown during a lesson, or the board where rhythmic and tonal patterns will be presented). In the secondary ensemble classroom, students with this accommodation often need to be seated near the conductor, piano, or front of the classroom to increase attention and focus during instruction. If a student has earned a "chair" in an ensemble, the first placement should be the one they have earned. Other placements may be considered as needed and in consultation with the student, parents, and other teachers.

5. Extra set of books at home for all subjects

Students in music classes are often asked to have materials in class and then to use those materials at home as they prepare for class. The transfers of this accommodation to the music classroom include recorders, music, octavos, instruments, music stands, lyres, and method books. If no additional materials are available and these are clearly needed by the student, the special education department may have funding to assist with providing these additional materials for a student.

6. Study guides should be provided

A student with this accommodation may have great difficulty inferring possible test questions, performance expectations, and may not be able to comprehend the information a teacher relays prior to an assessment. Before engaging in any assessment, it will be very important for this student to be aware of the exact knowledge, skills, and information she needs to succeed. This includes the exact scales (including the rhythm expected for the scale) or passages of music she will be asked to perform, a detailed outline of each subject to be included on a written assessment, and the type of questions on the test. This outline can include the way a question will be presented – for example, will the key signatures be listed and the student asked to name them or will a blank staff be listed and the student asked to write the key signature? This is a critical distinction for a student who needs this type of accommodation.

7. Extended time to take tests

Timed tests can be unfair for students who are not able to recall information quickly. When we ask students to do this, we are measuring the amount of time required to display their knowledge, rather than the knowledge itself. Students who need extended time to take tests may need un-timed scale tests, more time to complete singing or playing tests, more opportunities to respond to a rhythm or singing assessment in elementary music, and may need to perform the test in an adjacent room or bring the completed test back to class after finishing it by using a tape recorder (or burning a cd).

8. Use of calculator or multiplication chart

This accommodation can signify a challenge in the area of memorization of facts and other information. Students who have this accommodation listed on their 504 Plan may have difficulty recalling note names and patterns quickly (an example would be note names or the Circle of Fifths). They may need the use of mnemonic aids or outlines of information to use as they respond to classroom activities and assessments.

9. Write answers in booklet for all tests including the state standardized tests

This accommodation sometimes indicates difficulty with transferring information to other forms. A student may not be able to accurately complete an assessment on a blank piece of staff paper. She may need a template of staff paper to fill in the missing information. She may also do well if the format used for practice during class is exactly the same as the form used for assessment.

ATTENDING THE IEP OR 504 MEETINGS

As music educators prepare to attend IEP and 504 meetings for students with special needs, a review of existing paperwork, discussion with colleagues, and data/notes taken during class, provide excellent groundwork. This level of preparation may increase the perceptions other team members, and the school community at large, have of the individual music educator as well as the overall music program at school. It also will be greatly appreciated by students with special needs and their parents/guardians. Moreover, music educators will have then created the opportunity to be better teachers to students with special needs by being prepared to teach *all* students.

Another very helpful step to take as a meaningful member of the Child Study or IEP team is to attend the meetings. It can sometimes be difficult to ascertain when these meetings will be held. Information about students with disabilities is held in the strictest of confidence, and meeting times, etc. are not posted where the general school community may read them. A good strategy is to discuss concerns with a lead special education teacher, or the IEP Case Manager, and request to be involved in the IEP meeting. If release time cannot be scheduled during the meeting, it is certainly appropriate to send a letter or list describing the areas of strength and challenge observed during music instruction. It is recommended that this list begin with the strengths a student brings to a situation and the successes (even if they are small) the student has experienced in class (Duquette, 2001).

The possibility exists that music is an area of strength and success for a student with special needs. It is important for the team, including the parents of the student, to be aware of this. It is helpful to state, in a positive tone, the challenges a student is having and some suggestions of adaptive materials, alternate settings, or additional personnel that may make the experience a more appropriate learning environment for the student. Adamek and Darrow (2005) state: "Collaboration involves cooperation, meaningful communication, problem solving, idea sharing, information sharing, and planning and facilitating use strategies for students" (p. 56).

There are times when a student with special needs may still struggle in a music classroom. It is in these situations that a positive attitude and emphasis on being a valued member of the special education team will assist communication and the establishment of an appropriate "least restrictive environment" for students with special needs (Atterbury & Richardson, 1995; Hoskins, 1996). The data taken during class and active participation in IEP and 504 meetings (via written communication or personal presence) can now be of assistance as the problem-solving process begins for a student who is still struggling. It may be possible that the student has been placed in an environment that is not "least restrictive" and that a change in placement may be necessary. This change may be as simple as having the student come to music at a different time of day, or with a different group of students. A student's medication titration schedule (the levels of medication in a student's system sometimes change during the day) may be considered an issue for discussion. Sometimes a particular group of students will be better suited to a student with special needs. A student may need to be a part of a smaller class, or in a self-contained class, rather than in a general classroom. It may also be necessary for a student to have a paraprofessional during music, or additional adaptive equipment. These considerations are part of a possible change in placement for a student with special needs.

An initial strategy in this process is to discuss the struggles a student may be having in class. Meeting with the team may be necessary to discuss changes to the services a student receives in music. It is also important to make contact, either yourself or through the special/general education teacher, with the parents or guardians of a student who is having difficulty in the music classroom. Creating short-term behavior or academic plans with frequent parental (and team) notification is often an effective way to either correct a situation in a brief amount of time or to begin to pinpoint a more significant issue. Behavior plans will be discussed further in chapter 5.

It is sobering, yet empowering, to know that the music educator, as team member, has the right to ask for a full meeting of the team once all available procedures for identifying and ameliorating areas of academic and behavioral struggle for a student with special needs have been followed. If a meeting is requested, however, please be sure that appropriate data has been taken, and all suggestions made during communication with other team members have been implemented. Music educators who follow these guidelines will be in a position of strength and will have the support of the school team. A change in "least restrictive environment" can be made during the school year, and changes to the IEP or 504 Plan may be made at any time during the year by the team. The goal is to provide the most appropriate instruction for all students with special needs (Hammel, 2004).

UNDERSTANDING ADAPTATIONS, ACCOMMODATIONS, AND MODIFICATIONS

Once the inclusive music classroom has been prepared, IEP and 504 Plans have been reviewed, and relationships with members of the team have been established, music educators are ready to apply adaptations and accommodations for students with special needs. It is a legal responsibility to apply these strategies in the music classroom. More importantly, it is good teaching to treat each student as an individual and to give everyone the tools they need to be successful in the music classroom (those with special needs and those without special needs). This is the essence of "fairness" in education. Fair is not equal. Fair is providing every student in your classroom with the tools they need for success (Turnbull, Turnbull, Shank, & Leal, 2002).

Appropriate adaptations and accommodations are critical to success in the music classroom. Music educators are not limited to strategies listed in the special education paperwork. It is absolutely appropriate to find

Accommodations: Adaptations used when it is believed that a child can learn at the same level as the other students in the classroom.

Adaptations: Instructional tools and materials used to accommodate children based on their learning needs

Modifications: Adaptations used with different curricular goals in mind in order for the child to achieve at the highest possible level.

(Adamek & Darrow, 2005)

Figure 4.5 Accommodations

additional adaptations, accommodations, and modifications specific to your music classroom that will enhance the learning of your students. As music educators become more comfortable applying adaptations and accommodations listed as well as through creating new strategies, the process becomes easier and teachers may find that many of these strategies work for all students in the music classroom. "Universal design" is the term most often used to describe classrooms that are structured so that everyone has equal access (Avery, Johnstone, & Milligan, 2005; CEC, 2005; McGuire, Scott, & Shaw, 2006). That is one of the hallmarks of a truly successful inclusion classroom; all students can benefit from the strategies introduced to assist students with special needs (Van Garderen, & Whittaker, 2006).

INCORPORATING THE FIVE DOMAINS INTO CLASSROOM ACCOMMODATIONS

In chapter 1, five areas of challenge that affect students with special needs were introduced. These five areas are: cognitive, communication, behavioral or emotional, physical, and sensory. It is firmly believed that a classroom free of labels and designed to accommodate all students is the most respectful and successful environment for students with and without special needs. Many research-based and time-tested adaptations and accommodations for students with special needs have been considered and chosen and are listed at the end of this chapter according to the areas of challenge a student may experience. Remember that a student may often experience challenges in more than one area.

Please also note that many of these strategies may be employed with all students in the music classroom. The next section of this text will offer specific strategies for the music classroom as a well as small vignettes of successful lessons and techniques designed for readers to gain insight and inferences for their own classrooms. In addition, music teacher educators are encouraged to use these vignettes as an introduction to discussions in the methods classroom. The vignettes are posted as written by students and some do not contain person-first language as the students were still learning to consistently use this when speaking about students with special needs.

TEACHING MUSIC TO STUDENTS WITH COGNITIVE CHALLENGES

Vignette 4.2 Teaching Tempo to Students with Cognitive and Physical Disabilities

The Problem: The first class I see in the week are students in a mild cognitively impaired class. I needed to create a lesson that was visual based and involves movement in some manner for this group of students. This also brought to mind that the movement aspect of my lesson must either be obtainable for the severe class or must be modified to accommodate the needs of other students.

The Solution: When I thought about how I would make this lesson visual and movement based a thought of a high school earth science lesson came to me. The lesson I was thinking of was one where the teacher stretched a slinky out across the floor and showed us the way different kinds of waves looked. He moved one end of the slinky back and forth. I thought that this could be easily adapted to a music lesson. I decided to use a rope instead of a slinky and have the students make the waves in the rope to the speed of the song being heard. This filled both criteria of approaches because the wave is a very visual representation of the speed and also by the students moving the rope back and forth it engaged them kinesthetically. I also picked a rope that was somewhat colorful and stimulating to try to engage them further. I also liked this because with the severe students could see it and hold on to one end of the rope and I can move the other to the appropriate speed so they can feel the change in tempo. I had all the students sit in a semi circle and I passed the rope end from student to student. With the severe class I just gave the students an end of the rope and they stayed in their wheelchairs. The paraprofessionals helped the students that needed assistance in holding onto the rope.

I felt that all three classes responded well to this exercise. They were able to demonstrate the difference between tempos by moving the rope accordingly. They also seemed to get excited about the music and participating in the activity. This activity was a very effective approach to assessing student knowledge. I utilized a visual and kinesthetic exercise, which I feel made this lesson as effective with these groups of students.

(Adapted from Hourigan, 2007)

The above vignette (4.2) was written by a pre-service music teacher who was struggling to plan a lesson for students with cognitive and physical challenges. Students with cognitive disabilities typically struggle in three areas of learning: input (the way in which they receive and process sensory information), retention (the ability of students to commit knowledge to memory) and output (the ways learners can demonstrate and express their understanding of knowledge and skills, and generalize those concepts to other situations). Music educators who focus on cognition when teaching students with disabilities often consider enhancing the interactions between the learner and his environment (Wehmeyer, 2002). These learning strategies include the understanding that through this interaction "…the learner is an active component who makes the learning occur" (p. 61). In addition, the learner is encouraged to construct new meaning from these experiences.

As discussed earlier in this chapter, before adapting to the learning needs of a student, it is very important that music educators read the Individualized Education Program (IEP), Section 504 Plan or other legal document created for the student. Once the documents have been reviewed, the accommodation process can begin. In the music classroom, a student with challenges in the area of cognition may need multiple opportunities and response modes when participating in classroom and ensemble activities and assessments. This may include many repetitions of the material and their responses may be slower or uneven, and they may need to have information presented in all three modalities (visual, aural, kinesthetic). They may also receptively understand what is expected, but not be able to reproduce expressively. Once the music educator is aware of the preferred mode of learning, that modality can be stressed while the others may still be included to strengthen receptive skills and increase the possibility that a student may begin to learn in more than one (or two) ways.

TEACHING MUSIC TO STUDENTS WITH COMMUNICATION CHALLENGES

Vignette 4.3 Teaching "Fast and Slow" to Children with Cognitive and Communication Challenges: A Pre-service Music Teacher's Perspective

I was working with a class of students who are cognitively and physically challenged, which involves mostly children in wheelchairs. The children for the most part do not show their understanding or recognition of the music or activities, so it's challenging to plan lessons with the class because it is the teacher's job to do everything and not expect much feedback from the students.

(continued)

Vignette 4.3 (continued)

I was required to do a lesson based on fast and slow with the class. I made a CD of different pieces of music of varying tempos for them to listen to. I gave each student a maraca to shake when listening to the music. The students' aides were there to assist the students as needed. I wanted the students to shake the maracas fast when the music was fast and slow when it was slow. The aides had to help some of the students quite a lot in this activity, which I expected.

When the music was fast, it was easy to shake the maracas appropriately; however, when the music was slow, the maracas were not very useful. They did not represent a slower tempo very well. There was probably another instrument I could have used for the slower pieces; however, it would not have been wise to switch instruments for each piece with this class because it would have been too chaotic. In this situation, perhaps a different instrument in general would have been beneficial, but I was not aware this would be an issue until I experienced it.

Mrs. A, the cooperating teacher, assisted me in the lesson to help keep the students involved by having them move around and, whether it be walking or being pushed in their wheelchairs. This gave them a different physical experience with the music, which is always beneficial in a special education class. In addition, we used PECS (Picture Exchange Communication System) to allow the students to choose fast or slow from a choice of icons I learned that if something doesn't work as well as desired, then I should try to adapt my lesson as best as I can so that I keep each student involved.

(Adapted from Hourigan, 2007)

Vignette 4.3 was written by a student teacher that was faced with teaching a lesson to students who were either non-verbal or had severe communication challenges. Valdes, Bunch, Snow, Lee, and Matos (2005) state: "All teachers, regardless of the language backgrounds of their students, are directly and intimately involved with language" (p. 126). It is valuable for music educators to understand that language development is critical to success of students in the music classroom. If a student cannot understand instruction, their skills and understandings will not increase. It is imperative that music educators focus on language components when considering ways to deliver instruction to students with communication and language differences. As mentioned in the cognitive discussion, it is also important to observe the student, either in the music classroom or in other classes, to evaluate a student's receptive and expressive language skills as part of a formative data gathering opportunity. A recurring theme in this book has been the importance of frequent consultation with the group of professionals who serve with the music educator on the team in various areas of special education services. In this instance, the speech pathologist or speech teacher would be an excellent resource. They will be able to recommend specific teaching and learning strategies such as communication systems that are needed to assist a student who is in the music classroom.

One particular communication tool that many special educators use is the Picture Exchange Communication System (PECS) see (figure 4.6). This system allows many students who have communication challenges a visual and simplified way to communicate with teachers and other students. Many school districts already own the program Boardmaker. This program has many music icons available for use.

A Picture Exchange Communication System (PECS) can be used in the music classroom to express needs and choices for students with disabilities who have difficulty in the area of communication. If students are choosing an activity or instrument, pictures of the choices can be presented to the student who can then point, nod, or use a method of communication comfortable to them to express their choice. A PECS is also helpful when students need to signify understanding, or a lack of understanding, as well as when a student needs a break from instruction to rest or attend to personal care issues. Students can also indicate understanding of a concept. For example, if an early elementary class is working on the difference between beat and rhythm, a teacher can create a PECS with the two choices in picture form. The student can indicate whether the beat or rhythm is being demonstrated during an activity. In addition to Boardmaker, music educators often take pictures of choices and options available in their classrooms. These pictures can be laminated and presented as PECS for students with special needs. Special education teachers and staff members are acquainted with these systems and may have many PECS options available for use in the music classroom.

It is also important to consider the above information and the way it relates to a student's ability to receive, understand, and express music. There may

Figure 4.6 Picture Exchange Communication System (PECS)

or may not be a direct connection between the two. For example, a student with autism may be able to express herself musically; however, she may have considerable communication challenges otherwise. Music educators must consider both instructional and musical language challenges that may arise in the classroom and how to modify the classroom in a way that will remove barriers for students with special needs. A student's language ability may help or enhance their musical ability or vice versa. Working in tandem with the special education team may benefit the student in both language and music.

TEACHING MUSIC TO STUDENTS WITH BEHAVIORAL OR EMOTIONAL CHALLENGES

Student behavior can create unique obstacles for music educators. It is important to look at both positive and negative behavior. Specific adaptations, modifications, and accommodations in the area of behavior and music will be discussed in chapter 5. However, it is important (as it is with all areas discussed in this chapter) to determine whether the challenges associated with behavior warrant specific modifications to the way music is taught in a specific classroom. The fundamental goal of these changes to daily lesson plans is to increase the occurrence of appropriate behavior, decrease the occurrence of negative behavior, and teach appropriate behavior that is absent from a student's repertoire (Lewis & Doorlag, 2006, p. 267). This will ensure the best possible opportunity for *all* students to learn in the music classroom.

Students may also be diagnosed with severe emotional disturbance. When reflecting on an emotional disturbance, it is important for music educators to examine whether a student is internalizing or externalizing these emotions and if adaptations can be made to assist with these issues. The music therapy field has made great strides in finding ways to use music to assist with emotional needs (Davis, Gfeller, & Thaut, 1999). Music educators can learn strategies by consulting or contracting a music therapist for issues regarding students with emotional disturbance.

In the music classroom, a student with behavioral and/or emotional challenges may have difficulty with structure, rules, and social cues. Music classes are active and student-centered. Many students are initially not accustomed to this, and the perceived lack of structure can cause anxiety for a student with behavioral and/or emotional challenges. If the music classroom is structured so that each class begins and ends with the same song or activity, students may be able to self-calm, or redirect emotions, when they begin to feel angry, upset, or anxious. This also lets them know when a transition is to occur.

Positive reinforcement is one of the most critical elements for success when working with students who are challenged by behavior and emotions.

This includes musical reinforcers such as playing a drum or leading the group if those activities are, in fact, reinforcing for a particular student. The music educator who finds ways to positively reinforce good behavior, compliance, and academic success will be far more successful than a music educator who believes that all students should follow the same set number of rules to the same degree every day of the school year (remember fair is not equal). Social cues can be difficult for students with behavioral and emotional challenges. It is important for students to be seated near excellent role models who are able to serve as peer-advocates and buddies. Consistent positive interactions and a stable, sequential environment will increase the academic and behavioral success rate for students with behavioral and emotional challenges. An example of a positive reinforcement plan appears below (figure 4.7). These

---

Sequence suggestion:

1. Find out what activity (e.g. leading the group) or material (e.g. a drum or a book) the student really enjoys and would like to do as part of music time.
2. Ask the student what he or she is willing to "work for" to earn that choice.
3. Specify what needs to happen in music class that day in order for the student to be able to earn this choice time. Examples could but are not limited to either the behaviors that are causing learning interruptions or just the normal sequence of participation in the class.
4. Allow the student the structured choice time with the designated material or activity. It is very important that you provide the reward stated at the time promised. This will increase the possibility that the student will engage in this type of reinforcement activity again.

Please note: Positive reinforcement is about *earning* choices or privileges rather than taking these items away. Students either earn choice time or not. Therefore a checklist might need to be developed in order for the student to see exactly the choices he has made (either right or wrong). For example:

_____ Came into class and sat down without talking

_____ Participated without interruptions

_____ Treated others with respect and kept my hands to myself

_____ Did not interrupt the class or my teacher

_____ Choice time.

Figure 4.7 Positive Reinforcement Suggestions (choice time)

additive, rather than deficit, models are very effective with students who have challenges in this area.

STRATEGIES FOR MUSIC TEACHERS WHEN TEACHING STUDENTS WITH SENSORY CHALLENGES

Based on the onset of vision or hearing loss (e.g., from birth or later in life), or of another challenge that can cause sensory issues, students may have a range of complications regarding language, communication, and behavior. The primary challenge in the area associated with sensory disorders is communication (Davis, Gfeller, & Thaut, 1999). The onset of the sensory challenge will often determine the type of system needed to facilitate communication with a student. For example, a student may be able to use speech reading (i.e., reading lips) and standard oral communication. A student may also use American Sign Language (ASL) in addition to or instead of speech reading and oral communication.

A person who has visual impairments may also have communication challenges. These communication challenges may be overcome by using aural forms of communication to reinforce visual experiences. Davis et al. explain: "If we exclude concepts based on visual experiences, language development of children with visual impairments is not deficient" (p. 195). There are two misconceptions about students who have visual impairments. First, many believe that because a person is visually impaired, their other senses are heightened. Research does not support this. The second misconception is that persons who have sensory challenges also have cognitive disabilities. Davis et al. state: "Unless there are coexisting mental or physical disabilities, the development of children with visual impairments is more similar than dissimilar to that of normal sighted children" (p. 195). Students with vision loss may struggle in the areas of mobility (i.e., getting from one place to another) and orientation (i.e., establishing one's position in relationship to others and the environment).

Students with vision challenges benefit from increased aural input during instruction and assessment. An increased (perhaps greatly increased) font size, enlarged music, bolder and darkened visual materials, and accompanying aural stimuli are excellent strategies. Some students may be interested in learning to read braille music. A highly recommended source for information regarding reading braille music and preparing music for use by students with challenges in the area of vision is Dancing Dots (www.dancingdots.com). While use of these adaptations requires music educators to learn to read braille music, the benefits to students are lifelong and programs like Dancing Dots create a gateway for this valuable information.

Students who have sensory challenges often need accommodations to be successful in the music classroom. Students who have challenges in the area of hearing may need very specific accommodations. A hearing difference can range from very slight to profound. It is important for music educators to be aware of the degree of hearing loss, the adaptive devices used by the student (auditory trainer, cochlear implant, etc.), and the signs or behaviors a student exhibits when he is becoming overwhelmed by sensorial information. Again, this is why it is critical to consult special educators and observe students with hearing loss in other settings.

Students with some hearing and students with cochlear implants often have difficulty with distortion of sound. Music can compound this, particularly in an ensemble setting. Music educators who speak with the audiologist associated with the student can often find the appropriate level of sound, the level a hearing aid may be adjusted during classroom music or an ensemble, and the degree of difficulty a student may have with other ambient sounds in the classroom.

Seating preferences are important for students with hearing challenges. If possible, these students should be seated near the music educator and in the center of the classroom so that visual cues, lip reading, and the use of visual materials (chalk, white, or Smart Board) can be optimized.

Instruments that readily carry vibrations (eg., guitar or harp) can be good choices for students who have hearing challenges and wish to play instruments. Many students may also have excellent experiences with clarinet and saxophone because of the large frequency range and resonant capabilities. The most important consideration when choosing an instrument, however, is student interest. If a student has a sincere interest in an instrument, it is recommended that he be allowed to learn his instrument of choice.

The use of frequent visual cues during instruction and for academic and behavioral directions is valuable for students with these differences. It is helpful if the teacher and students learn some American Sign Language (or other method of signing used by the student) to assist with communication.

Students with sensory difficulties can also have challenges in the area of perceiving sensory information. These students are often overwhelmed by the amount of sensory information in the classroom and throughout their school day. Many are hyper-sensitive, however, some are hypo-sensitive to the same stimuli in the classroom. Caution in the use of colors, sounds, and textures in classroom materials, bulletin boards, and lesson planning can assist students who are challenged in this sensory area.

TEACHING MUSIC TO STUDENTS WITH PHYSICAL AND MEDICAL CONDITIONS

An important consideration when teaching a student with a physical or medical condition is that he may not have any other challenges. Teachers can often make mistakes in assuming when they meet a student with a physical disability that he also has a related cognitive challenge. It is very beneficial to conduct a complete assessment of a student's potential for success in music. Again, it is recommended that teachers observe students in other classes and that strategies be discussed with parents and other special educators. It is essential to focus on adaptations that will provide an opportunity for the student to make the most meaningful contribution, with dignity, in the music classroom.

Another caveat relevant to music educators that cannot be overstated is the importance of the awareness of the specific needs (physical and medical in particular) of students in the classroom. These students will also have specific needs that will require accommodation in the area of movement and accessibility to classroom instruments, stands, chairs, and risers. They may be absent from school for periods of time as health conditions necessitate and it is the responsibility of the music educator to modify expectations and create appropriate accommodations. These accommodations may include a simplified part or partial participation in performances as the student may not be strong enough to perform an entire program or may have missed school and not been able to learn enough music well to be confident in playing all repertoire in a performance. When students with challenges in this area travel with musical ensembles, their needs and the possibility of intervention on the part of the music educator, or other staff member who travels with the music ensemble, could be critical. Creating accommodations that honor the student and his needs as well as his musical strengths is another example of "fair is not equal" and of considering the person rather than the disability.

PUTTING IT ALL TOGETHER

Successful teaching of students with special needs requires an extensive knowledge of the subject matter (in this case, music), a willingness to participate as a member of a team, a philosophy that places the students first, and a great deal of time and effort as we seek to provide each student with what they need to have the opportunity to succeed. It is an endeavor worth undertaking, and our students deserve nothing less. We encourage you to develop an inclusive philosophy as part of your overall philosophy of music education and to remember that music is for every child—not just for a few. The table listed below is a compilation of many successful adaptations,

CG = Cognitive
CM = Communication
B/E = Behavioral/Emotional
P = Physical
S = Sensory

Accommodations and adaptations	CG	CM	B/E	P	S
Use an overhead projector or computer-enhanced image to enlarge materials (music, books, sheet music) as much as possible and provide written materials for all spoken instruction. A "picture" schedule is good for non-readers and students with autism.	X	X	X		X
Allow students a hands-on examination of all new materials, equipment and instruments during introduction of a concept. This kinesthetic approach combined with the visual and aural instructional elements will help students learn according to their modality.	X	X	X	X	X
Allow students to tape record rehearsals or lectures and tape record a test or assignment. Allow students to respond to tests or assignments on the tape, orally, or in writing.	X	X		X	X
Provide music or reading materials in advance to allow time for arrangements to be made for students with special needs.	X	X	X		X
Use velcro strips to help students hold mallets or small instruments. Sticks can also be wrapped with tape or foam rubber to facilitate handling.			X	X	X
Jingle Bells, or cymbals can be sewn onto a band or ribbon and tied to the wrist. Straps and cords can be used to attach rhythm instruments to wheelchairs or walkers for students who may drop them during class.			X	X	X
Code music, or instruments with colors or symbols to help students remember notes, or rhythms. A highlighter or colored pens/chalk can be used to help a student focus on a specific part of the music or book.	X	X	X		X
A felt board, or other raised texture board can be used with heavy rope to demonstrate the concept of a staff to students who learn kinesthetically, or are visually impaired.	X	X		X	X
Provide a written rehearsal schedule for students to follow. These can be on the chalk or bulletin board or placed in folders.	X	X	X		X
Individualize some assignments for students who may not be able to complete the quantity of homework other students can. Check the IEP to make sure you are following the modifications listed.	X	X	X	X	
Make use of computers for students who need extra drill and practice.	X		X		X
Separate rhythmic and melodic assignments until students with special needs can combine the two.	X			X	X
Limit the use of words not yet in the student's vocabulary and be consistent with the terminology you do use.	X				X

Figure 4.8 (Continued)

Accommodation/Modification/Adaptation					
Allow students to help plan their own instructional accommodations and be a partner in the process.	X	X	X	X	X
When preparing music for use by students with special needs, several adaptations can be made. The teacher can indicate tempo and meter, mark the student's part, allow students to highlight music, Write measure numbers and breath marks in the student's part, create visual aids for difficult words, and provide visual cues for score markings and phrase lengths.	X	X	X		X
When using written assessments with students with special needs, provide accurate and complete study guides. Help focus study efforts on important events, ideas, and vocabulary. Use this tool to help students organize and sequence information.	X	X	X		
Use short tests at frequent intervals to encourage students to work at an even pace rather than postponing the study of a large amount of material until just before a long exam. This also provides a student "some room" to perform poorly on a single test without significantly compromising the grade for the entire marking period.	X	X	X		
Allow students to use a word bank. They may remember concepts, but have difficulty recalling spelling.	X	X	X		
Vary the style of test items used. Using a variety of test items will prevent a student from being unduly penalized for having difficulty with a particular type of question.	X	X	X		
Place a rubber strip on the back of a ruler or use a magnetic ruler to help students measure or draw lines without slipping. Use adhesive-backed velcro to attach items to a desk or wheelchair laptray.	X			X	
Allow students to use pens (felt tip) or pencils (soft lead) that require less pressure or use a computer to complete assessments or assignments.			X	X	X	X
Wait to prompt students for verbal answers to questions after least 5 seconds have passed. They may need a longer period of time to process the question and determine an appropriate response. It may help to "call on" the student only when his/her hand is raised. This may lower any possible frustration level and prevent student embarrassment.	X	X	X		
If an accommodation or modification is listed in the IEP, it must be followed by all teachers.	X	X	X	X	X
Create a special seat or seating area so that a student knows and can expect where he will sit during class (chair, disc or carpet square, taped area, special mat).		X	X	X	X
Allow movement during class from one chair or special seating place to another.			X	X	X
Allow a student to participate for a small amount of time. Increase this time slowly as the student is acclimated to the classroom routine. This may begin with the start of class or the end of class depending on the student and her preferences.			X	X	X

Figure 4.8 Examples of Accommodations, Modifications, and Adaptations for the Music Classroom

accommodations, and modifications for use as examples in music classroom (figure 4.8). It is organized according to the five domains discussed in this chapter. There are many other adaptations and accommodations that may be used in the classroom. The strategies you find most successful will be the ones you develop and use when considering the needs of the individual students who are in your classrooms and ensembles.

DISCUSSION QUESTIONS

1. What are some of the most important strategies a music teacher can use to be part of the team at her school (discuss at least four)?
2. What are the similarities and differences between an IEP and a 504 Plan?
3. Please choose five accommodations and discuss how those may be beneficial for an entire music class or ensemble?
4. Based on what you have read in this chapter, what are some specific adaptations, accommodations, or modifications that you could use in your classroom (or future classroom)?
5. Have you worked with students in any of the categories mentioned above? If so, what were some of the challenges or successes that you noticed?

REFERENCES

Adamek, M. S., & Darrow, A. A. (2005). *Music in special education*. Silver Spring, MD: The American Music Therapy Association.

Ansuini, A. M. (1979). *Identifying competencies for elementary school music teachers in planning learning experiences for children with learning disabilities* (Doctoral dissertation, S.U.N.Y. at Buffalo, 1990). Dissertation Abstracts International, 40-10A, 5299.

Atterbury, B. W. (1993). Preparing teachers for mainstreaming. *Quarterly Journal of Music Teaching and Learning, 4*(1), 20–26.

Atterbury, B. W., & Richardson, C. P. (1995). *The experience of teaching general music*. New York, NY: McGraw Hill Publishers.

Avery C., Johnstone, C., & Milligan, C. (2005). Using universal design to unlock the potential for academic achievement of at-risk learners. *Teaching Exceptional Children, 38*(2), (22–31).

Coe D., Matson J., & Fee, J. 1990. Training nonverbal and verbal play skills to mentally retarded and autistic children. *Journal of Autism Developmental Disorders, 20*, 177–187.

Dalrymple, N. (1993). *Competencies for people teaching individuals with autism and other pervasive developmental disorders* (ERIC Document Reproduction Service No. ED 363 980).

Davis, W.B., Gfeller, K. E., Thaut, M. H. (1999). A introduction to music therapy. Silver Spring MD: The American Music Therapy Association.

Duquette, C. 2001. *Students at risk: Solutions to classroom challenges*. Portland, ME: Stenhouse Publishers.

Gfeller, K., Darrow, A. A., & Hedden, S. K. (1990). Perceived effectiveness of mainstreaming in Iowa and Kansas schools. *Journal of Research in Music Education, 58*, 90–101.

Gilbert, J., & Asmus, E. (1981). Mainstreaming: Music educators' participation and professional needs. *Journal of Research in Music Education, 29*(1), 31–37.

Hart, B., & Risley, T. R. 1975. Incidental teaching of language in the preschool. *Journal of Applied Behavior Analysis, 8*, 411–420.

Hammel, A. M. (1999). *A study of teacher competencies necessary when including special learners in elementary music classrooms: The development of a unit of study for use with undergraduate music education students* (Doctoral dissertation, Shenandoah University, 1999) Dissertation Abstracts International, 40–10A, 5299.

Hammel, A. M. (2004). Inclusion strategies that work. *Music Educators Journal, 90*(5), 33–37.

Heller, L. (1994). *Undergraduate music teacher preparation for mainstreaming: A survey of music education teacher training institutions in the Great Lakes region of the United States* (Doctoral dissertation, Michigan State University, 1994). Dissertation Abstracts International, 56–03A, 858.

Hoskins, B. (1996). *Developing inclusive schools*. Bloomington, IN: The Forum on Education.

Hourigan, R. M. (2007) Teaching Music to Students with Special Needs: A Phenomenological Examination of Participants in a Fieldwork Experience. Doctoral Dissertation, The University of Michigan (ISBN # 9780549174868/VDM Verlag (2008) ISBN#: 978-3-8364-7663-8).

Lewis, R. B., & Doorlag, D. H. (2006). *Teaching special students in general education classrooms*. Upper Saddle River, NJ: Prentice Hall.

McGee G. G., Almeida M. C., & Sulzer-Azaroff, B. 1992. Promoting reciprocal interactions via peer incidental teaching. *Journal of Applied Behavior Analysis, 25*, 117–126.

McGuire, J. M., Scott, S. S., & Shaw, S. F. (2006). Universal design and its applications in educational environments. *Remedial and Special Education, 27*(3), 166–175.

Nocera, S. D. (1979). *Reaching the special learner through music*. Morristown, NJ: Silver

Ozonoff, S., Rogers, S. J., & Hendren, R. L. 2003. *Autism spectrum disorders: A research review for practitioners*. Washington, DC: American Psychiatric Publishing, Inc.

Pierce K., & Schreibman, L. 1997. Multiple peer use of pivotal response training to increase social behaviors of classmates with autism: Results from trained and untrained peers. *Journal of Applied Behavior Analysis, 30*, 150–160.

Pressley, M., Raphael, L., Gallagher, J. D. & DiBella, J. (2004). Providence-St. Mel School: How a school that works for African American Students works. *Journal of Educational Psychology, 96*(2), 216–235.

Prizant, B., & Wetherby, A. 1998. Providing services to children with autism (0–2 years) and their families. *Topics in Language Disorders, 9*, 1–23.

Rowan, B., Chiang, F. S., & Miller, R. J. (1997). Using research on employees' performance to study the effects of teachers on students' achievement. *Sociology of Education, 70*, 256–284.

Section 504 and the ADA: *Promoting student access (second edition)*. Council of Administrators of Special Education, Inc. 1999. Washington, DC: CASE, Inc.

Shellard, E., & Protheroe, N. (2000). *Effective teaching: How do we know it when we see it? The Informed Educator Series*: Arlington, VA: Educational Research Service (monograph).

Stronge, J. H. 2007. *Qualities of effective teachers* (2nd ed.). Alexandria, VA: Association for Supervision and Curriculum Development.

Thorp, D. M., Stahmer, A. C., & Schreibman, L. 1995. Effects of sociodramatic play training on children with autism. *Journal of Autism Developmental Disorders, 25*, 265-282.

Turnbull, A., Turnbull, R., Shank, M., & Leal, D. (2002). *Exceptional lives: Special education in today's schools*. (3rd ed.). Upple Saddle River, NJ: Prentice Hall.

Universal Design for Learning (2005). Council for Exceptional Children. Upper Saddle River, NJ: Merrill Prentice Hall.

Valdes, G., Bunch, G., Snow, C., Lee, C., and Matos, L. (2005). Teaching diverse learners. In L. Darling Hammond & J. Bransford (Eds.), *Preparing teachers for a changing world* (pp. 126-168). San Francisco: Jossey-Bass.

Van Garderen, D., & Whittaker, C. (2006). Planning differentiated, multicultural instruction for secondary inclusive classrooms. *Teaching Exceptional Children, 38*(3), 12-20.

Wagner, S. 1999. *Inclusive programming for elementary students with autism*. Arlington, TX: New Horizons.

Wang, M. C., Haertel, G. D., & Walberg, H. J. (1993/1994). What helps students learn? *Educational Leadership, 51*(4), 74-79.

Weiss, I. R., & Pasley, J. D. (2004). What is high-quality instruction? *Educational Leadership, 61*(5), 24-28.

Wehmeyer, M. L. (2002). *Teaching students with mental retardation*. Baltimore, MD: Brooks Publishing.

Williams, D. (1988). *Regular classroom teachers' perceptions of their preparedness to work with mainstreamed students as a result of preservice coursework* (Doctoral dissertation, Indiana University, 1988). Dissertation Abstracts International, 49-09A, 2622.

PART III

PRACTICAL CLASSROOM ADAPTATIONS, MODIFICATIONS, AND ASSESSMENT TECHNIQUES FOR TEACHING STUDENTS WITH SPECIAL NEEDS IN THE MUSIC CLASSROOM

Chapter 5

Developing a Student-centered and Inclusive Music Classroom

Classroom behavior is a common concern among many music educators. This is particularly true for music educators who teach in inclusive settings. This chapter is designed to provide effective tools and strategies at the micro-level (e.g., behavior and management techniques), and the macro-level by informing the reader of philosophical underpinnings that encompass a successful inclusive classroom. The socialization and lasting relationships that all students develop in school are also of considerable importance. Therefore it is imperative for music educators to strive for a caring, inclusive environment that is conducive for all students to learn. The practical strategies suggested at the end of this chapter are presented to encourage music educators to create a tolerant, caring classroom that is conducive for music teaching and learning. Many of the techniques discussed in this chapter are just examples of good teaching regardless of what population of students you are teaching.

CLASSROOM MANAGEMENT AND STUDENTS WITH SPECIAL NEEDS: FOUR IMPORTANT CONSIDERATIONS

Effective classroom management begins long before the students enter the music room. A well-prepared environment is essential for optimal instruction and is particularly important when teaching music to students with special needs. This groundwork can be time-consuming and requires a thoughtful approach to the classroom setting; however, it is well worth the planning when the classroom becomes an inclusive and student-centered environment.

Conroy, Sutherland, Snyder and Marsh (2008), explains that specific teacher interventions can lead to improved student behavior. These interventions include: (a) close supervision and monitoring, (b) classroom rules, (c) opportunities to respond, and (d) contingent praise. As music educators, we can apply these principles to music classrooms. The next section of this chapter is designed to relate these interventions to music teaching and learn-ing, and to provide strategies for music teachers.

Close supervision and monitoring. Conroy et. al found that close super-vision and monitoring can by implemented in the music classroom in the following ways: (a) student proximity to the teacher; (b) a music teacher's ability to visually monitor all students; (c) active engagement with students; (d) student access to teacher; and (e) ratio of adults to students that is con-ducive to close supervision.

The proximity of the student (especially one who has the potential to disrupt class) to the music teacher is an important first step in managing behavior. In the beginning, it is often helpful to place students with spe-cial needs near an excellent student who can model appropriate behaviors. These interactions can then be monitored by the music educator. In addi-tion, ensuring that students with special needs are actively engaged with other students may lessen the severity or frequency of outbursts and other inappropriate behaviors. It is important for students to have access to teach-ers and for students to know they can communicate with the adults at school in a manner that is comfortable and appropriate for them. If peer support is not effective, it may be beneficial to place the student near you (the music teacher). It is also helpful for the music educator to be aware of the student-to-teacher ratio in classrooms and ensembles, and to advocate for additional adult assistance when necessary.

Classroom rules. Classroom rules should be developed in collaboration with students, school-wide standards of conduct, and the behavior goals of the IEP. As part of this collaboration, students should express their willing-ness and ability to comply with rules and standards. Creating a classroom culture that includes a regular and efficient manner of communicating and enforcing rules is important.

Class and ensemble rules can be developed with students each year. This provides a sense of ownership in the classroom climate and students are often more willing to comply with a system they created. In environments of mutual respect, students are more likely to create rules that are simple and easy to understand. Music educators should regularly review the rules (or have student leaders review the rules) and communicate their willingness to apply consequences when necessary. This includes a consistent application of consequences when rules are not followed. When students are aware that the application of behavioral consequences is consistent and fair (remem-bering that fair is not equal), they know they are in a classroom where their behavioral efforts are honored.

In addition to using plans that coordinate with a school-wide initiative, as well as plans put in place by general classroom teachers, it is important to have a clear set of expectations for students (Zahorik, Halbach, Ehrle, &

Molnar, 2003). Some teachers create class rules that are too vague, ask too much or too little of students, or compile a lengthy list of rules that are difficult to remember, comply with, and enforce. Begin with a few rules that are general enough to be adapted to many situations and are easy to remember. If a student is having great difficulty following the class rules, write or draw a picture of the rule on a note card and have the student put the card in his or her pocket to assist in remembering that rule. Some students will only be able to follow a few rules (or one rule) at the outset. In this case, hold the student accountable for the agreed-upon rule and be consistent in enforcement of that rule (Marzano, Marzano, & Pickering, 2003).

At times, a student can exhibit a behavior that is distracting or counter to the classroom culture and not be aware this is occurring. In these cases, create a special signal or gesture to let this student know that his or her behavior is not appropriate. Many students who are less affected by their disabilities respond well to this quiet and specific reminder regarding the rules (Kohn, 1996; Cotton, 2000). This honors the student, respects the place this student holds within the classroom environment, and allows instruction to continue without time spent redirecting the student during class time. If the quiet attempts to redirect the student are not successful, the teacher may then choose to create a more specific behavior plan (Shellard & Protheroe, 2000). This method is often successful and can also improve the relationship between student and teacher as respectful and student-centered strategies are put in place.

Students who are developmentally able and less affected by their disabilities often appreciate the opportunity to participate in the creation of their own behavior plans, expectations, and consequences. This honors the personhood of each student and creates a partnership between teacher and student that can strengthen the nature of a student-centered classroom and relationships necessary for student success (Wharton-McDonald, Pressley, & Hampston, 1998). Students often are keenly aware of their own limitations and of what strategies will assist them to be more successful during instruction.

Opportunities to respond. Allow opportunities to respond during instruction that include time allotted for visual, kinesthetic, and oral responses. In addition, use an instructional model that allows students to respond individually, in small groups, and as a whole. Give students many opportunities to demonstrate their knowledge (academic and social) and allow them to respond in the method that is most comfortable for them (visual, kinesthetic, and oral). Assess students frequently and in a variety of environments to ensure their learning and response modes are honored.

Contingent praise. Students need regular praise for appropriate social and academic behaviors. Specific praise offered within a system that includes the above three interventions is a powerful and empowering experience. Students know they have worked well and to the best of their ability. They are also aware that you are aware of their efforts. "Catch them being good" is the old adage. It is not only applicable; it is an achievable goal in our music classrooms.

INITIAL PREPARATION AND PLANNING

Once a music teacher is aware of the students who will be in a specific class or ensemble, she should develop a preliminary strategy for managing behavior. Many students with special needs have behavior plans and management systems already in place (see IEP). It is very effective to follow the same strategies used by other teachers and staff members. Consistency is important in that it lessens the number of transitions required during the school day. Music educators will find it very helpful to talk with other team members and colleagues to define a set of expectations and possible consequences prior to the first day of school.

CONTINUED COMMUNICATION

Once the student has begun participating in the music classroom, continued communication with special education teachers and staff members is essential (Howard, 2002). Many students with moderate to severe special needs will attend music class with a paraprofessional or aide. These staff members are key stakeholders in the educational process because they often know the student with special needs very well (Mitchell, 1998; SECTQ, 2003). Paraprofessionals are with the student all day and are aware of any changes in schedule or activities that may upset or overexcite a student. They can also be great partners in instruction. Music educators should treat paraprofessionals as team members in classrooms and provide them with information prior to class time to allow them to learn the lesson and prepare to participate in instruction. This allows paraprofessionals the opportunity to share any additional information that may assist in the teaching and learning process, and shows them that their participation in the process is valued.

Students with more moderate to severe disabilities may be coming to music from a self-contained classroom. Music educators may be assigned to teach students either in a self-contained classroom or who come to music as a class. In either situation, the lead special education teacher is a valuable resource as they have important insights into classroom management and behavior that may be useful in music classrooms (Sokal, Smith, & Mowat, 2003; Emmer, Evertson, & Anderson, 1980).

PHYSICAL ARRANGEMENT

Students with special needs often benefit from a consistent place to sit (Bain & Jacobs, 1990). Seating charts can be useful when planning for effective classroom management. Planning for appropriate seating may include proximity to a paraprofessional or student helper, as well as any instruments and music used during class. In elementary general music settings, place students near the teacher and also near any instruments or materials that may be used during class to lessen the number of transitions required. In ensemble settings, the use of a paraprofessional or student helper can ease transitions and anxiety that may arise during rehearsal. To promote effective socialization, do not physically or socially isolate a student from peers: place students near positive models (behavioral and academic). Not only can these students be great help, they often may be of assistance with a student who has challenges.

It is also important to place students with special needs away from extraneous visual materials that can be distracting (bulletin boards that are not needed during the current lesson, posters, or other colorful art), or areas of the room (i.e., ventilation systems, lighting that is audible, areas of high glare) that can decrease student attention either through visual, kinesthetic, or aural stimuli. Careful planning regarding seating can demonstrably increase on-task behaviors (Walls, Nardi, von Minden, & Hoffman, 2002).

PARENTS AND CLASSROOM BEHAVIOR

Parent support and communication is valuable when creating a classroom environment that is positive and student-centered. At the beginning of the school year, or when the student first becomes a part of class, communication (written or oral) with the parents is essential (Brophy & Good, 1986). Speak with parents to discuss their goals as well as the goals you have for their child. Discuss the musical and social goals for the student in specific terms. Allow parents to share the ways they feel their child's disability may manifest itself in the music classroom (Hamre & Pianta, 2005). Create a notification system and timetable and make sure parents are aware that you as the music educator are truly vested in the success of their child. This initial contact is also very important if behavioral or academic issues arise during the year (Boyle-Baise, 2005). With a clear communication system in place, parents can be a part of the process, and classroom management issues can be ameliorated in a time-efficient manner (Langer, 2000).

ANXIETY

Some classroom management issues can stem from anxiety. Many students with special needs are anxious during class because they are unsure about teacher expectations and what will be asked of them that day (Zeichner, 2003). It can be very helpful to have a written or pictorial schedule of activities or a rehearsal order for students to use as a guide. This alleviates anxiety regarding performance expectations. It also gives students an idea regarding the amount of time they will be asked to sit still, move about the classroom, pay close attention, or work in groups. Perry, Marston, and Hinder (2001) explain that the teacher should honor the time, attention span, and behavior limits of students, and allow them to attempt to monitor their own anxiety during class. Special educators and paraprofessionals can assist with information regarding ways this strategy is implemented in other classes.

The music classroom or ensemble setting can be very exciting as students work together to create music. This type of environment, however, can be overstimulating for some students with special needs. Be alert to the sensory limits of students (see the special education team) and provide a quiet place in the classroom for students who need a break. Use hall passes for students who need to leave the classroom at various intervals to decrease anxiety or sensory overload. This pass can be to another teacher or to a guidance counselor who signs the pass, and the student comes back to class without other classmates being aware of the reason for the brief absence. Strategies that honor the personhood of students with disabilities can benefit the entire school community (SECTQ, 2003).

Intent is also an important consideration when determining consequences for inappropriate behavior. It may not be the intent of a student to be disruptive. She may be trying to communicate her anxiety, overstimulation, or overall uneasiness with the class (Ozonoff, Dawson, & McPartland, 2002). She may have had an experience earlier in the day that is coming to fruition or she may not be feeling well. Many students with disabilities have communication delays. This leads them to act out to express dissatisfaction with their surroundings. That does not mean that she should not face consequences; however, teachers have been known to label a child as a "bad kid" when in fact there is a simple communication barrier or misunderstanding within the classroom. Again, when disruptive behavior occurs, it is important for the music educator to follow up with other team members (e.g., special education teachers, paraprofessionals, parents, etc.). They may have seen similar behaviors and be aware of the triggers that cause such disruptions. They also may have strategies for curtailing such behavior.

Ultimately, the goal of effective classroom management is to allow students and teachers to work together in a community free from anxiety, negative personal interactions, and detrimental language and behaviors that are counter to an inclusive and positive environment. In addition to the strategies previously discussed, one of the most important elements in developing classroom management skills is to make sure the students are aware that they are all of equal value to the class or ensemble. Everyone seeks to be of value, and students with special needs may feel they are of lesser value than their peers. Frequent reminders using multiple strategies will help create an environment where acceptance is prized and all participation is appreciated.

MODERATE INTERVENTION PLANS

There are times when even the most prepared music educator can face behaviors that are more difficult than expected. There are times when more information and intervention are necessary. If we begin each year by becoming familiar with the student's educational paperwork, behavior plans, and by engaging in discussions with other colleagues, it will be easier to approach other members of the educational team to request assistance when needed (Rogers, 1998). The first step to take when a student is demonstrating difficult behaviors in a music classroom is to collect data. Data can include very short statements as to what was happening in the classroom before the behavior occurred, what the specific behavior included, and what you did as a result of this behavior (Anderson & Romanczyk, 1999). This type of data collection is sometimes referred to as a Functional Behavioral Analysis and the three steps may be called "ABC" or Antecedent, Behavior, and Consequence (Koegel, Koegel, & Hurley, 1992).

Taking data is important and can be powerful when presented to colleagues. Having specific information regarding your classroom environment, what is happening, and how it is affecting the class are very useful tools. When case study or grade-level teams are able to read specific information, it is much easier to begin planning interventions (Horner, Strain & Carr, 2002).

If a plan is put in place, there should be a definite beginning and ending date as well as a method for notifying all team members (parents included) of the successes and challenges encountered. A specific date for evaluation of an intervention plan will assist the music educator in that he or she is no longer alone in data collection and interpretation regarding behaviors. If the plan is not successful, the team now has more information and can take the next step together in defining expectations and consequences for the behavior of a student with special needs (Koegel, Koegel & Dunlap, 1996).

SCHOOL-WIDE POSITIVE BEHAVIOR SUPPORTS SYSTEMS

Another set of goals used often in schools is the School-wide Positive Behavior Supports (SWPBS) system (American Institute for Research, 1999). This system, noted by Sugai, Simonsen, and Horner (2008), involves initial, secondary, and tertiary interventions that apply to all students in the school, is monitored by all teachers and staff members, and is positive in nature. Parental involvement is critical in this system and all stakeholders are invited to participate in the creation of and support for positive behaviors in school (Onikama, Hammond, & Koki, 1998). With school-wide participation, all adults in the building are equal stakeholders in the behavior and interactions of all students. This positive and collegial process can create an environment where all persons in the school culture are seen as valuable and equally responsible to each other (Marzano, 2003).

Music educators are integral to the success of School-wide Positive Behavior Supports as the continuity of behavioral expectations expands to music classrooms and ensembles. By being aware of the specific behavior expectations for all students as well as specific students who have challenges in the area of behavior, music educators will increase the possibility that SWPBS goals are met. This type of collegial participation also increases the perception by school and administration personnel that the music educator and music program are supportive of school-wide efforts that reach beyond the music classroom.

THE SOCIALIZATION OF STUDENTS WITH SPECIAL NEEDS

Music is by nature a social, interactive subject. Unfortunately, students with special needs are typically delayed in social development and may not be equipped to make connections with other students. Students who are not challenged with disabilities may have difficulty understanding how to engage or interact with students who are new or have challenges. The result can be serious for students with special needs. As they get older, they may fall farther into isolation. Research suggests that students who are challenged with special needs are more likely to suffer from social isolation, depression, and mental illness (Goldson, 2001). Inappropriate behavior, if left unchecked, can lead to students with special needs being abused and serious life-changing events. As music educators, it is our responsibility to promote a positive social environment for all of our students, regardless of the challenges they face.

THEORETICAL FRAMEWORK FOR SOCIALIZATION AND INCLUSION

In working with music teachers regarding how best to approach the social integration of students with and without special needs into music classrooms, three basic theoretical frameworks have emerged. These frameworks include: (a) *Caring: A Feminine Approach to Ethics and Moral Education* (Noddings, 1984); (b) *Social Identity Processes in Organizational Contexts* (Hogg & Terry, 2001); and (c) The Zone of Proximal Development ZPD (Vygotsky, *Mind and Society,* 1934/1978). Each theory provides assistance in understanding how students in grades K–12 interact socially and how best to approach problem situations at all levels of instruction.

CARING: A FEMININE APPROACH TO ETHICS AND MORAL EDUCATION (*NEL NODDINGS, 1984*)

In our current educational environment, teachers are often challenged to teach social morals and ethical responsibility. Slogans, acronyms, and themes that encourage appropriate ethical behavior are often found on the walls of many schools. It can be difficult, however, to teach students to care about their peers. According to Noddings (1984), "As humans we want to care and be cared for" (p. 7). She explains that while students instinctively care about their peers, this instinct may not be motivation enough to act in a caring way toward others. As teachers we must integrate the value of caring into our approach to music education, especially for students who are challenged with disabilities. Having compassion for those who are disadvantaged is a life lesson that students can carry with them throughout their lives and can be taught as part an overall philosophy in the music classroom.

In the music classroom, this may include a very low threshold of tolerance for negative behavior (e.g., teasing or tormenting). In addition, an intervention that is planned by the music teacher and the rest of the team may be needed in order to establish an atmosphere of compassion within the classroom. Students may need to be instructed on such things as person-first language, how to engage and help a student, or how to express their concerns. This also may include organizing an intervention when negative behaviors persist. Figure 5.1 is an example of how this might work in a music classroom.

1. Identify behaviors that you would like to change and the student that you would like to support.
2. Speak with special education staff about appropriate terminology to use in describing the students challenges
3. Plan a day when the student in question can be diverted to another class or activity during this time (if needed).
4. Have special educators, parents, and your students sit together in an uninterrupted environment and make this the topic of the day.
5. Ask the students for help including what specifically they can do to assist you in teaching music.
6. Reestablish rules for conduct and what you expect.
7. Establish a clear conduit of communication for when adjustments need to be made.

Figure 5.1 Steps to Organizing a Classroom Intervention for Positive Behavioral Support in an Inclusion Classroom

SOCIAL IDENTITY PROCESSES IN ORGANIZATION CONTEXTS

Social identity theory is one theoretical underpinning by which researchers examine relationships and power within social groups. This theory specifically addresses how social structures can have a negative affect on individuals. The fundamental understanding of social identity theory is that a person's self-perceived value to a group can directly affect his overall self-worth and self-identity. Hogg and Terry (2001) explain that "a social category within which one falls, and to which one belongs, provides a definition of who one is" (p. 7). Music students can construct a social identity based on their experience within their music classroom in several ways. This identity can manifest itself within a social group, a section within a performing ensemble, or in ways their self-perceived success relates to the overall goals or class expectations. Because a student's self-worth is a critical part of this identity, particular attention needs to be paid to those who are challenged, and how the student and the rest of the class perceives those challenges.

One co-author recently worked with a student who was challenged by traumatic brain injury and played trumpet in band. Because he struggled in band socially and academically, he had difficulty understanding that these challenges did not make him a bad musician, or more important, a bad person. It was just as much work as a teacher to convince him otherwise as it was to get him ready for a concert. At times he wanted to give up. His parents and the co-author worked very hard to separate the academic, personal, and social challenges in his instruction as well as to encourage him to improve in all areas. This can be very challenging for music teachers. However, it is critical for a student with special needs to understand that his academic and social challenges do not make him "stupid" or "bad." It is obvious how these implications can snowball into larger mental health concerns.

RISKS (LESSONS LEARNED FROM VYGOTSKY)

Even as adults, forming relationships in a group setting requires risk. We must take chances not only to reach out and form a relationship but also to foster and continue a relationship. This can be uncomfortable for all students, especially students with special needs. In our classrooms, a student may have tried to initiate and reinitiate contact and failed. Other students may have attempted to initiate conversation with a student who has a communication challenge and also failed. The combination of both behaviors can result in a "downgrade" of a student's place within a group (see social identity theory above). In addition, these events may discourage a student from attempting to connect in the future.

The Zone of Proximal Development (ZPD) developed by L. S. Vygotsky is often used to explain the benefits of group learning within a social context. The basic premise is that students often learn more from capable peers than they would learn if left alone. Cooperative learning, peer-tutoring, and modeling are all examples of where the Zone of Proximal Development (ZPD) can be applied. The most important part of this theory regarding students with special needs is to understand their need for a "comfort zone." Students with disabilities often struggle with many aspects of everyday life that cause them to retreat into their "comfort zone." Students can have a social, physical, sensory, or academic "comfort zone." It is apparent that students with certain disabilities at an early age already demonstrate a lack of interest in engaging with their teacher or with their peers. It is important for teachers, therapists, and parents to keep students with disabilities interested in existing and learning with their peers.

Students who are not challenged by special needs also have a "comfort zone." It is often easier for them to retreat into their established social network than to take the risk to reach out to a student who may appear to be different. The key is to encourage students (with or without disabilities) to take risks in order to make a connection with other students. As music educators it is vital to encourage both groups to take the risk to interact.

Music teachers may ask: How do we encourage students to take risks in socializing with students? Ice breakers at the beginning of the year are great for this. For example, have students choose a number. Have them sit according to this prescribed number (to mix them up and not allow students to sit by their friends). Have your students interview the person sitting to their right. Questions could include items like what is your favorite food? Or what kind of music is on your iPod? Students will then realize that they have more in common than they think. This is just one example. There are also other ways of encouraging positive socialization such as pre-assigning group projects (with students that you think would work well together), pre-assigned seating (as mentioned before), and mentoring (older students with younger students). Figure 5.2 is a list of print resources for music teachers to develop a deeper understanding of this phenomenon.

Astor, R. A., Meyer, H. A., & Behre, W. J. (1999). Unowned places and times: Maps and interviews about violence in high schools. *American Educational Research Journal, 36*(1), 3–42.

Baxter, M. (2007). Global music making a difference: themes of exploration, action, and justice. *Music Education Research, 9*(1), 267–279.

Bradley, D. F., & Switlick, D. M. (1997). From isolation to cooperation in teaching. In D. F. Bradley, M. E. King-Sears, & D. Tessier-Switlick (Eds.), *Teaching students in inclusive settings: From theory to practice* (pp. 109–128). Boston: Allyn and Bacon.

Cipani, E., & Spooner, F. (1994). *Curricular and instructional approaches for persons with severe disabilities.* Boston: Allyn and Bacon.

Colorose, B. (2004). *The Bully, the Bullied, and the Bystander: From Preschool to High School—How Parents and Teachers Can Help Break the Cycle of Violence.* New York: Harper Collins.

Cook, L., and Friend, M. (1995). Co-teaching: Guidelines for effective practices. *Focus on Exceptional Children, 28*(3), 1–16.

Didden, R., Duker, P. C., & Korzilius, H. (1997). Meta-analytic study of treatment effectiveness for problem behaviors with individuals who have mental retardation. *American Journal of Mental Retardation, 101*, 387–399.

Emmer, E. T., Evertson, C. M., & Worsham, M. E. (2003). *Classroom management for secondary teachers.* Boston: Allyn and Bacon.

Fay, J., & Funk, D. (1995). *Teaching with Love and Logic.* Golden, CO: Love and Logic Press, 1995.

Glasser, W. (1990). *The quality school.* New York W.W. Norton & Co.

Glausser, W., & Glasser, C. (1999). *The Language of Choice Theory.* New York: Harper Collins.

Hammel, A. M. (2004). Inclusion Strategies that Work. *Music Educators Journal, 90*(5), 33–37.

Hoover, J. H., & Oliver, R. (1997). *Bullying Prevention Handbook: A Guide for Principals, Teachers, and Counselors.* Bloomington, IN: National Education Service.

Hourigan, R. M. (2008). Teaching Music to Performers with Special Needs. *Teaching Music, 15*(6), 26–29.

Hourigan, R. M. (2009). The Invisible Student: Understanding Social Identity Within Performing Ensembles. *Music Educators Journal, 95*(4), 34–38.

Figure 5.2 (Continued)

Ilmer, S., Snyder, J., Erbaugh, S., & Kurtz, K. (1997). Urban educators' perceptions of successful teaching. *Journal of Teacher Education, 48*(2), 279–284.

Kozulin, B., Gindis, V., Ageyev, V & Miller, S. (2003). *Vygotsky's Educational Theory in Cultural Context.* Cambridge, UK: Cambridge University Press.

Lewis, R. B., & Doorlag, D. H. (2006). *Teaching Special Students in General Education Classrooms.* Upper Saddle River, NJ: Prentice Hall.

MacLeod, J. (1987). *Ain't No Makin' It: Aspirations & Attainment in a Low Income Neighborhood.* Boulder, CO: Westview Press, 1987.

Olenchak, F. R., & Renzulli, J. S. (1989). The effectiveness of the schoolwide enrichment model on selected aspects of elementary school change. *Gifted Child Quarterly, 33*(1) 37.

Prizant, B. M., & Wetherby, A. M. (1998). Understanding the continuum of discrete-trial traditional behavioral to social-pragmatic developmental approaches in communication enhancement for young children with autism/pdd. *Seminars in Speech and Language, 19*(4), 329–353.

Varene, H., & McDermott, R. *Successful Failure: The School America Builds.* Boulder, CO: Westview Press.

Wolk, S. (2002). *Being good: Rethinking classroom management and student discipline.* Portsmouth, NH: Heinemann.

Figure 5.2 Resources for Understanding Student Socialization

PRACTICAL STRATEGIES FOR MUSIC EDUCATORS

This section is designed to offer pragmatic suggestions for music educators in creating an inclusive social structure within their classrooms. These suggestions will be presented in a broad sense to be generalizable to as many situations within music education and music teacher education as possible. It is hoped that both pre-service and in-service music educators as well as music teacher educators will develop a "tool box" of techniques to promote a positive social atmosphere in music classrooms. This is essential in order to provide a pedagogically sound, inclusive learning environment for all students.

BE AWARE OF THE SOCIAL ENVIRONMENT IN YOUR SCHOOL

Music educators tend to be isolated within the public schools. They are often the only or one of few music teachers within a school building. Many travel between buildings. This can be a disadvantage in understanding the social structure within a school. Create opportunities to get out of classrooms and offices, and visit other parts of the school to get a sense of the social conditions that exist. The hallway, the lunchroom, the playground, sporting events, and other school-related social activities are all places to gather such information. In addition, just talking with students and parents at these events will provide a sense of which students are friends, which seem isolated, and which students may be more likely to assist in establishing a positive social atmosphere in the music classroom.

It is important to know the social groups among students in a school. These groups may be created according to geographical boundaries (neighborhoods or portions of neighborhoods), socioeconomic status, academic standing, sports teams, extracurricular activities, and clubs. Unfortunately, sometimes race and gender can be factors in these groups as well. Having an awareness of the social strata within a school can be powerful information when creating groups within a music classroom or ensemble. An empowered music educator can use this information to create an inclusive and "clique free" classroom environment.

Eckert (1989) explains that the atmosphere students create can be encouraged by the school environment, and sometimes by teachers themselves. She explains: "Adults do not impose their class system and ideologies on adolescents; they provide the means by which adolescents can do it themselves" (p. 6). Music educators can unintentionally encourage unhealthy social structures with their students. Music educators should self-evaluate and look at the big picture regarding how social groups in music classrooms function and how they relate to the overall school environment.

In your own self-evaluation, it may be helpful to examine how you may contribute to an unhealthy atmosphere. Questions may include:

- Do I (intentionally or not) play favorites?
- Do I gossip with students?
- Is my classroom an inviting place (from both the student and the teacher's perspective)?
- Are there "cliques" in my classroom?
- Are they positive or negative in nature?

Other questions may come to mind. The goal is to be critical and objective in understanding the nature of the social atmosphere within the music classroom and ensemble setting.

Music educators play an important role in the lives of music students, and teacher attitudes and actions are powerful indicators of whom we are. They also provide a great deal of insight into the behaviors our students may wish to emulate (Fullan & Miles, 1992). If music educators model inclusiveness, acceptance, and kindness, students will demonstrate these qualities as well. Because teachers allow all students to participate equally in classrooms and posit a "fair is not always equal" philosophy, students are taught that everyone deserves to be treated fairly within a community (Stainback &

Stainback, 1990). This may mean that some students get extra turns or get to choose more often. Some students may receive preferred seating in class. All of this may appear to other students to be preferential treatment. This may be a moment to teach students that these accommodations are a part of the overall teaching and learning process for everyone, and that some students need these accommodations to be successful. It is also helpful to state that if any student in the class or ensemble ever needs something new or more to learn, the music educator will ensure that student receives what he needs. It is important to assure students that true equity and fairness permeate the learning environment.

SYNERGY

Students often make choices in groups that they would not necessarily make on their own. These choices can be positive or negative. Students with special needs may not understand these social situations and are then unable to protect themselves from the malicious scrutiny of their peers (Dewey, 1991; Gustein, 2000). We have found that students with high-functioning skills who have special needs can fall victim to such situations without understanding the larger implications. Often students with special needs can unintentionally perpetuate the unwanted scrutiny (Marriage, Gordon, & Brand 1995; Mesibov, 1984). Students who lack understanding about students with special needs may think they are having harmless fun without understanding the larger picture. Moreover, inappropriate behavior within a crowd can be a protective structure for a dominant leader within the group. If the group displays such an inappropriate behavior it is more difficult to "pin down" the individual to correct the situation.

Based on recent events in today's society, the implications can be critical. Bullying or hazing of individuals, if left unchecked, can lead to abuse and retribution. In these cases, students with disabilities need to be protected. It is important to be proactive in these situations (Ozonoff & Miller, 1995).

A MORAL/ETHICAL CODE

Hogg and Terry (2001) explain that the longer a teacher waits to provide information and model appropriate social behavior, the more vulnerable the group is to forming an unhealthy social hierarchy. In other words, "cliques" begin to form where students demonstrate power over those who don't belong within a self-identified group. This may seem a little extreme; however, the social dynamic within a music class may be indicative of a larger school problem. A student's music classroom can be a safe haven where everyone feels as though he or she belongs.

When the synergy of a classroom or ensemble is structured to promote acceptance and inclusiveness, reflection among students can be quickly channeled to a positive course even when students make errors in judgment. It is our consistent cultural mores and code of ethics that eventually envelop even the largest of music programs. If those mores and ethics are positive and inclusive, the resultant actions of our students will be positive and inclusive as well.

Establish a code of ethics and moral behavior within your classroom rules. This may be in a guidelines and procedures handout or a handbook. Send a copy home to parents to be signed. This sends a message that inappropriate behavior will not be tolerated. Most importantly, follow through with the guidelines established. This will make the message very clear that such behavior is not tolerated. Consistency is crucial in this area as students are not only learning from what we tell them—they are also learning from what we do (Colvin, Ainge, & Nelson, 1997; Johns & Carr, 1995). Having a clear and consistent set of guidelines for behaviors and interactions is important for students with and without special needs. Even more important is to monitor and act upon these guidelines. Students will honor these actions more readily than a vague listing of behavioral outcomes and procedures that are stated once at the beginning of a school year.

BEING PROACTIVE IN YOUR APPROACH TO SOCIALIZATION

For a student with special needs, creating and maintaining relationships with other students can be a challenge. Students with disabilities may be coming to music from a self-contained classroom or even another school. The following suggestions are intended to encourage music educators to be proactive in their approach to creative a positive social environment in the classroom.

As mentioned in part I, in the days and weeks prior to the start of a new school year, it is critical that teachers take the time to read and comprehend the IEP (Individualized Education Program) and 504 (Section 504) Plans or Summaries for their students. As we know, this is a legal responsibility. However, more importantly, it is part of an inclusive philosophy to know the students in our classrooms. Taking the time to read the paperwork regarding a student with special needs is a helpful first step in integrating students (with and without special needs) within the music classroom.

After reading the paperwork, it is also advisable to talk to the teachers closely involved in the educational planning for students with special needs.

If some students follow a specific behavior plan (see part I), it is very helpful to make that plan a part of daily, or weekly, interactions with them. Consistency is imperative when defining parameters for classroom expectations and behaviors. These conversations are also important as they set the tone with other professionals regarding attitudes and levels of participation in the overall inclusive culture of schools. When colleagues are aware that music educators are prepared and willing to actively include all students in instruction, they will often be willing to assist with creating strategies to educate students with special needs (Ainscow, 1999; Hobbs & Westing, 1998).

In planning for the first few days, assist students in breaking down social barriers. Oftentimes, students simply do not know each other. Students can have a tendency to separate from those who are different. In this instance, being proactive is the best approach. Take class time to allow students to reveal information about themselves to their peers. This may require assistance for a student with special needs. In some cases it is advisable to involve a special educator or parent to explain the challenges a student faces. Try to move the focus away from a disability and to the common interests among students. For example, Andrew may have autism. With the appropriate permission and support, it may be acceptable to reveal the diagnosis and the challenges involved. Do this without dwelling on the diagnosis. Move to the fact that Andrew likes to play basketball or guitar. Students will attach themselves to those commonalities when they attempt to interact. Other techniques that are often used include: icebreakers, wearing of name tags and other techniques to initiate contact. Remember, information will promote acceptance.

In elementary music classroom settings, playing partner games and dances early in the school year will assist in introducing students to others they may not know. It also reminds students that we all have relative strengths and weaknesses. For example, Bruce may not be able to read notes on the staff quickly; however, he is one of the first to remember all the steps to a new folk dance. It is also important to choose partners carefully for students and to allow them to practice choosing partners themselves. A common approach is to have a student ask, "Will you please be my partner?" The other student then will say one of two things: (a) "Yes, I would be happy to be your partner"; or (b) "I'm sorry—I already have a partner. Maybe next time?" This simple set of steps, taught early in the school year, and reinforced throughout the year, may lead to increased positive interaction in the music classroom.

Seating for Socialization

As mentioned in part I, strategic seating is essential for effective classroom management. Seating is also an easy, nonthreatening way to encourage students to interact. It is effective, even in performing ensembles, to vary seating arrangements. Another strategy is to create opportunities to encourage students to work together. Music educators can also be strategic in placing gregarious students with students who are reserved or placing students who are farther along academically with those who need assistance. All of these seating approaches, if well considered, can make a meaningful difference in encouraging students to work together.

When planning classroom instruction, consider placement of students with special needs near students who are good academic and behavioral models. These students may serve as formal or informal "buddies" for students with special needs. A small caveat to this strategy is to not use the same students for each class meeting. "Buddy burnout" can be a negative factor among students who are consistently asked to partner with students with special needs. Also, consider only using a student helper for the portion of class when a student with special needs will need assistance. Another successful strategy is to ask a student with special needs to assist someone else. This has been a powerful reminder to all students that those with special needs have areas of strengths as well.

When placing students in semipermanent seating, such as a secondary ensemble, consider the needs of the student, the ensemble, and the recommendations on the IEP (Individualized Education Program) or 504 (Section 504) Plan. Often, creative thinking can lead to finding a place for all students that fits their academic, emotional, and social needs. It is hoped that the suggestions mentioned above will assist in providing a learning environment that is conducive to learning for all of your students.

Travel

Whether it is a field trip to an orchestra concert, a trip to a local festival, a day trip to perform at an amusement park or a trip across the country, music groups often travel. Trips can often be times when students with social challenges have difficulty. Trips can also be an environment for inappropriate behavior such as bullying or abuse. It is our job as responsible educators to curtail these behaviors and protect those who are vulnerable.

Allen (2004) explains that an unsupervised group in certain situations can attempt to exert group control over an individual. A familiar example of this type of situation is hazing. As mentioned above, the synergy of a group can outweigh the logical and caring judgment of the individual. Again, this may seem extreme. However, with the excitement of the trip, students can find themselves in a situation that they will regret.

Be careful of such things as rooming lists and bus lists when traveling. Students with social challenges will struggle (if they attend at all) in these circumstances. Travel often requires students to take initiative to find people to room or sit on the bus with during the trip. Signing up for a bus list or a rooming list often reminds them of the fact that they do not have friends within the ensemble with whom they feel comfortable.

Consider the following rules for such occasions: (a) assign bus and rooming lists yourself; (b) if you want students to sign up themselves, require students to have representatives from different groups (sections, classes, etc.); or (c) if you are on a longer trip, have a different rooming list every night. Some of these suggestions require more work and attention by the music teacher. These strategies can limit the possibilities of isolation and force students to ask other students to be a part of their travel plans. Again, model acceptance and zero tolerance of inappropriate behavior. This includes the willingness to accept anyone into a group. Students can learn valuable life lessons from situations where positive behaviors are modeled.

Free time at a festival, park, or museum is an optimum time for students with special needs to become isolated. Students who are socially challenged may attempt to stay with the adults instead of exploring with other students. It is easier to remain with adults instead of attempting to make a connection to a peer group. Remaining with adults on a trip defeats the purpose of experiencing such opportunities with peers. When this occurs, consider having a "buddy system" rule and require students to travel in groups. If someone is left out of a group, hold the "buddy" accountable. Students can learn the life lesson of caring about the well-being of *everyone* in a group by abiding with this system. Sometimes by adhering to these rules students can connect with others who they would not otherwise know. Again, establishing rules such as the ones suggested above allow you to model acceptance and community building among your students.

Leadership

Leadership opportunities can be considered out of reach for students with special needs. It can often be challenging enough to be in class and participate. In secondary programs, leadership positions often go to students who are chosen, at least in part, by their peers. Students who are coming into music programs from self-contained classrooms or even from other schools may not, for whatever reason, be chosen. In elementary general music classrooms, music teachers can find themselves in a bad habit of choosing the most outgoing students for leading the class or passing out instruments.

Music may be a subject where a student with special needs can demonstrate and develop leadership skills. One co-author recently met a young man named Sam who was diagnosed with autism and was elected president of his high school band. This was due in part to some assistance from his band director. His director nominated him. Sam probably would not have been nominated otherwise. Because of this nomination, Sam gained confidence, gave a good "pitch" to his peers, and won the position. In fact, his band director has expressed that Sam was the most organized and dedicated leader he has ever had. The students were so inspired by him that they had one of the most productive years in recent memory. In addition, his classmates nominated him for student of the year at a local television station.

The point of this example is that Sam needed some help in the initial nomination process. By nominating him, Sam's band director instilled a dose of confidence into Sam that allowed him to shine. In other words, Sam's band director forced his hand to integrate him into the social structure of the band by setting up a positive scenario for Sam to succeed. It is also important to point out that this required risk taking by all parties involved.

We would caution that Sam was ready for this. Some students are not. The same sort of situation could have happened on a smaller scale. For example, Sam could have been elected to a position of less responsibility (i.e., section leader). It is up to the teacher to know the student well enough to understand what he or she can handle.

Collaborative Performance Opportunities

Performance opportunities can be an excellent way to encourage interaction among a group of students. Music can be the catalyst to encourage communication between students who would not ordinarily collaborate. Examples include: collaborative performances between classes (e.g., self-contained classroom and general education classroom), group composition projects, and chamber music. The challenge is to not always group these performances by ability level. It is sometimes useful to group students together based on other outcomes. For example, you may place a student who is challenged into a chamber group with a student who is exceptional to achieve an instructional goal. Another example is to have a combined performance with a self-contained classroom (with students assisting each other) in order for the outcome to be more about teaching or building personal relationships. A student from another culture may have unique insights to share as an ensemble prepares a piece of music or a lesson from his culture. These students, who have often recently immigrated, sometimes have limited means to express themselves to their classmates. As music *educators*, it is important to step out of usual routines and take a look at the larger picture of what a performance could mean.

CONCLUSION: CRITICAL ISSUES FOR STUDENTS
WITH SPECIAL NEEDS

There is more at stake in assisting students with special needs than just creating an atmosphere of acceptance. Thompson and Cohen (2005) state: "Victims of chronic harassment are at serious risk for poor mental and physical health, as well as academic achievement" (p. 16). In the current school environment, it is important for teachers to set forth expectations in music classrooms that abusive behavior will not be tolerated. Report any suspected behavior and immediately inquire about any potential abuse. Do not hesitate to bring in outside help from school counselors and social workers and parents (i.e., a team approach). As mentioned earlier, the music educator is the model of appropriate behavior. If the model is zero tolerance, the students will follow this lead. The positive steps taken, however small, can have a lasting effect on a student's well-being.

It should be every music educator's goal to establish an inclusive, compassionate, safe, and productive teaching and learning environment. This includes strategies that allow all students to learn, including those with special needs. Understanding how the accommodations in this chapter may assist a student with special needs is a great beginning. It is also imperative for a music educator to know when and how to advocate for support when negative behavior is hindering the ability of students to learn (i.e., intervention plans). It is important that music educators consider how students develop their personal identity through socialization. Music can be the catalyst for students to develop healthy self-concepts and establish positive relationships throughout their time in public school. These concepts and relationships continue with students (with and without special needs) as they leave public school settings and continue their lives as adults.

DISCUSSION QUESTIONS

1. How will you, or do you, model compassion in the music classroom? What specific steps are necessary to achieve this goal?
2. What are some ways to honor the "comfort zone" of a student while encouraging that student to step beyond these behaviors and into the mainstream of a classroom?
3. What are some practical ways to develop positive relationships with students? What are some practical ways to develop positive relationships with colleagues?

4. How can you promote behavior inclusiveness among all students in your music classroom?
5. What are some creative ways to promote leadership within the music classroom or ensemble?

REFERENCES

Ainscow, M. (1999). *Understanding the development of inclusive schools.* Studies in inclusive education series. London: Falmer Press.

Allen, B. (2004). *Difference matters.* Long Grove, IL: Waveland Press.

American Institute for Research. (1999). *An educator's guide to schoolwide reform.* Arlington, VA: Educational Research Service.

Anderson, S. R., & Romanczyk, R. G. (1999). Early intervention for young children with autism. Continuum-based behavioral models. *Journal of the Association for People with Special Handicaps, 24*(3), 162–173.

Bain, H. P., & Jacobs, R. (1990). The case for smaller classes and better teachers. *Streamlined Seminar-National Association of Elementary School Principals, 9*(1).

Boyle-Baise, M. (2005). Preparing community-oriented teachers: Reflections from a multi-cultural service-learning project. *Journal of Teacher Education, 56*(5), 446–458.

Brophy, J., & Good, T. L. (1986). Teacher behavior and student achievement. In M. C. Wittrock (Ed.), *Handbook of research on teaching* (3rd ed., pp. 328–371). New York: Macmillan.

Conroy, M., Sutherland, K., Snyder, A., & Marsh, S. (2008). Classwide interventions: Effective instruction makes a difference. *Teaching Exceptional Children, 40*(6), *24nd burnouts: Social categories and identity in high school.* New York: Teachers College Press.

Colvin, G., Ainge, D., & Nelson, R. (1997). How to defuse confrontations. *Teaching Exceptional Children, 29*(6), 47–51.

Cotton, K. (2000). *The schooling practices that matter most.* Portland, OR: Northwest Regional Educational Laboratory and Alexandria, VA: Association for Supervision and Curriculum Development.

Dewey, M. (1991). Living with Asperger's Sundrome. In U. Frith (Ed.), *Autism and Asperger's Syndrome.* Cambridge: Cambridge University Press.

Eckert, P. (1989). *Jocks and burnouts: Social categories and identity in the high school.* New York: Teachers College Press.

Emmer, E. T., Evertson, C. M., & Anderson, L. M. (1980). Effective classroom management at the beginning of the school year. *The Elementary School Journal, 80*(5), 219–231.

Fullan, M., & Miles, M. B. (1992). Getting reform right: What works and what doesn't. *Phi Delta Kappan, 73*(10), 745–752.

Goldson, E. (2001). Maltreatment among children with disabilities. *Infants and Young Children, 13*(4), 44–54.

Gustein, S. E. (2000). *Autism: Asperger's: Solving the Relationship Puzzle.* Arlington, TX: Future Horizons.

Hamre, B. K., & Pianta, R. C. (2005). Can instructional and emotional support in the first grade classroom make a difference for children at risk of school failure? *Child Development, 76*(5), 949–967.

Hobbs, T., & Westing, D. L. (1998). Promoting successful inclusion through collaborative problem solving. *Teaching Exceptional Children, 34*(2), 12–19.

Hogg, M. A., & Terry, D. J., (2001). *Social identity processes in organizational contexts.* Philadelphia: Psychology Press.

Horner, R., Strain, P., & Carr, E. (2002). Problem behavior interventions for young children with autism: A research synthesis. *Journal for Autism and Developmental Disorders, 32,* 423–446.

Howard, T. C. (2002). Hearing footsteps in the dark: African-American students' descriptions of effective teachers. *Journal of Education for Students Placed at Risk, 4*(4), 425–444.

Johns, B., & Carr, V. (1995). *Techniques for managing verbally and physically aggressive students.* Denver, CO: Love.

Koegel, L. K., Koegel, R. L., Dunlap, G. (1996). *Positive behavioral support.* Baltimore, MD: Brookes.

Koegel, L. K., Koegel, R. L., & Hurley, C. et al. (1992). Improving social skills and disruptive behavior in children with autism through self-management. *Journal of Applied Behavior Analysis, 25,* 341–353.

Kohn, A. (1996). What to look for in a classroom. *Educational Leadership, 54*(1), 54–55.

Langer, J. A. (2000). Excellence in English in middle and high school: How teachers' professional lives support student achievement. *American Educational Research Journal, 37*(2), 397–439.

Marriage, K. J., Gordon, V., & Brand, L. (1995). A social skills group for boys with Asperger's Syndrome. *Australian and New Zealand Journal for Psychiatry, 29,* 58–62.

Marzano, R. J. (2003). *What works in schools: Translating research in to action.* Alexandria, VA: Association for Supervision and Curriculum Development.

Marzano, R. J. with Marzano, J. S., & Pickering, D. J. (2003). *Classroom management that works: Research-based strategies for every teacher.* Alexandria, VA: Association for Supervision and Curriculum Development.

Mesibov, G. B. (1984). Social skills training with verbal autistic adolescents and adults: A program model. *Journal of Autism and Developmental Disorders, 14,* 395–404.

Mitchell, R. D. (1998). World class teachers: When top teachers earn National Board certification, schools-and students-reap the benefits. *The American School Board Journal, 185*(9), 27–29.

Noddings, N. (1984). *Caring: A feminine approach to ethics and moral education.* Los Angeles: University of California Press.

Onikama, D. L., Hammond, O.W., & Koki, S. (1998). *Family involvement in education: A synthesis of research for Pacific educators.* Honolulu, HI: Pacific Regional Educational Laboratory.

Ozonoff, S., Dawson, G., & McPartland, J. (2002). A parent's guide to Asperger Syndrome and High-Functioning Autism: How to meet the challenges and help your child thrive. New York: Guilford.

Ozonoff, S., & Miller, J. (1995). Teaching theory of mind: A new approach to social skills training for individuals with autism. *Journal of Autism and Developmental Disorders, 25,* 415–433.

Perry, D., Marston, G., & Hinder, S. et al. (2001). The phenomenology of depressive illness in people with learning disability and autism. *Autism, 5,* 265–275.

Rogers, S. L. (1998). Empirically supported comprehensive treatments for young children with autism. *Journal of Clinical Psychology, 27*, 167–178.

Shellard, E., & Protheroe, N. (2000). Effective teaching: How do we know it when we see it? *The Informed Educator Series.* Arlington, VA: Educational Research Service.

Sokal, L., Smith, D. G., & Mowat, H. (2003). Alternative certification teachers' attitudes toward classroom management. *The High School Journal, 86*(3), 8–16.

Southwest Center for Teaching Quality (SECTQ). (2003). Alternative certification teachers' attitudes toward classroom management. *The High School Journal, 86*(3), 8–16.

Stainback, W., & Stainback, S. (1990). Facilitating peer supports and friendships. In W. Stainback & S. Stainback (Eds.), *Support networks for inclusive schooling* (pp. 51–63). Baltimore: Paul Brookes.

Sugai, G., Simonsen, B., & Horner, R. (2008) Schoolwide positive behavior supports: A continuum or positive behavior supports for all students. *Teaching Exceptional Children, 40*(6), 4.

Thompson, M., & Cohen, L. (2005). When the bullied must adjust. *Education Digest: Essential Readings Condensed for Quick Review, 70*(5), 16–19.

Vygotsky, L. S.. (1934/1978). *Mind in society.* Cambridge, MS: Harvard University Press.

Walls, R. T., Nardi, A. H., von Minden, A. M., & Hoffman, N. (2002). The characteristics of effective and ineffective teachers. *Teacher Education Quarterly, 29*(1), 39–48.

Wharton-McDonald, R., Pressley, M., & Hampston, J. M. (1998). Literacy instruction in nine first-grade classrooms: Teacher characteristics and student achievement. *The Elementary School Journal, 99*(2), 101–128.

Zahorik, J., Halbach, A., Ehrle, K., & Molnar, A. (2003). Teaching practices for smaller classes. *Educational Leadership, 61*(1), 75–77.

Zeichner, K. M. (2003). Pedagogy, knowledge, and teacher preparation. In B. Williams (Ed.), *Closing the achievement gap: A vision for changing beliefs and practices* (2nd ed., pp. 99–114). Alexandria, VA: Association for Supervision and Curriculum Development.

Chapter 6

Curriculum and Assessment for Students with Special Needs

Every successful music educator has a curriculum that contains a scope (overarching goals) and sequence (how we will achieve our goals and in what order) that are critical to reaching meaningful educational goals within the music classroom. Walker and Soltis (2004) state: "Working with the curriculum is an integral part of all teachers' daily lives" (p. 1). When specific curricula are not mandated (by the state, or federal government), most music educators use a set of standards or guidelines to devise a scope and sequence for classroom teaching (i.e., the National Standards).

It is important as music educators to consider their curriculum when preparing to teach all students, not just students with learning challenges. This is what separates an educator from a therapist or a service provider. The questions that we will address in this chapter include: How do music educators maintain a focus on their own curricular goals while adapting that same curriculum to the individual needs of students? And how do we assess and reflect on these goals to make adjustments in our curriculum?

These are difficult questions to answer. In fact, this has been a challenge for teachers since the inclusion of students with special needs began following the passage of P.L. 94-142 more than 35 years ago. Walker and Soltis explain, "While many teachers supported the goal, many were offended that rigid regulations were imposed on them without their consent" (p. 84).

All these issues require a thoughtful and sequential approach when preparing, presenting, and assessing instruction in the music classroom. However, the stronger the underlying curricular focus is, the easier it will be to adapt and modify your existing curriculum to individualize instruction for students who have learning differences.

Your specific curriculum, if not mandated by your state or school system, will be a result of your philosophy of music education. Even when utilizing prescribed curricula, your choices in scope and sequence will reflect your values in the classroom. These same values will be reflected in the choices you make in modifying your curricula for students with special needs.

FUNDAMENTALS OF CURRICULUM DESIGN AND STUDENTS WITH SPECIAL NEEDS (A QUICK REVIEW)

The first priority in addressing the curricular needs of a student with special needs is to once again examine the IEP or 504 Document. These documents will include all mandated curricular goals and assessments for determining curricular outcomes. There are many inferences that can be made by examining the choices of other teachers in your building as they adapt their curriculum for a specific student or group of students. Speaking with other teachers who work with your students with special needs is also often a valuable strategy. Next, reevaluate the fundamental model of your curriculum design at the school level and in your classroom. Consider the needs of your students and the goals stated in their special education documents as you adapt your curricula and the expectations you have for a student with special needs. Your modifications can include musical, extramusical, and social elements that can be observed and assessed in your classroom.

In order to situate our discussion, we offer a quick review of basic curriculum strategy. Yes, there are many ways to design your curriculum. The four different types described below assist us in offering suggestions for adaptations and modifications within the music classroom. This discussion is also aimed at allowing you as a teacher to make connections to the curricular focus in your own classroom.

A materials-centered curriculum is centered on the selection of a basic set of materials (e.g.. a general music textbook series or a method book series) and the design of lesson plans around this material (Labuta & Smith, 1997). Many general music classrooms and performance-based music education classrooms use the materials approach. These curricula often include a guide to a scope and sequence that teachers may follow throughout the year.

A content-centered music curriculum stems from the music literature. Many of our performance-based classrooms use a content-centered approach. Teachers who use this approach choose a piece of music, a style of music, or a composer and build their curriculum accordingly. This type of curriculum usually requires a music educator to consider the skills necessary as prerequisites to learning or performing the material chosen.

A method approach in music education stems from an establish method or ideology (i.e., Orff, Kodály, Music Learning Theory). Each method leads music educators to create a scope and sequence for students. There are ways to adapt or modify methods for teaching music to students with disabilities within each approach while maintaining the basic tenets of the curriculum.

An experience-based curriculum or constructivism is another approach to music teaching and learning. This approach is centered on learning experiences of the student. The teacher acts a facilitator, concentrating on knowledge acquisition in an active and engaged environment. This will be discussed at length in this chapter.

CONSTRUCTIVISM AS A CURRICULAR MODEL TO ASSIST WITH INCLUSION

While practical and fundamental modifications to curricula are important (e.g., the Four Teaching Practices), the musical meaning and aesthetic experience of a musical education is also essential. There has been much written and discussed in music education regarding a constructivist approach to teaching and learning (Steffe & Gale, 2006). A constructivist approach to curriculum can be defined as a learning theory that emphasizes learning as a social process in which students construct meaning through their own experiences (Dewey, 1929).

The constructivist philosophy of teaching is not always considered when working with students with special needs. Often this approach is reserved for students who are at grade level or above. It is important for music teachers to consider the musical experiences from the student's perspective in working with a modified constructivist curriculum for students with special needs. Moreover, a fundamental value of constructivism is that "learning is a social act where students interpret new understandings of their worlds in relation to previous knowledge and experience" (Scott, 2006, p. 19).

Music enhances the quality of life of all people. Many adults with special needs find social and spiritual identity and purposeful experiences in the arts that they cannot find through other experiences. Therefore, enhancing their understanding will widen their ability to consume and participate in musical activities as an adult. Due to delays in social development, many people with special needs require practice in interpreting their own understandings of music and its relationship to the world. Music can be the vehicle that will assist them as they make lasting relationships with peers, social groups, and the community.

Teacher-directed learning (the opposite of constructivism) approaches a musical topic or concept from one learning perspective at a time (e.g., aural or visual). Conversely, music educators who explore constructivism may uncover many techniques that will enhance the ability of students with special needs to engage the musical material and concepts within the curriculum. This multimodal effort vastly increases the possibility that students will access and achieve the curriculum, or modified curriculum, in your classroom.

Constructivism allows teachers to create experiences for students as they enter a learning community from various levels of previous knowledge.

Teacher-directed or Traditional Approach	Constructivist or Student-centered Approach with Modifications for a Student with Special Needs
Objectives: 1. Students will demonstrate their understanding of notation by composing a piece of music within the guidelines provided.	Objectives: 1. Groups of students will demonstrate their understanding of notation by composing a piece of music of any style of their choice based on their experience.
Procedures: 1. Students will work individually (with teacher assistance) in class. 2. Students will be required to finish their work at home.	Procedures: 1. Groups of three will be established and asked to contribute equally to the composition based on their ability. **Modification:** Tim (student with special needs) will contribute based on his skill set. Students in his group will be informed of a potential role for Tim in the group. 2. Student groups will perform their composition and field comments from the class in order for them to reflect, revise, and resubmit their composition. 3. The instructor will also ask reflective and guiding questions (including questions directed at Tim's portion of the assignment) in order to probe deeper into their experience and to unlock the potential of this assignment.
Assessments: Instructor will grade each assignment with an established rubric.	Assessments: 1. Students will perform their compositions for the class. 2. Peer feedback forms will be used. 3. Student-constructed rubrics will be used. 4. Modified rubric for Tim will be used based on his skills and progress.

Figure 6.1 An Example of a Constructivist-based lesson for Students with Special Needs 6th Grade Composition

Within the concept of constructivism, music teachers are seen as facilitators, collaborators, and co-learners in the music classroom. The experience is crucial to a successful lesson that allows students to discover knowledge through social experiences in which they share inquiry into a topic with their peers. This is an effective approach for students with special needs. Figure 6.1 offers two examples of the same lesson. One is conceived via a traditional approach and the other within a constructivist approach. Vignette 6.1 was written by an Indiana music educator who was successful in his constructivist approach with a child on the autism spectrum in instrumental music. This was included to offer a real-life example of constructivism in practice.

Vignette 6.1 Mike and the Didgeridoo

Mike is a percussionist in my junior high band. He is in eighth grade and is on the autism spectrum. I assess students using portfolios. As part of the portfolio they choose projects to complete. I have worked closely with Mike's special education teacher to make accommodations for his assignments. We decided Mike would research instruments from around the world. He would write the information on note cards then tell the information to me.

His first report was on the didgeridoo. I happened to have a didgeridoo at home. I brought the didgeridoo to school and lent it to Mike's special education teacher. Mike told me about his research of the didgeridoo. He brought the didgeridoo back to the band room when he gave his report. Mike used his note cards to tell me about the didgeridoo. Mike was so excited about the didgeridoo he would not put it down when he brought it back to me. The students in the band wanted to know about the instrument Mike had. Mike then told the other band students about the didgeridoo with my help. He was so excited. The students were very gracious toward Mike even clapping when he was finished.

For whatever reason, I did not take the didgeridoo home right away. I left it in my office. Every day Mike would get the didgeridoo and take it back to the percussion section. He would twirl it around and dance with it. He also would play it with the band mostly during warm-ups. Mike was playing the didgeridoo during Anne McGinty's "English Folk Trilogy" one day. I stopped the band and asked Mike what instrument he was playing for "English Folk Trilogy." He told me he was going to play the didgeridoo. I explained to Mike the didgeridoo would not work for English Folk Trilogy. I then told Mike that it might be cool to find a

(continued)

Vignette 6.1 (continued)

piece that had didgeridoo in it. I regretted telling Mike this immediately. I knew there no band pieces featuring the didgeridoo.

I decided I would teach the Australian folk song "Kookaburra" to the band and we would arrange it as a group, making sure to feature the didgeridoo. The band learned the melody and bass line of "Kookaburra" all while Mike was blowing away on the didgeridoo. We then began arranging. The students came up with ideas, then we voted on the ideas we liked the best. I asked for three ideas of which section or sections would play the melody and the bass line. Or if the students wanted to play "Kookaburra" in a round and in what order the instruments would enter.

The arrangement turned into theme and variations. Between each variation was a pause where Mike would play the didgeridoo. The percussion came up with Australian sounding effects. The band had notation with the name of our band as the arranger. The students loved seeing the band listed as the arranger on the notation.

We learned about the Kookaburra bird and Australian culture. As part of the junior high curriculum students study Australia. The lessons meshed well with their social studies classes. We watched video of aboriginal musicians. As a result of these lessons we decided to add the Kookaburra's laugh as well as some aboriginal drums.

We performed the arrangement at our fall concert. It was the crowd's favorite piece of the concert. Mike's parents were thrilled with his performance. Mike told me he was proud of his performance. Mike's Mom was very excited and proud of him.

Written by James Byrn, Caston Public Schools, Indiana

FOUR PRIMARY TEACHING PRACTICES TO CONSIDER WHEN TEACHING STUDENTS WITH DISABILITIES IN A MODIFIED OR ADAPTED CURRICULUM

Any of the above approaches to curricula can be adapted for students with special needs. However, there are certain overarching teaching techniques to consider when adapting curricula. These four techniques include modality, pacing, size, and color. By considering these techniques in the way we adapt or modify our curriculum and instruction with students with special needs (with obvious consultation with the special education documents and personnel), students will have more opportunities to learn in our classrooms. We realize that each of the four are also considered teaching and accommodation techniques; however, in teaching students with special needs, *these practices* should be considered when adapting or modifying curriculum.

Modality

When teaching any students, particularly students with special needs, it is critical to introduce each concept and skill through all modalities (aural, visual, kinesthetic). Everyone learns differently, and students with special needs sometimes have great preferences, or limited options, for the modality they use to process information. In preparing to adapt a curriculum for students with special needs, an effective strategy is to brainstorm the number of ways a concept can be taught. This list is universal, meaning it can be used for all students in your classroom, and all students will benefit from being introduced to material through multiple modalities.

Whether you use a material-, content-, experience-, or method-centered approach, your lesson planning can be enhanced through the use of multimodal approaches. It may be helpful to list the modality choices aural (A), visual (V), and kinesthetic (K) on your scope and sequence charts and lesson plans to guide your use of multiple modalities in teaching.

Pacing

Our lives as music educators move very quickly. We often speak, walk, and teach at a rapid pace because we have a great deal of material to teach, have numerous performance deadlines, and want to give our students the very best (both in quality and quantity) that we have to offer. For some of our students, our pacing will still be considered too slow! Many of our students will be able to follow our scope and sequence well. Conversely, some students will not be able to learn the amount of music studied in a class or ensemble, and may become frustrated by the pace of instruction, amount of materials, performance expectations, and sheer sensory overload (visual, aural, and kinesthetic).

For those students who need adjustments to the pace of materials, instruction, and overall curriculum, consider modifications to pacing. These modifications require careful consideration, as it is important that the needs of all students in classes and ensembles are honored, and that the alternative pacing procedures put in place are effective and appropriate for everyone.

Size

Processing time and effectiveness can be compromised by the size of materials. When students with special needs are working very hard to process information, the relatively small size, faint font, and large amount of material on

- Use raised textured board (perhaps a rope on a board to show a five line staff) for students to touch as they are introduced to the concept of lines and spaces. This adds a kinesthetic element to a primarily visual concept.
- Use movement activities to accompany some listening experiences. Many students learn best when their bodies are in motion and concepts such as tempo, style, dynamics, and genre can be practiced through movement. Using this to accompany the aural experience of listening can be very effective. These activities are enjoyed by students of all ages and do not need to be considered elementary in nature.
- Have students track measures in their parts or a score (possibly via a projected image) while listening to a recording. We often do this with beginning performance groups and with elementary students; however, this is still a useful activity with more experienced students as well. Score study is a complex, yet extremely useful skill, and a multi-modal approach can be an enriching experience for all students.
- Create three-dimensional figures to represent abstract concepts (notes, rhythms, solfege, dynamic and artistic markings). Some students must touch a three- dimensional object to grasp the meaning of some higher-level concepts.
- A picture or written schedule to accompany the aural directions and procedures in class can ease student frustration.

Students may excel when given the choice of modality for response to a quiz or performance test. They may also perform best when given the choice to respond in two or more ways to a question or task.

Figure 6.2 Modality Examples for Music Teachers

one page can be frustrating. When material is made larger, bolder, and when information that is not essential at the moment is removed, students often find they are more able to understand and respond to instruction.

Color

It can be very difficult for some students to read music or books that are black and white. These two colors are very stark, and the contrast can create issues within the eyes that cause the processing of information to slow. Color softens this difference and can drastically improve the ability of a student with special needs to read music. Color is also an excellent modification to

- Part revisions may be necessary. Some students will be unable to read a part as written by the composer. It may be necessary to simplify a part (use bass line, chord outlines, first note of each measure, etc.) to meet the musical needs of a student. As the student improves, these modified parts may be adapted.
- A student may need to begin with a "blank score" that is filled in slowly as his abilities increase. For some students, the amount of ancillary information on a page (title, composer, tempo and dynamic markings, pictures) can be distracting and frustrating. Placing only the amount of information a student actually needs to perform successfully may be very effective.
- Some students may need to learn less material than others. For example, learning the A section of a piece, memorizing the chorus rather than the verses, practicing the rhythm only rather than the rhythm combined with the melody, or mastering one movement instead of four may be the most beneficial way to begin with a student.
- For students who have sensory issues, partial participation in class or a performance may be necessary. If the pace of a class becomes too fast or the amount of sounds, sights, and textures overloads a sensory system, a student may need to participate in music for a shorter amount of time, or learn less material for the concert and only perform the portions of music learned.
- Student assistants (buddies) can be valuable in the pacing process as they can repeat directions, refocus attention, and answer questions a student may have if the pace of class/rehearsal is too fast. We suggest having several buddies take turns working with a student to avoid "buddy burnout" among our assistants.
- Wait time is another important element of pacing. Some students take up to 10 times the amount of time we need to process a question or a piece of information. When asking a question of a student, wait at least five seconds before re-prompting or redirecting. If a student has difficulty with aural questions, try a modality and pacing accommodation and write the question on a piece of paper or draw a picture of the question or information. This combined with a longer wait time honors the student, and the process of teaching and learning.

Figure 6.3 Pacing Examples for Music Teachers

Remove all extraneous material from a page and create a large space for the staff and musical notation.

- Use a large and bold font. You may also wish to use a card or piece of paper to cover the words or notes not needed at that moment. The card or paper may move along the page to assist the student as she reads the notation or words.
- Project material onto an overhead or LCD projector and allow students to stand near the projected image or touch the information as you are teaching.
- Use a font that is simple and has no decorative elements.

Figure 6.4 Size Adaptations for Students with Special Needs

- Colored transparencies placed over music or written pages may assist students in reading. Another option is to cut strips of colored transparencies for students to use as they track their reading.
- Music and text can be highlighted for ease in score and staff reading. For students who are learning to play band and orchestra instruments, specific notes may be highlighted for practice. For example, a beginning flutist who is learning to play D, Eb, and F may only be able to finger D at first. Highlighting all the Ds in a line can help her track and play the note she is practicing. Some highlighters have erasers at the opposite end. These can be used to erase notes and highlight new notes if needed, or to erase highlighted lines for use by other students who do not need highlighted materials.

For students who have difficulty remembering the note name, fingering, and playing procedure in the amount of time allowed in an ensemble setting, notes may be color coded at first to remove some of the steps required for this type of reading. For example, a beginning recorder student may be learning B, A, and G. B may be highlighted in blue, A may be highlighted in red, and G may be highlighted in green. As a student learns to read the notes, the colorcoding may become less frequent and then be phased out altogether. A teacher may further this modification by adding paper hole reinforcers around the holes. The reinforcers can then be color coded to match the highlighted notes in case a student needs to remember the color that matches the fingering.

Figure 6.5 Color Adaptations for Students with Special Needs

draw student attention to details and to items of importance. Finally, the use of color in photographs, diagrams, and pictures can improve student understanding of concepts presented during instruction.

CURRICULAR MODIFICATIONS IN MUSIC EDUCATION FOR STUDENTS WITH DISABILITIES

Often special educators consider different curricular models when defining the least restrictive learning environment (LRE) for students with special needs. More often this includes constructing a parallel curriculum to the existing general education curriculum. A parallel curriculum follows the path of the existing grade level or subject matter of a student's regular education counterpart with modifications or adaptations as needed. In a sense, the IEP is also a curricular document in itself. However, it does not include the specificity of units and assessments, or a scope and sequence, necessary for a strong curriculum.

A parallel curriculum can be designed using two potential threads. First, a modified curriculum follows the subject and approach (see above), but does not have the same expectations (i.e., level of difficulty). An adapted curriculum allows for the same expectations; however, issues such as time, size of assignments, and physical adaptations are made to accommodate the student or students. Modifications and adaptations to curricula work together throughout the preparation, presentation, and assessment cycles in a classroom. Figures 6.6 and 6.7 are included to compare what different modified curricular expectations look like in a instrumental (6.6) and a general music class (6.7). It is hoped that these might spark ideas for your own music classroom.

Evaluating your curriculum and determining best practice (through modifications and adaptations) for students with special needs and individual learning differences is really just good teaching. This process follows the same principles used with all students. The difference is that students with special needs require an intensification of good teaching practices (modality, pacing, size, and color).

INCORPORATING IMPORTANT ELEMENTS OF MUSIC THERAPY INTO THE MUSIC EDUCATION CURRICULUM (CONTRIBUTED BY AMY M. HOURIGAN MT-BC)

Children have similar needs that are necessary to address for success in their everyday lives, they are: communication, social, and cognitive needs. These areas are continually developing in our students and can be addressed in the music classroom.

"A Hymnsong on Phillip Bliss," David Holsinger   (Content-centered): Eight Weeks

Nonmodified or Adapted Curricular Goals	Modified Curricular Goals (for an included individual in the same band)	Adapted Curricular Goals (for an included individual in the same band)
• Students will be able to sing the Hymnsong in the key of E-flat (National Standard 1).	• Student will be able to match pitch on an E-flat.	• Student will be able to buzz (on their mouthpiece) the Hymnsong in the key of E-flat (modification for a student with normal cognitive function and vocal or speech disability).
• Students will demonstrate their understanding of all musical terms in this piece.	• Student will be able to demonstrate their understanding of at least two musical terms from this piece.	• Student will demonstrate an understanding of all musical terms in this piece. However, student will be given as much time as he needs to complete the task.
• Students will perform their part individually with good tone, pulse, and rhythm.	• Student will perform a modified-rewritten part individually with good tone, pulse, and rhythm. (This could also be a portion of a piece of music.)	• Student will perform the part individually with good tone, pulse, and rhythm. However, student will be given as much time as he needs to complete the task and will be given a proctor to assist him during the playing exam. Length of material may be shortened (with some standards).

Figure 6.6 A Modified Parallel Curriculum for Eighth-grade Band

- Students will understand all key relationships.

- Students will understand the significance of Phillip Bliss and his contribution to the arts and culture.

- Students will attempt to improvise in the key of concert E-flat within the context provided by the instructor.

- Student will demonstrate an understanding of the "home" key.

- Student will be able to understand when and where Phillip Bliss lived.

- Student will improvise rhythmic patterns while playing an E-flat.

- Student will be able to play, sing, write, or use any means possible to demonstrate an understanding of all key relationships.

- Student will be given multiple means to demonstrate understanding of this topic (oral exam, paper, traditional test with more time, etc.).

- Student will improvise rhythmic and tonal (separately) patterns in the key of E-flat.

Figure 6.6 (Continued)

Sol-Mi Notation—Quarter-eighth Notation (Presentation Stage) (Method-centered) Four Weeks

Nonmodified or Adapted Curricular Goals	Modified Curricular Goals	Adapted Curricular Goals
• Students will sing sol-mi patterns using neutral syllables.	• Student will approximate higher and lower pitches following individual prompt by teacher.	• Student will sing sol-mi patterns using neutral syllables at a tempo of his choosing.
• Students will derive quarter-eighth patterns from chants that are well-known to them.	• Student will tap the rhythm with words to chants that are well-known to him.	• Student will derive quarter-eighth patterns using popsicle sticks given as much time as necessary.
• Students will show higher and lower with their hands and with the use of icons.	• Student will show higher and lower through any modality he prefers.	• Student will demonstrate higher and lower using icons and/or body motions.
• Students will discover the two pitches (sol and mi) and their similarities as noted in several folk songs well-known to them.	• Student will sing folk songs that contain sol-mi with other students.	• Student will discover sol-mi in at least one folk song well-known to him.
• Students will apply new rhythm syllables to chants well-known to them.	• Student will chant rhymes that contain quarter/eighth patterns with other students.	• Student will chant using rhythm syllables at a tempo of his choosing.
• Students will apply new solfege syllables to chants well-known to them.		• Student will apply new solfege syllables to at least one chant well-known to him.

Figure 6.7 A Modified Parallel Curriculum for a First-grade General Music Class

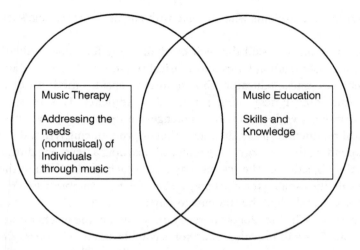

Figure 6.8 Music Therapy and Music Education

As mentioned in chapter 3 (and shown in figure 6.8), music therapists are interested in meeting the individual goals (nonmusical) of individuals. Music therapists assess their clients by identifying strengths and needs in the areas of communication, socialization, motor function, emotion and cognition before beginning to create goals and objectives for therapy. While music educators are not music therapists, being aware of the strengths and needs of students before planning a lesson is a technique that can adopted from the music therapy profession. The next section is designed to shed light on how these disciplines can enhance each other. These are just broad examples. Obviously each child is different. The National Standards for Music Education will be used as a framework to discuss these theories and to put these techniques into practice within the music classroom. The concepts offer a large framework of ideas. Music teachers are encouraged to modify these suggestions within their own classroom.

1: Singing, Alone and with Others, a Varied Repertoire of Music.
Challenges: Varied Repertoire

When choosing a "varied repertoire of music," consider the text. Music educators primarily make literature choices based on the musical concepts that can be taught. To assist students with special needs consider using a smaller collection of songs or songs with fewer words that can teach a larger number of musical skills and concepts. In addition, do not be afraid to rewrite music to simplify concepts and lyrics. The sheer number of words in a song may be daunting for students who struggle with cognitive processing, speech, or attention.

Singing songs is a skill that will be challenging for some students (e.g., simultaneously reading lyrics and musical notation). When making litera-ture choices, music educators should always consider the breadth of con-cepts (including lyrics) being presented to students. This consideration allows students with processing challenges an opportunity to concentrate on vocal production rather than decoding or pronouncing lyrics. If students are expending their energy struggling with learning a new song during each class, the objective of the lesson may not be achieved. Dividing the lyric responsibilities among the class may be helpful. For example, when teaching an ABA song, ask all of the students to sing the A sections. The teacher sings the B section. When students are ready, they can join the teacher during the A section. This will provide a sense of accomplishment. *Consider offering a varied repertoire consisting of fewer songs and allow students to be responsible for musical content/skills rather than spending their time processing how to pro-nounce lyrics.*

2: Performing on Instruments Alone and with Others a Varied Repertoire of Music. Challenges: Equipment Choices, Structure of Playing Experiences

Choosing appropriate instruments is essential to an effective instrumen-tal music experience. Before planning an instrumental music lesson for a class, which contains students with special needs, there are additional considerations to be made. For instance, students who are working to improve fine motor skills or have impaired vision may have difficulty play-ing instruments. When accessing these pieces of equipment make neces-sary adaptations that will provide a positive musical experience for the student.

The amount of cognitive processing necessary to read music and partici-pate in playing music in an ensemble is staggering. Music educators should be aware that students with disabilities need an access point that matches their processing ability. Reducing the amount of information that students will be responsible to comprehend will reduce frustration for students. Is the objective of the lesson to play the instruments in an ensemble? If the answer is yes, try iconic representation, using pictures rather than notes and rests, or consider limiting the amount of visual material presented to the student, by using paper to cover up what is not being read. *Consider the instrument and the precise fine motor skills that are necessary to play it and reduce the amount of information students are deciphering during the activity.*

3: Improvising Melodies, Variations, and Accompaniments.
Challenges: Providing Structure in Improvisation

This is an area where students with special needs may excel. In order to provide a successful improvisation experience, support is necessary. This can be scaffolded. At first, ask students to echo tonal and rhythm patterns. This provides the students an opportunity to play or sing what is heard and to perform alone. In the next stage, have students "pass" a given rhythm around the class (each student performs the rhythm given to them by the previous student in turn). Next, combine a group playing the given rhythm with students performing their own rhythms. This type of improvisation provides scaffolded choices. Students are aware of how long they will improvise and when they have to start and stop. This will alleviate anxiety in some students and offer them the opportunity to be musically creative.

Ostinati can be used to provide access points for students with special needs. Often, an ostinato is the simplest element of the structure for the improvisation experience. Peer-assisted ostinati can allow students to participate and, as they gain confidence, attempt an improvised pattern with the group.

Tonally, providing a limited set of pitches or pitches "that work" no matter what, (i.e. pentatonic scale), can assist students in gaining confidence and building improvisation skills. Instruments (i.e., Orff instruments) can be adapted for use in these situations. *Consider providing a nonverbal and musical beginning, middle, and end to musical improvisations as well as multiple access points.*

4: Composing and Arranging within Specified Guidelines.
Challenges: Providing Structure When Composing

With the numerous choices music provides, composing presents its own set of difficulties. For students that struggle with fine motor skills and attention, composing may be a greater challenge. One solution for students with fine motor difficulties is to use technology. If the technology is available at school, some adaptations may still need to be made (e.g., keyboards, standard computers or computers with touch screen capabilities). If technology is not available, having an aide or paraprofessional assist in the notation (scribe for them) for the student is essential. We want the lesson to be about composition not about notation skills.

In order to give structure to teaching composition, provide a limited number of choices. For example, provide students with a pre-written composition that leaves out the last pitch in a phrase. Provide the student with three choices, and then allow them to choose a final pitch. This last pitch will not only give them the opportunity to begin to make their own musical choices, but will give insight to their musicality. Using the same pre-written composition, add additional phrases leaving different sections of the phrase for the students to make choices. This will give students the opportunity to create beginnings, middles, and ends. *Consider giving students a limited number of musical choices to start and then add concepts as they develop skills.*

5: Reading and Notating Music. Challenges: Reading and Notating Music

These are especially difficult skills for students with special needs. Practice daily. Go slowly. Be patient. When approaching new material, start in small chunks. There is a great deal of cognitive processing required to read music. Take out as many extraneous factors as possible such as lyrics and artwork. Students may benefit from using a pointer, reading with a partner, and/or using paper to cover up material that is not being read. All these ideas assist students in focusing on exactly where they should be looking.

With notation, the same guidelines apply. Practice daily. Go slowly. Be patient. Notation can be accomplished with pre-written cards. These cards can have a selection of rhythm patterns on them. Let students piece the cards together like a puzzle. The objective with notation is to visually represent what is heard. Pre-written material just cuts out the middleman. *Consider presenting these tasks in the smallest chunks possible.*

6: Listening to, Analyzing, and Describing Music. Challenges: These Are Abstract Concepts

When teaching this content standard, think creatively and remember that this is often considered one of the most challenging standards. Music educators may not consider that listening, analyzing, and describing music are not concrete concepts; they are very abstract. This may be where the struggle lies for children with special needs. Many students with special needs (especially with cognitive challenges) do not understand abstract concepts such as those that come through description and analysis of music.

These skills will need to be practiced. As you do this, start small, use visuals, provide choices, and continue to apply new strategies until the standard is achieved. For example, play a recording of *The 1812 Overture*. Give students instruments and a visual of a cannon to use while listening. While the students listen to the recording, they will play their instruments. Tell them when they hear the cannons to lift their picture in the air. When the cannons stop, the students will resume playing their instruments.

The above is an example of first steps in the development of critical listening skills. Analyzing may consist of creating a class listening map. The map may have two elements…cannons and no cannons. When describing the music, provide choices. Start with timbre. Provide pictures of one person singing, a singing ensemble, one instrument playing, and an orchestra. Ask students to choose which best represents what they have heard. Choose other elements of music that can be represented concretely in order for students to have access to the concept. Be sure to support visually impaired students with tactile representations whenever possible. *Consider providing choices that can assist with the understanding of abstract concepts.*

7: Evaluating Music and Music Performances. Challenges: Pairing Concrete and Abstract Concepts

To address this content standard, students must be able to comprehend the elements of music. This standard is similar in its challenges to standard #6. The objective is to have students speak about the piece using music vocabulary. Begin the evaluation process with one element at a time.

Choosing the appropriate music to evaluate is critical. Pieces with pronounced examples of the elements will work best. For example, allow students to listen to *Trepak Dance* from *The Nutcracker*. The first time through, just listen. For the second listening, use a parachute. Ask the students to demonstrate the rhythm of the piece of music by manipulating the parachute. Is it bouncy or smooth? Try listening to other pieces of music at the other end of the rhythmic spectrum to compare, such as *Aquarium* from *Carnival of the Animals*. By the end of class, the students can create a sentence that describes the piece. Continue this process that includes pairing concrete with abstract concepts. *Consider your choice of music carefully.*

8: Understanding Relationships between Music, the Other Arts, and Disciplines Outside the Arts. Challenges: Funds and Planning

The best way to understand the relationship between music and the other arts is to experience them first hand. For most of us, identifying artists willing to come to the music classroom may not be as difficult as expected. Be sure to plan a hands-on experience with the artist; this will be invaluable to your students. Not only is this a fabulous experience for all students, but you may learn something as well. Another strategy is to plan one week a year to have an artist-in-residence come to your classes. This type of access will benefit your students with special needs, and quite possibly, the entire school (teachers included). If an artist is not available to come to class, technology may be a good alternative. Music educators can communicate via computer screen and get a glimpse of artists in other fields. *Consider bringing artists to your classroom.*

9: Understanding Music in Relation to History and Culture.
Challenges: Abstract Concepts

Fortunately, music is part of practically every element in our lives. To assess students' understanding of music in relation to our culture, pair visuals with music. Provide students with pictures of weddings, birthday parties, and holidays. Then, play music that fits the events and environment at each of these events. Ask students to point to the picture that matches the music. Determine what students are studying in their other classes: especially in subjects like social studies. Attempt to find music that reinforces their understanding of those subjects. Do not count them out. Many students may understand this concept more than they express in music class. *Consider choosing music that reinforces understood cultural events and time periods.*

A music therapist can assist a music educator in accessing content, adapting and accommodating material, and understanding the nuances and challenges of providing meaningful musical experiences for students with special needs. To summarize the discussion above (as shown in figure 6.9), providing structure, pairing abstract with concrete concepts, and sequencing in small steps are all music therapy concepts that can be applied to music education. The most important consideration from the perspective of a music therapist is to think outside the box when teaching students with special needs. A music therapist can be an excellent partner when providing these types of suggestions within the music classroom.

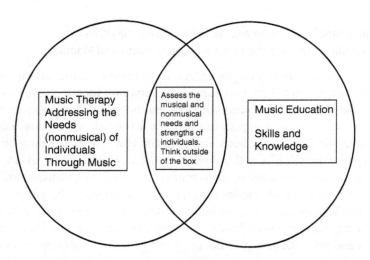

Figure 6.9: Combining Music Therapy Concepts with Music Education

ASSESSMENT AND STUDENTS WITH SPECIAL NEEDS

Assessment is the third essential principle (accompanying preparation and instruction) of an effective curriculum, including the self-evaluation of teaching practices and is a necessary aspect of teaching in the public schools. By the time a student finishes high school, he has taken hours and hours of tests. Students with special needs sometimes take many tests to just determine eligibility for special education. In order for a student to have an IEP or 504 Plan, they often are given a series of tests to determine the degree of eligibility and disability. It is important to understand that assessment can sometimes be confused with testing. The assessments we conduct in the music education classroom, even with students who have special needs, center on the curriculum we teach and provide feedback for self-reflection and self-evaluation. Music educators are rarely asked to participate in assessments as part of special identification. Music educators are rarely asked to participate in the testing procedures as part of special education identification and classification. However, quality assessment based on music literacy and content goals (including the individualization of assessment) is one element that separates a music educator from a music therapist.

In the following section of this chapter, we will review basic assessment techniques and how these can be modified or adapted for students with special needs. In addition, we will provide examples for you to adapt for use in your own classroom.

MEASUREMENT, ASSESSMENT, AND EVALUATION FOR STUDENTS WITH DISABILITIES

Oosterhof (2001) defines educational measurement as "the process of determining a quantitative or qualitative attribute of an individual or group of individuals" (p. 6). Measurement is used to evaluate learnable characteristics of students within your classroom. Pitch, rhythm, tone, and understandings of musical concepts are all potential attributes that can be measured.

Evaluation "is concerned with the outcome of the measurement" (Oosterhof, 2001, p. 5). Evaluations can also be informal and based on your own day-to-day interactions with a student.

Assessment is the tool used to measure the learnable characteristics of students within the classroom (e.g., tests, demonstrations, etc.). The following section will focus on assessment tools and techniques for students with special needs.

The reason for the review above is to give you an opportunity to consider the ways you currently use these terms. Do you establish objectives in your curriculum that can be adequately assessed (and that are attainable by students with special needs)? Are these objectives consistent with your curriculum and with the National Standards in Music (or another set of standards put forth by your state or school district)? Do you regularly evaluate these objectives and determine their relevancy to the individual needs of your students (including those with special needs)? Do these objectives need to be modified? These are important questions for consideration. They become especially important when deciding to modify or adapt a curriculum for students with special needs.

FORMATIVE ASSESSMENTS FOR STUDENTS WITH SPECIAL NEEDS

Formative assessment occurs as we are beginning instruction and is incorporated into teaching practice. Garrison and Ehringhaus (2009) explain that "When incorporated into classroom practice, it provides the information needed to adjust teaching and learning while they are happening" (p. 1). As music educators, we find ourselves determining the ability of our students by assessing them in the moment. For example, a teacher may begin a lesson by singing a song. After singing this particular song (depending on how well it is performed), he may determine whether or not the song requires rehearsal or if the class will move on to another activity. This is formative assessment.

When teaching students with special needs in music in an inclusive setting, the music educator may need to conduct many formative assessments to monitor the learning of an individual. This information will be used to evaluate whether instruction should continue down a certain path, a student will be sent with an aide or helper to reaffirm the subject matter, or instruction will cease on a topic altogether (because it is simply too difficult). All these are formative assessments that are part of a music teacher's day.

ESTABLISHING A BASELINE OF UNDERSTANDING

The first step in understanding the kind of assessments you will need to use or adapt in your classroom is to construct a baseline assessment in your classroom. A baseline assessment occurs prior to instruction. This can be informal testing either with the entire group or with a small group of individuals. This can be done without causing anxiety or stress that may exacerbate the possible skill deficit present in some students with special needs. However, it is also important to determine what skills and understandings a student brings to the classroom.

Some examples of formative assessments are:

Elementary

Students can be seated in a circle facing outward. The teacher sings a short pattern and the group students can repeat the pattern. As the teacher walks around the outside of the circle, she can hear the students who are matching pitches and can note this on a chart as a formal formative assessment.

Beginning Band

Students can play the "tag game" with each other. One student performs a rhythm on one of the notes the band has learned (e.g., Concert F). His partner then echoes the rhythm pattern (they will self-select for level of difficulty by choosing the patterns comfortable for them). The teacher can walk among the partners listening and noting the patterning successes and challenges of the students.

Beginning Choir

Students stand in a circle facing outward. The teacher has them improvise and sing known notes in a pentatonic scale (do re mi so la). The students show hand signs and improvise the solfege they know well (they are self-selecting for level of difficulty by choosing the patterns comfortable for them). The teacher walks around the circle noting the students who are maintaining the tonal center, singing the correct solfege syllables, and showing the correct hand signs.

Beginning Orchestra

Students sit in sections with their instruments (no bows). The teacher calls or plays open strings. The students play the pattern indicated by the teacher. The teacher notes students who are playing the correct open string patterns. Students may also do this in a circle as a section taking turns calling and playing the open string patterns.

Secondary Instrumental

Have a beginning of the year basic playing exam (either on SmartMusic or in-person). Try to be as positive as possible. Look for motor skills, embouchure issues, and music literacy challenges that may affect the student. This will assist in adaptations and modifications.

Secondary Choral Music

Conduct a beginning of the year vocal warm-up to establish parts (formative assessment). Check for things such as pitch matching ability and music literacy. You can do these warm-ups in small groups in order not to embarrass the student you are assessing. In both secondary areas, good communication with previous music teachers is recommended.

WRITING CLEAR, OBTAINABLE OBJECTIVES FOR STUDENTS WITH SPECIAL NEEDS

After establishing a baseline of skills and knowledge, it is time to write clear and obtainable objectives for your students with special needs. It is recommended that music educators create very specific objectives that are observable and measurable. The following are examples of objectives that have been modified for students with special needs:

7th Grade Choir

Objective: The students will solfege unfamiliar patterns using only notes in the diatonic major scale (steps—no skips), and rhythms that include quarter, paired eighth, and half notes, and equivalent rests.

Many seventh-grade choir students will be able to achieve this goal. Students with excellent preparation at the elementary level will find this objective easily attainable. Some students with special needs, however, may find this objective to be very difficult. When students are having particular difficulty with an objective, expectations can be modified while noting student progress toward the goal. These expectations are then charted for students with special needs, and the charts are used to document progress toward achieving the stated objective (figure 6.10). An added benefit of creating alternative assessment charts is that this allows the music educator an opportunity to revisit the many steps required to perform a sometimes seemingly easy objective.

Music educators may prefer to use a different adapted assessment tool with students who have special needs to record the incremental progress on a long-term objective. Many elementary school students learn to read quarter, paired eighth, half, four sixteenth, one eighth, two sixteenth, and two sixteenth eighth note patterns as part of their rhythm literacy objectives. Some students may be able to echo or pattern all of these rhythms, yet only be able to create or derive quarter and eighth note patterns. A chart that shows student progress over time can be used as part of the overall documentation of learning in the music classroom. Some teachers attach these as ancillary

Pitch matching

Sing major scale on neutral syllables, ascending   ☐

Sing major scale on neutral syllables, descending   ☐

Sing major scale with solfege, ascending   ☐

Sing major scale with solfege, descending   ☐

Sing pitches on a staff with solfege   ☐

Find and sing "do" using a "do key"   ☐

Reading

Recognize staff   ☐

Recognize treble and bass clefs   ☐

Understand line and space notes   ☐

Name the line in both clefs   ☐

Name the space in both clefs   ☐

Identify notes on lines and spaces in both clefs   ☐

Recognize rhythms: half, quarter, eighth, and equivalent rests   ☐

Recognize bar lines and measures   ☐

Recognize time signatures 2/4, 3/4, and 4/4   ☐

Rhythm readiness

Maintain steady beat   ☐

Chant and clap   ☐

Perform half notes and rests   ☐

Perform quarter notes and rests   ☐

Perform paired eighth notes   ☐

Figure 6.10 (Seventh-grade Choir)

data on report cards, or share these with parents and classroom teachers during IEP and 504 Meetings or at parent/teacher conferences. Figure 6.11 is an example of an adaptive assessment tool for a student with special needs in an elementary music classroom.

ASSESSING NONMUSICAL GOALS

Some students experience difficulty with transitioning to the music classroom or ensemble. It can be difficult to assess the progress of a student with-

Rhythm sequence	♩	♫	♩	♬	♬	♬
ECHO Neutral						
Syllable						
Transfer neutral to syllable						
IDENTIFY In a rhyme or song – aurally						
Visually						
DERIVE From a rhyme or song						
CREATE New rhythms that contain						
Anderson & Hammel (2007)						

Figure 6.11 Rhythm Reading Sequence: Elementary School Rhythm Reading (Adapted Sequence)

out creating a task analysis of all the elements necessary for that student to perform the stated objective. An example for a cellist in a high school orchestra is below (Figure 6.12):

High School Orchestra

Objective: The students will perform Peter and the Wolf *expressively (with peers) as part of a varied repertoire of music.*

For a student with moderate communication and cognitive challenges, this typical high school orchestra objective requires many discrete skills that we may not notice unless we list the steps required to perform this task. For some students, the nonmusical skills required are equal in challenge to the musical skills. Below is a chart listing the steps in this process. These steps stop at the point the music begins to illustrate the skills necessary for this student to be prepared for a downbeat or tuning note.

Finish task in previous classroom	☐
Put materials away and walk with aide to door	☐
Walk from classroom to orchestra room	☐
Walk into the orchestra room	☐
Go to the instrument storage room	☐
Find cello	☐
Take cello, bow, and resin from case	☐
Walk to folder cabinet	☐
Find folder	☐
Carry all materials (with assistance of aide) to collect chair and stand	☐
Place folder on stand	☐
Sit in chair	☐
Place endpin in chip on the floor	☐
Prepare bow with resin and tension	☐
Check space for arms	☐
Open folder	☐
Choose "Peter and the Wolf"	☐
Place music on stand	☐
Put pencil on stand	☐
All ready!	☐

Figure 6.12 High School Orchestra Objectives

As you can imagine, it can be exhausting to complete all the steps necessary for success in a high school orchestra when you have moderate communication and cognitive challenges!

The next step is to begin the modification or adaptation process as the music educator creates an assessment to chart progress toward achievement of the musical objective. These modifications would perhaps include a tape or CD of the orchestra performing *Peter and the Wolf*, an individual recording of the cello part (or a modified cello part if the student needs this modification), color coding, directions to assist the aide as he works with the student, and time on-task (or time allowed for rest and quiet off-task) behaviors. Be sure to allow "brain breaks" as you remember the skills that student is demonstrating just to be in the room with the other students.

ALTERNATIVE ASSESSMENTS FOR STUDENTS WITH SPECIAL NEEDS

Often, as teachers, we focus on the product instead of the process. This can be a difficult quest for both the teacher of a student with special needs and the student herself. A student may exhibit an extraordinary amount of effort; however, for whatever reason, she may not be able to demonstrate her understanding on the day of a test or an evening performance. Student portfolios are a way for students to demonstrate their work over a long period of time rather than a one-chance performance either on an exam, classroom evaluation, or a concert. Student portfolios can also be adapted or modified for the student based on his ability to meet the stated objectives. The portfolio can include student written work, photos of the student working toward objectives, playing tests, exams, recordings (made by the student), reflections, or any class material that can be archived within a portfolio.

SUMMATIVE ASSESSMENTS AND STUDENTS WITH SPECIAL NEEDS

After determining your goals for an individual you must also determine how you will know if you have attained these goals and how your curriculum might change to enhance learning. We have discussed formative assessments, created a task analysis of elements required to perform an objective, and given examples of alternative assessments in the music classroom. The final type of assessment is summative assessment. This is the assessment that takes place at the end of instruction when you are evaluating whether the students have met the goals set based on your formative (or baseline) assessment.

Oosterhof (2001) explains that "summative evaluations follow instruction and typically involve unit tests, midterm and final exams, and projects, or other end of unit assignments" (p. 22). In music this may involve experiences that show mastery of content (curriculum mastery), music theory exams, music terms tests, singing or playing tests, district or mandated music skills testing, and other types of summative assessment. All these are important to a successful curriculum and for an educationally successful classroom experience.

There are many questions a music teacher should ask before establishing a fair summative assessment for a student with special needs These questions include:

- What can be gained by assessing this student with special needs?
- What am I looking for with this assessment?
- How will this assessment inform my teaching of this student with disabilities?

Music teachers must be aware of the ways a summative assessment may impact a student (academically, socially, and emotionally). Remember, a student with special needs has spent a great deal of time being tested. Whether it is to determine a diagnosis, eligibility, or establishing a baseline in language or speech, they have been through batteries of exams. Many students with special needs understand what these tests are and are sensitive to the outcomes.

It is important for students with special needs to know they have done well and have learned. It is not useful for music educators to remind a student (again) that she is different or that she is unable to complete an objective obtained by her classmates. By deriving and teaching achievable objectives, every student can succeed at an individual level in your music class or ensemble. Remember that fair is not equal in the music classroom. Fair is ensuring that every student has the opportunity to succeed. By adapting and modifying your curriculum and assessment procedures, you are creating fairness for your students.

CONCLUSION

This chapter provides instructionally appropriate strategies for music teachers as they modify curricula and assess students with special needs. Students with special needs often engage in modified or adapted curricula in other subjects. In fact, the IEP itself is a document that contains these modifications. The challenge for music educators is to create similar opportunities for students with special needs in the music classroom and ensemble. In addition, it is important to continue to assess students regardless of their age or stage of development. Students with special needs are often omitted from assessments. This can create a false sense of your teaching ability as well as an inaccurate portrayal of the learning capability of an individual with special needs. This, in turn, will inhibit the potential acquisition of skills and understandings for students with disabilities in your music class. As stated in earlier chapters, you are the music educator. You understand the different ways students learn music. It is up to you to create the modifications to your curriculum design and assessment procedures to create the opportunity for every student, including students with disabilities, to be successful in your music classroom.

DISCUSSION QUESTIONS

1. A student with communication challenges has been included in your middle school orchestra program. She is having great difficulty remembering the exact placement of her fingers (even with the tape

placed for the finger placements). A playing test is in two weeks that will require her to know these placements without stopping to look at her fingers and move to the next note. Do you think this student would benefit more from modifications or adaptations to the objectives for the playing test? What can you do to modify or adapt her objectives to make the test "fair" for her and to give her an opportunity to succeed?

2. There is a new percussionist in your high school marching band. Previously, he has only played bass and snare drum. He is resistant to playing mallet percussion and absolutely refuses to play the cymbals because they are too loud. Your band curriculum specifies that all percussionists learn to play all instruments and there are specific objectives for mallet percussion skills. What can you, as the band director, do to adapt or modify the curriculum for this student?

3. Your fifth-grade music class on Wednesday mornings includes a student with severe cognitive challenges. In reviewing your curriculum for fifth-grade music, you see that every student is to demonstrate mastery of sixteenth note rhythms in all variations (duple and compound). You are sure that this student, whom you have taught since kindergarten, is going to have a difficult time achieving this district-mandated objective. What can you do to modify or adapt the curriculum for this student?

REFERENCES

Dewey, J. (1929). My pedagogic creed. *Journal of the National Education Association, 18*(9), 291–295.

Garrison, C., & Ehringhaus, M. (2009). *Formative and summative assessments in the classroom.* Westerville, OH: National Middle School Association. Retrieved on April 9, 2009, from http://www.nmsa.org/Publications/WebExclusive/Assessment/tabid/1120/Default.aspx.

Labuta, J. A., & Smith, D. A. (1997). *Music education: Historical contexts and perspectives.* Upper Saddle River, NJ: Prentice Hall.

Oosterhof, A. (2001). *Classroom applications of educational measurement.* Upper Saddle River, NJ: Prentice Hall.

Scott, S. (2006). A constructivist view of music education: Perspective for deep understanding. General Music Today, *19*(2), 17–21.

Steffe, L., & Gale, J. (2006). *Constructivism in education.* Hillsdale, NJ: Lawrence Erlbaum Associates Publishers.

Walker, D. F., & Soltis, J. F. (2004). *Curriculum and aims:* New York: Teachers College Press.

Chapter 7

Teaching Strategies for Performers with Special Needs

Vignette 7.1 Allison

My name is Allison and I would like to share my story with you. I grew up in a rural area of the Midwest. During my sixth-grade year, I was faced with the same things that every other student my age had to deal with, such as peer pressure, friends and just feeling accepted. I was a pretty good student and was involved in a lot of activities, including music.

In sixth grade, I decided that I would like to join band. Although I didn't know much about music at the time, I decided I wanted to try. However, there was one glitch. I didn't know what I could play because I only had one arm. I was born without part of my left arm, below the elbow. My teacher said trumpet would work just fine. Hardly knowing what a trumpet was, I said ok! I don't think I could have been any more excited.

After one day on trumpet, we moved to another town and were faced with whether I should continue with band. I decided to join and did my best for being a few months behind the others. However, a few days into class, my new director informed me that he thought trumpet might be a bad choice for me because of my arm. He thought maybe a baritone could work. At that point though, he wasn't even sure that band was best for me because he wasn't sure I could hold up the instrument correctly. I decided that if I couldn't play what I wanted, then I wouldn't be in band. I joined choir instead.

The next year came around and I decided to try again. I joined band and chose trumpet. I was first chair within two weeks and only lost it for one year in high school to a senior. I know that it was my stubborn streak and determination that motivated me to be successful, at least at the beginning. Music became everything to me. As a high school student I began to consider a career in music. In preparation for such a career,

(continued)

Vignette 7.1 (continued)

I considered trying to become a drum major. When I talked to my high school director about this idea, she said that it would be too difficult for others to follow me because of my arm. Unfortunately, I accepted that answer and didn't try out. At the end of my junior year, I decided to try getting into college anyway to study music. I am very happy to say that I have been a music educator for 10 years now and have taught all areas of music grades kindergarten through 12. I even got to go back to teach with my middle school director before he retired. We both learned a lot through our experience together.

Here's what I would like for you to take from my story. Both of my directors were very good directors who just didn't know how to adapt in a way to best meet my needs. My middle school director simply made assumptions that I couldn't hold an instrument because of its size. The fact wasn't that I couldn't hold the instrument correctly. I was just a nervous, sixth grader, new to a school, who was worried about what others would think about me and my arm as I was holding up my trumpet. As for the high school director, I just felt that she gave the answer that she thought was best.

As educators we want to see our students succeed. Today, our students come to school with a wide variety of physical, mental, and social needs. We must really think out of the box in order to meet them where they are at and help them to be successful at meeting their goals. I have learned that we each have what it takes to help others be successful in reaching their goals, especially in the arts. Focus on what they can do. Ask questions about what is making it difficult for them to succeed. Have a teachable heart and that will help instill patience in both you and your students, allowing for multiple successes. Also realize that success comes in many different forms other than the expected. Be willing. Remember, those same teachers that didn't necessarily say or do the right things at times, were still the ones that taught me and helped instill into me a love for music.

Discussion Questions:

1. What are the larger implications of Allison's participation in band?
2. Should band and orchestra students be allowed to choose whatever instrument they want regardless of physical challenges?
3. What would you have done (as the director) in this situation?

Because of previously discussed changes in philosophy and policy, the demographics of our performing ensembles are constantly changing. Many school districts have moved toward a policy of full inclusion of students with special needs. This has led to an increased number of students with special needs in performing ensembles and has challenged many conductors to find ways to include many students with disabilities who were not previously a part of performing ensembles. In addition, this has forced many conductors to reexamine their underlying philosophy of what it means to be a successful ensemble conductor.

The purpose of this chapter is to offer techniques for choral and instrumental conductors who teach performers with special needs and to suggest ideas for consideration for those who are preparing to conduct performing ensembles. These strategies come from extensive work researching, consulting with ensemble conductors, and working with parents of performers with special needs. This chapter is designed to alleviate any anxieties conductors and conducting students may have and to provide confidence when teaching students with disabilities.

THE HIDDEN CURRICULUM IN TRADITIONAL PERFORMING ENSEMBLES (EQUAL ACCESS)

Typically the percentage of students with disabilities in performing ensembles is far less than the overall percentage of students with disabilities in a school. This is anecdotal data, however; the open challenge exists to those who teach performing ensembles to truly examine this phenomenon throughout their school system (Pre-K through 12).

Band, choir, and orchestra directors can inadvertently discourage participation of students with special needs in their ensembles in many ways. For example, many band and orchestra programs have an entry point in or around fifth grade. However, after that point, students are not allowed to join. Unfortunately, many students with special needs are not developmentally ready to join an instrumental or choral ensemble in fifth grade. Many of these same students would be extremely successful if given another point of entry later in their school career. Small curricular nuances such as a floating entry point to beginning band, choir or orchestra can make a meaningful difference in developing an inclusive performing ensemble program in a public school.

Another hidden discouragement is the mere fact that students, as a requirement for participation, are required to be "put on the spot" regularly. Auditions, playing tests, and informal demonstrations of achievement are common in the typical rehearsal. The authors have even seen conductors do these types of exercises on purpose to "weed" students out of their program. For some students with disabilities, this is just one more way to feel that they are not as capable as their peers. It is easier for them to not participate and to choose something else.

Parents of students with disabilities can learn from other parents about how participation works in performing ensembles. In some communities, parents form subcultures through their work with support groups, similar participation in activities, and fund-raising organizations. It is very easy for a conductor to be known as an inclusive, accommodating teacher or a discouraging, noninclusive teacher just by the way his or her program is designed and implemented.

For those music educators who are currently conducting ensembles in the public schools, a further challenge is to look at the entire music education program objectively and consider whether or not the program is accepting of all students regardless of their abilities. For the music education student preparing to conduct ensembles, the challenge is to consider your philosophy and the way the changing demographics in schools may be reflected in performing groups in future music education programs.

PARTICIPATING IN THE SPECIAL EDUCATION PROCESS

Many music educators, including many conductors, do not understand their rights and responsibilities as a teacher of students with special needs. This was discussed at length in chapters 1 and 2. However, many also do not understand the IEP or 504 documents and the meetings that take place in order to meet the needs of an individual student (this process will be discussed later in this chapter). This section of the chapter is designed to give further understanding into the special education system as it relates to performing ensembles.

As mentioned earlier in this book, the first step in understanding a performer's disability is to contact or consult with members of a student's IEP or 504 Plan "team." Attending these meetings as part of participation in the special education process is a valuable activity. Much can be learned about a student's talents and capabilities. Many conductors of school ensembles have stated anecdotally that they have never attended (or in some cases have never heard of or about) an IEP or 504 Plan meeting. The same directors also explain they feel unsupported and misinformed about their students. These meetings are "ground zero" for information that leads to a better understanding of a student's capabilities.

If attending an IEP or 504 Plan meeting is out of the question, seeking the document (that results from these meetings) is an acceptable replacement.

It is also the law. There are a few areas in the document that are of particular importance and are critical to understanding a student's needs. The first is called the present level of academic function section (terminology varies by state). This statement is a narrative that is put together by a special educator about a student's capabilities. By reading this section, conductors can gain insight into the challenges they may face when teaching this student in a performance setting.

The second area of the IEP or 504 Plan that conductors may want to consider is the academic goals established by other teachers. This may also assist efforts to understand the strengths and weaknesses of a performer with special needs. This becomes even more valuable when designing assessment opportunities for students with special needs (discussed later in this chapter). These portions of the legal documents may help conductors design ways to adapt instruction for students with disabilities. Further ideas for adapting instruction will be presented later in this chapter.

UNDERSTANDING THE DISABILITY (SEEKING RESOURCES)

It is the responsibility of ensemble conductors to know the students that are in each ensemble. Yet, it is perplexing to hear of an ensemble director who spends hours and hours programming music, organizing trips, and preparing for contests, and yet fails to seek background information regarding a student. There are many publications in the music education literature that focus on students with disabilities (see chapter 9). Seeking these resources (see sidebar) and reading about the needs of a student takes a small amount of time.

Suggested Resources

Damer, L. K. (2001). Inclusion and the law. *Music Educators Journal, 87*(4), 17–18.
Finale: www.finalemusic.com.
Hammel, A. M. (2004). Inclusion strategies that work. *Music Educators Journal, 90*(4), 33–37.
Lewis, R. B., & Doorlag, D. H. (2006). *Teaching special students in general education classrooms.* Upper Saddle River, NJ: Prentice Hall.
Menlove, R. R., Hudson, P. J., & Suter, D. (2001). A field of IEP dreams: Increasing general education teacher preparation in the IEP developmental process. *Teaching Exceptional Children, 33*(5), 28–33.
Pontiff, E. (2004). Teaching special learners. *Teaching Music, 12*(3), 51–58.
SmartMusic: www.smartmusic.com.
Zdzinski, S. F. (2001). Instrumental music for special learners. *Music Educators Journal, 87*(4), 27–29.

The relatively small amount of time spent consulting with special educators, reading available articles in music education (or music therapy) regarding a certain disability, and talking with parents can make the difference. An important part of this consultation should be to determine whether the student is at grade level academically. Sometimes disabilities can be deceiving. If the student is not at grade level, find out if he is on track to receive a regular diploma at the end of high school. This will help determine some of the possibilities for this student.

Knowing the transition plan in place for a student (college, vocational school, supervised work training) is of value when considering the specific ensemble placement and set of accommodations that may be employed when teaching a student with special needs. This information is important because it lets you know the expectations other team members have for the student. Conductors can use this information as they design accommodations, adaptations, and modifications for a student and plan for inclusion in specific ensembles. For example, a student who will be placed in a supervised work training environment may not be able to participate in marching band or show choir because both of these activities may have responsibilities at a certain time of day, or after school. Students who are working toward supervised work employment will be required by the school (and their employer) to work a set number of hours at specific times of day. This may limit the ensemble choices and consultation with the team (including the parents) is advisable.

Remember that most students with special needs will have a transition plan in place during their high school years. This is a part of their IEP or 504 Plan. Knowing this information will take some time but will be rewarding in the end. Remember, all students are different. Articles and books can provide a broad sense of a student's capabilities. Yet, it is the special educators and parents that can be of the most assistance in understanding the specific needs of a student with special needs who is part of an ensemble.

ADAPTATION OF INSTRUCTION FOR PERFORMERS WITH SPECIAL NEEDS

The previous information leads us to the question: How do I begin to teach a performer who has a disability? In general, most music educators are much more qualified than they realize. The following section is designed to remind ensemble conductors of techniques that may not have been considered. Many of these ideas may have already been put in place without knowledge of the value for students with special needs.

The first priority for a music educator who is adapting instruction is to understand that they are the expert music educators (or future music educators). Music educators should be confident in their previous music experience and realize that they do understand the many ways students learn music. It is surprising when music educators, especially ensemble directors, forget this premise when attempting to teach a student with special needs. Even though the music educator is the expert, teaching a performer with special needs may require an examination of ideas about how students really learn music and a sincere effort to be creative when accommodating performers.

The next step in adapting instruction is to determine how a specific student learns best (see previous chapters in this text). He may be an aural learner rather than a visual learner. This may require him to learn music by ear first; therefore, he may need recordings of the music to help him with his practice. She may struggle with the routine of the rehearsal. The music educator may need to provide a list of what will happen on a daily or weekly basis to aid this student in rehearsal. Just like many curricular decisions in music, all strategies are individualized for each student and may be defined as the result of trial and error during rehearsals. All students are different and require some individualized thought, and it is always acceptable to continue to try new ideas and techniques when others are not meeting the needs of the students with and without special needs in ensembles.

THE USE OF TECHNOLOGY

There are many ways that technology can be used to assist students when practicing. The conductor can record an individual part or example using digital recorders (that can be downloaded to a CD). Digital video recorders can allow conductors or private instructors to model appropriate performance practice. These video clips not only assist with the audiation of musical passages, but they also allow students to constantly see correct posture and breathing while practicing.

In addition, SmartMusic is an excellent tool to extract parts, make recordings, and choose appropriate literature for a student with special needs. SmartMusic can also be used to modify assessments for students with special needs. SmartMusic allows students who have anxiety about performing in front of an instructor the opportunity to go home and complete the assessment in private online.

Notation programs (e.g., Finale) can be used in a variety of ways to extract, modify, and simplify parts for individual performers. In addition, these notation programs can be used to highlight or increase the font of passages for performers who will benefit from this accommodation. Many conductors overlook these devices as tools for accommodation when in fact they are

Adapting music to fit the student's needs

- Use a notation program to simplify parts
- Require only portions based on the student's ability
- Change range or tessitura
- Highlight passages of importance

Assisting a Student with Practice

- Videotape or record examples of what you expect
- Practice with a buddy
- Provide music and a recording far in advance

Adapting Equipment

- Make larger grips (mallets, sticks, etc.)
- Change lead-pipe to favor opposite hand
- Use tape to mark targets (strings for fingers, percussion)

Rehearsal Routine

- Pre-write a schedule for a student
- Provide a student assistant
- Let the student explore the rehearsal room without their peers

Performance

- Let student explore the stage without people
- Go over what is expected before the performance
- Assign a student assistant
- Provide an escape route if for times with over-stimulated

Figure 7.1 General Adaptation Ideas for Performing Ensembles

very appropriate tools to enhance performance. Figure 7.1 was assembled to provide suggestions for adaptations for students with special needs in performing ensembles.

LARGE GROUP PERFORMING ENSEMBLES: ARE THEY THE APPROPRIATE PLACEMENT FOR STUDENTS WITH SPECIAL NEEDS?

It is often a surprise to music educators when the statement is made that large-group music may not be for all students. Some specific students with special needs have a very difficult time with large groups and loud music.

It can be that the parent is pushing the student to participate in a large ensemble rather than the initiation coming from the student. Many successful ensemble conductors begin by offering small group music experiences such as lessons or chamber groups in place of the large group setting to a student with special needs. If the student becomes interested (notice we said student), it may be helpful to slowly orient him to the large ensemble as a way to determine whether this is the best current option for the student.

Making an appropriate placement into an ensemble is imperative for the success of a student with special needs. Select ensembles should be for select students who qualify. Again, this is often a surprise to many when stated this directly. The authors are tireless advocates for students for special needs. However, with advocacy comes responsibility. As explained before, students with special needs should be placed in a situation that offers the most potential for success (a free appropriate public education in the least restrictive environment). As long as there is a place for all students in a music program (a second or third ensemble as well as a select ensemble) it is okay for there to be a place for select students who may or may not have special needs. A teacher would never place a student in trigonometry if he could not understand algebra. Conversely, it is also worth noting that when a student has mastered the content and objectives of that second or third ensemble, he should be considered for a more select ensemble based on his past performance and current skill level.

MEANINGFUL PARTICIPATION

Vignette 7.2 Kevin

My son, Kevin, attends a local public school that houses several special education classrooms. Kevin's classroom is classified as a moderate room, and the kids vary in age.

One morning, as I was dropping Kevin off for school, I was on the phone with a friend who mentioned the annual end-of-year school music program that was going on that evening. Instantly, I panicked, thinking I had missed something in the newsletter because this was the first I had heard of it. I called Kevin's classroom teacher to get the details of when Kevin was to be there that evening, show time, etc.

(continued)

Vignette 7.2 (continued)

His teacher was very angry but thankful that I had called as she explained to me that the special education children were not included in the program. She had been waiting for a parent to notice because she knew then the complaints would start pouring in. I was just aghast. In my mind, I kept trying to reason why my kid was being left out of a school function.

Kevin had just finished participating in the Prism Project, a musical for students with special needs, as had a handful of other kids from the very same school. The experience had been beyond words and so rewarding for Kevin that it made this act of exclusion that much more intolerable and hurtful.

My first phone call was to the music teacher himself who refused to take my call. He knew it was time to duck and cover. My second call was to the principal who was totally caught off guard. She had assumed that the special education students were part of the production. She said she would get back to me. My third approach was to drive directly to the Special Education Cooperative Office to file a complaint in person.

As the day progressed, I found out that the music teacher had been given a direct order to include the students with special needs but had chosen to ignore it. The principal had assumed that he would follow orders. She was very embarrassed, apologetic, and angry. In the end, the music teacher was disciplined by the administration building and an improvement plan was put in his personal file.

Sadly, the program continued that night. I wondered how the music teacher felt about the performance after purposely leaving children out of it. I don't know how he could have felt a sense of satisfaction or accomplishment. Later, I found out that one parent wore a homemade T-shirt to the program that read: MY SPECIAL ED. STUDENT WAS LEFT OUT OF JEFFERSON'S MUSICAL!

To me, the issue was much larger than Kevin and his peers being left out of a musical. It represented an incredible failure in the school system as a whole for all of the "electives"—music, art, library, and gym—and the curriculum that was or in most cases wasn't provided to our kids.

Special education students rotate through these classes just as typical children do; however, they are not treated as though these classes have anything to offer them. Even worse, they are treated as if they have nothing to offer these subjects. The teachers of these subjects are not required to make lesson plans related to goals held by special education children, nor do they have to report on anything they are doing in the classroom. The grade cards/progress reports for special education children never makes mention of music, gym, library, or art class. Kevin can spend an entire year in music class, and I have no idea what he has done in there.

Because of this, a lot of the time spent in these classrooms is a waste of time for special education children. It makes it very easy for teachers to pass out plain paper and crayons or pop in a video to pass the time. This is incredibly heartbreaking when this time could be so constructive! Endless concepts could be taught, and many things being taught in the classroom could be reinforced. Not to mention, our kids love music, art, and gym. They just need teachers who are willing to think outside of the box and invest in them.

The entire situation left me feeling very sad because our kids are often not treated with equal value and worth. I was left wondering: Why is a direct order (that was ignored) needed to include special education children? What would have happen if he left all the Hispanic children out of the musical? Would the protest have been more than a T-shirt?

(Contributed by Nancy, a parent of a child with special needs)

The key to participation by a student with special needs is that it must be meaningful. Each student should make a contribution to the ensemble. Recently, a university supervisor observed a student teacher in a junior high band setting. The cooperating teacher had a student with special needs in his band class. The student was a percussionist who stood in the back corner of the room playing on a practice pad instead of a real drum. However, it was obvious (by the skill level demonstrated as the student played on the practice pad) that he could handle something expressive within the percussion section such as a cymbal part or a "toy" part. His participation did not contribute musically to the ensemble, and it was obvious that he knew it. This was disheartening to watch. It was just laziness on the part of the conductor.

The previous paragraph, as well as vignette 7.2, highlights the fact that some ensemble conductors assume students with special needs cannot contribute. Some conductors may not want to take the time to consider ways a student can contribute to the musical ensemble in a meaningful way. Many students can be fully functioning members of an ensemble with the assistance of the music educator. This may include rewriting a part to reduce the complexity of their contribution or limiting the number of pieces a student may play on a concert. However, it is important that what they perform represents an authentic contribution to the ensemble. The adaptations created to help a student are the beginning of their success in an ensemble. Remember, the music educator is the musician and, therefore, the expert in that performing genre. Ensemble conductors (through their own experience) can be very creative in creating adaptations and accommodations for music ensembles.

Creating adaptations may also require a music educator to assist a student with practice techniques. For example, Jason has difficulty (because of his disability) with written material. His teachers realized that most of his music was learned by rote. In the beginning a music educator was videotaped playing the student part. The student then practiced with the videotape by copying what the music educator was doing. However, the ability to learn to read music was always a goal. After he learned his part aurally, the music was used as a guide for practice. Jason, and many others students like him, have the ability to learn basic music reading skills. Jason also learned a great deal from repeated viewing of the videotape. These can be powerful visual reminders of sitting (or standing) posture, breath support, and vowel placement for singers. These kinds of adaptations to practicing strategies are a necessity for early success. As music educators know, students can leave programs out of frustration. Helping a student with special needs learn to practice can be of vital assistance as she finds success in an ensemble situation.

Some students may have physical special needs that will require some accommodations. Again, be resourceful. Many music dealers are willing to make physical adaptations to instruments. In addition, federal law requires that all rehearsal spaces be accessible. Therefore, school districts should provide these accommodations.

Many ensemble conductors leave students with special needs out of the assessment process assuming they are exempt. Holding students with special needs accountable is part of the teaching and learning process. This is where it is advised that the IEP or 504 Plan be reviewed again. Look at the goals in some of the other subject areas such as math or English. See what kind of adaptations or accommodations that student receives in other classes. The student may be able to learn the same music but may need more time to complete an assignment. A music educator may need to simplify directions or ask for assistance in administering a singing or playing exam. Review the adaptations and accommodations listed earlier in the text. Many of these are appropriate for an ensemble situation as well. Formative assessment strategies may need to include reading or writing help for students. These options will become clear after seeking the IEP or 504 document and consulting with a special educator.

CONCLUSION

The suggestions provided in this chapter are designed to help ensemble conductors prepare to teach music to students with special needs. This process challenges music educators to participate in the special education system and to be resourceful in learning about their students with special needs from special educators, documents, and parents. It is hoped that the suggestions mentioned above will help music educators understand performers with special needs and help them to be more confident in their attempt to provide a worthwhile performing experience for students with special needs.

DISCUSSION QUESTIONS

1. How would you address the inclusion of students with special needs in your choral ensemble when recruiting students at a local elementary school? What strategies can you employ that will ensure that every student knows that he or she is welcome to join your program? How can those strategies be demonstrated during your recruiting performance?
2. What adaptations and accommodations do you think would be most appropriate for a student with cognitive and communication challenges who wants to play the cello? Be sure to consult the strategies suggested in previous chapters. Also, what is the next step to take if your initial attempts are unsuccessful?
3. What are some strategies for including a student with physical challenges in a marching band setting? How can your music, drill, and rehearsal time be adapted to meet the needs of this student?
4. Is there a way to appropriately include a student who struggles with loud sounds and large groups of students in a performing ensemble? Please list some strategies and rationale for discussion.

Chapter 8

Teaching Music to Students Who Are Intellectually Gifted

Vignette 8.1 Hannah

11-year-old Hannah was very excited when her mother told her that the band director at Blue Middle School had agreed to work with her after school on Wednesday. Hannah had begun middle school the month before and had been waiting to play her flute for the band director since the orientation night when she learned that the school had three bands (beginning, intermediate, and advanced). She had practiced very hard and was hoping to be told she was good enough to be placed in the advanced band, even though she was only in sixth grade. She wasn't able to be in the band class during school because she had been promoted to eighth-grade academic work and was taking three high school credits this year. There was no room for band in her schedule.

On the day of the advanced band audition, Hannah practically ran to the band room with her flute in her hand after school. The band director had said she would meet with her and a few other students who wanted to audition. They all sat nervously on the front row waiting for Ms. Harvey to enter. While waiting, Hannah looked at all the shiny trophies that sat on shelves around the room. She counted them. There were 27 in all. She thought they looked beautiful and really liked the shiny gold and other metal that designated the category of awards.

Finally, Ms. Harvey was ready to hear the students play. Hannah waited patiently while the other students played some scales and their chromatic scale for the band director. She knew they played pretty well, and she also knew she was better. When Ms. Harvey asked her to play, Hannah played the most difficult scales she knew as many octaves as the fingering charts had shown in her flute book. She also played her chromatic scale very, very fast. The band director didn't seem to know what else to say to her

(continued)

Vignette 8.1 (continued)

except to tell her she did well. Ms. Harvey had never heard a sixth-grade student play a three octave chromatic scale with sixteenth notes at MM = 120. That was a great performance level for a high school student. She was a little relieved that Hannah would not be in the band on a regular basis because she wasn't sure how she would be able to teach her much, let alone challenge her. Ms. Harvey then began working with the other students and told them that they all played well enough to play in the advanced band. Hannah looked at the clock and saw that she still had 30 minutes until her mom would be there to pick her up. She looked at the trophies again and suddenly realized that maybe they weren't metal at all. They might be made of plastic instead. Then, she began to count the pillars on them and created algebraic equations based on color, size, and shape. It would be a long 30 minutes.

INTELLECTUAL GIFTEDNESS IN THE MUSIC CLASSROOM

There are students like Hannah in our public schools. They are inquisitive, questioning, exceptionally interested, and have a distinct look about them as they learn new information. They are the students who learn difficult concepts instantly and completely. They are the students who can comprehend an entire scope and sequence of a topic, seemingly in an instant. They are also at great risk in our classrooms that are often designed for the average student and offer accommodations for students with other types of special needs. The special needs of students who are intellectually gifted are often delayed, ignored, and denied. For these students, the promise of tomorrow and a teacher who will finally challenge them begins to fade. This reality often sets in during the late elementary and middle school years.

UNDERSTANDING THE SPECTRUM OF SPECIAL NEEDS (GIFTED AND TALENTED)

While the philosophy of this text has placed importance on encouraging "label-free learning" for students with special needs, there are times when a distinction is necessary. One of these distinctions is in the cognitive area. Most often, music educators adapt teaching to accommodate students who learn at a slower rate; however, it is important to also consider adapting our teaching for those students who learn at a faster rate than their peers. These students are often identified as being gifted. The philosophical premise that students learn best and teachers are most prepared when a label-free environment is established remains a hallmark of this book. We (the co-authors) consider the decision to briefly digress as we discuss students who are gifted as necessary to understand the specific special needs of students whose cognition capabilities are vastly increased. We will return to our label-free approach at the end of the chapter as we summarize the information gleaned from this area of students with special needs.

A BRIEF BACKGROUND OF HOW STUDENTS ARE IDENTIFIED AS "GIFTED"

The identification of students who are gifted has had a long and circuitous journey. Alfred Binet was the first to develop a measure for judgment or mental age to screen and provide educational barriers for children not considered intelligent enough for a formal education (Binet, 1894). He designed his intelligence test for these purposes, yet he did consider intelligence to be educable and stated that intelligence can be improved and enhanced over time (Walker, 1991).

Lewis Terman standardized Binet's test at Stanford University. It then became known as the Stanford-Binet Intelligence Scale (Winner, 1996). Through the standardization process, Terman determined that intelligence is fixed and will not change over time (Terman, 1925). He was the first person to use the term gifted (Terman and Oden, 1959; Walker, 1991). Terman defined giftedness as the top 1% level in general intelligence ability as measured by the Stanford-Binet Intelligence Scale or a comparable instrument (Terman and Oden, 1947).

Renzulli (1977) noted that superior intellectual ability alone does not necessarily identify a student with extraordinary capabilities. He posited that students who demonstrate above-average intellect, high task-commitment, and high creativity skills create the profile of a gifted student. His model of giftedness has been widely used to identify students who may not otherwise receive gifted services (Webb, Meckstroth and Tolan, 1994). He also distinguished two types of giftedness termed "Schoolhouse giftedness" and "Creative-productive giftedness." Renzulli spent much of his career encouraging schools to include more creative and artistic opportunities for students who were gifted (Renzulli, 1986).

THE CURRENT IDENTIFICATION PROCESSES

Many students in elementary schools are given group IQ tests to identify those students who may be eligible for gifted education services. These tests are not as accurate as small group or private testing, particularly when identifying younger-age elementary students (Walker, 1991). School systems set their own benchmarks for IQ testing and services. Generally, the baseline IQ range for services is between 125 and 145. Some research has shown that students from diverse backgrounds and socioeconomic levels are disproportionately absent from gifted programs, particularly those programs that use group IQ testing as the primary assessment vehicle for acceptance (Webb, Meckstroth, and Tolan, 1994; Winner, 1996).

INDIVIDUAL IQ TESTING AND OTHER IDENTIFICATION PRACTICES

Individual IQ testing is much more expensive and time consuming than Group IQ testing. It is, however, much more accurate (Silverman, 1993). Some argue that IQ testing only measures academic aptitude within the dominant culture, rather than a pure measure of intelligence (Walker, 1991).

Students who are gifted are also sometimes identified through Standard Achievement Testing (academic), teacher nomination, and parent nomination (VanTassel-Baska, 1998). Teacher and parent (Kerr, 1994) input is seen as important as their anecdotal information can be very accurate and sometimes augments data received through standard IQ testing (Winner, 1996).

Creativity testing is also sometimes used to identify students with strong divergent thinking skills. Further ancillary methods of identification include student-derived products and performances, the top percentile of honor roll listings, individual pupil motivation for learning, and peer nomination (Webb, Meckstroth and Tolan, 1994; Walker, 1991).

CATEGORIES OF GIFTEDNESS

Highly/Profoundly Gifted
Hollingsworth (1931) stated the following regarding students who are gifted:

> Where the gifted child drifts in the school unrecognized, held to the lockstep which is determined by the capacities of the average, he has little to do. He receives daily practice in habits of idleness and daydreaming. His abilities are never genuinely challenged, and the situation is contrived to build in him

expectations of an effortless existence. Children up to about 140 IQ tolerate the ordinary school routine quite well, being usually a little young for the grade through an extra promotion or two, and achieving excellent marks without serious effort. But above this status, children become increasingly bored with school work, if kept in or nearly in the lockstep. Children at or above 180 IQ, for instance, are likely to regard school with indifference, or with positive distaste, for they find nothing to do there. (Winner, 1996, p. 401)

Students who are highly gifted may find themselves waiting after assignments are completed for as much as 50% of their school day and students who are profoundly gifted may "waste" 75% of their school day (Webb, Meckstroth and Tolan, 1994). Figure 8.1 delineates the categories of giftedness as determined by IQ. These designations are often included in literature regarding students who are intellectually gifted.

A DISCUSSION OF VARIANT NEEDS AND SERVICES PROVIDED TO STUDENTS WITH SPECIAL NEEDS

Most of the general population falls within one standard deviation of the norm (IQ 85-115) when tested. Figure 8.2 shows the standard deviation model as applied to IQ scores. Much of the energy, time, resources, and discussion regarding students with special needs have a focus on the students who perhaps have IQs that are less than 85. The lowest 2–3% of students, when viewed according to IQ scores, receives the bulk of services, personnel, and funding to facilitate their education (Winner, 1996). Students who have IQs ranging in the top 2–3% often experience very little in the way of services and supplementary aides (Winner, 1996).

Students who have IQs that fall in the bottom two standard deviations are enrolled in special education programs and receive services, often extensive services. Students who possess IQs that fall in the top two standard deviations are often not provided services at all (VanTassel-Baska, 1998). If services are provided for students who are gifted, they are often not individualized to differentiate their respective level of giftedness

Mildly (or basically) gifted	115–129
Moderately gifted	130–144
Highly gifted	145–159
Exceptionally gifted	160–179
Profoundly gifted	180+

Figure 8.1 Giftedness as measured by IQ Scores

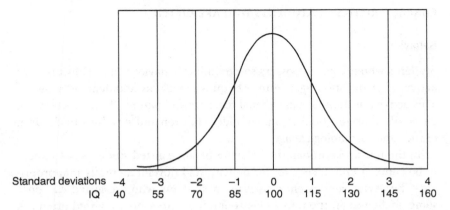

Standard deviations	−4	−3	−2	−1	0	1	2	3	4
IQ	40	55	70	85	100	115	130	145	160

Figure 8.2 [bell curve]

(gifted, moderately gifted, highly gifted, profoundly gifted) (Winner, 1996). Often, students with IQs of 130 are offered the same level of services as students with IQs of 180 (VanTassel-Baska, 1998). If we look at the other end of the bell curve, we see that students with IQs of 70 receive a vastly different educational experience than students with IQs of 20 (Winner, 1996).

ELITISM VS. EGALITARIANISM

The discussion of elitism vs. egalitarianism is one often repeated when discussing appropriate services for students who are gifted. The concept that giftedness is an elitist value is as absurd as proposing that mental retardation is not worth serious discussion within the educational community. Some gifted education experts call for the same level of individualized education and changes in the Least Restrictive Environment (LRE) for students who test at three and four standard deviations above the norm as for those who test at three and four standard deviations below the norm (VanTassel-Baska, 1998). It is unlikely that a student with an IQ of 50 would be in an inclusion classroom with no services or accommodations. A student with an IQ of 150, however, is often in an inclusion situation with no services or accommodations. Their IQs are equally different from those students who are considered average (IQ = 100), however, the attention paid to their educational needs is vastly unequal (Silverman, 1993). Webb explains: "Gifted children are not simply decorated normal children—they are, indeed, fundamentally different. A child with IQ 145 is as different from the normal IQ of 100 as the child of IQ 55" (Webb, 1994, p. 31).

CHARACTERISTICS OF STUDENTS WHO ARE GIFTED

Behavior

Students who are gifted possess some similar behavior traits. They are very active, often questioning, continue to question all day and demand answers. This active questioning can exhaust teachers and parents. Students who are gifted often prefer the company of older children and/or adults to children of the same chronological age.

In the music classroom, the behavior of some gifted students can appear to be rude, attention seeking (or deficit), and developmentally inappropriate. The asynchronous characteristic in students who are gifted can pose some challenges in the music classroom. Students who are gifted often ask very detailed questions that may not seem pertinent to the lesson or activity. They may blurt responses even when no question has been asked. Or, their responses may be seemingly unrelated to the question asked.

It is important for music educators to know the relative strengths and challenges of their students who are gifted. Once these specific needs are known, it becomes easier to be aware of possible behavioral triggers for a specific student as well as ways to lessen the effect these behaviors may have on other students in the music classroom. It will be helpful for those who teach students who are gifted to either be ready with responses to questions and concerns posed by a student or to set an appropriate time to work with these students in an individual or small group setting. Developing meaningful relationships with students who are gifted can greatly enhance the teaching and learning relationship with the individual students as well as preserve class and rehearsal time for the musical goals necessary for the development of all students in the classroom.

Learning

Students who are gifted often possess an extreme attention span when engaged in activities that interest them. They learn material faster, earlier, and remember information without review. They can comprehend and manipulate concepts that are too abstract and complicated for others that are the same age. They are passionate about one or more areas of interest or study and spend a great deal of time working and studying in their area of interest. They multitask and multiprocess at a greater rate than other students (Sousa, 2003; Winebrenner, 2001).

It can be fascinating, and slightly disconcerting, to observe a highly gifted student encounter a new intellectual challenge in the music classroom. The amount of time necessary for mastery of a concept is often a fraction of the time needed for students who are not gifted. Once a student who is gifted has learned the concept, the rest of the time needed by others in the music classroom to absorb, apply, and master is often wasted for this student.

For example, the amount of time a student who is gifted needs to memorize the names of the lines and spaces on the treble clef may be miniscule. If this lesson is being taught with a visual focus on a staff at the front of the classroom, students who are gifted will begin to tune out the lesson shortly after learning the concept. To continue to engage students who are gifted, new challenges will need to be posed (e.g., ledger lines, bass clef notes, or alto and tenor clef). Using centers, or small group work, can greatly increase the amount of class time that is actually useful for students who are gifted.

Differentiating educational experiences in the music classroom can benefit all learners. When planning lessons, activities, and rehearsals, considering the variant needs of students with special needs is essential. Many music educators who are successful when differentiating instruction write essential questions that are appropriate for various levels of understanding and comprehension. By preparing these questions and experiences in advance, music educators can begin the process of truly teaching to the variant needs of all students in the classroom.

Creativity

Students who are gifted have an almost limitless capacity for creativity in their area of giftedness. They often enjoy discovery and can create many items or products as a result of their creative interests. They can easily generate and develop ideas, are able to elaborate and add detail to their creations, and often challenge others to practice divergent thinking skills (Winebrenner, 2001).

Music educators who teach students who are gifted are sometimes challenged by the depth of creativity and divergent thinking presented by students during instruction. Providing regular opportunities for students who are gifted to develop these strengths may lead to benefits for all students in the music classroom. These opportunities can be created in the areas of composition, improvisation, performance, recording and technical creativity, literary arts, and the relationships between music and other art forms.

An example of an extension opportunity for students who are gifted is to ask them to research repertoire chosen for a concert. Students who are gifted may enjoy creating CDs or DVDs of compositions, performances, or rehearsals. The possibilities are as divergent as the creativity of the students. A caveat to offer is for the music educator to ensure that students who are gifted are invested and interested in these additional opportunities. Oftentimes, teachers assume that a greater workload equals a challenge for students who are gifted. More work does not necessarily mean a student is learning or is engaged. Students who are gifted can begin to feel their giftedness is a punishment if they are consistently asked or required to complete a greater quantity of work. Choosing quality opportunities that match the interest of students will truly be of benefit to students who are gifted.

Emotion

Hollingsworth (1975) stated, "To have the intelligence of an adult and the emotions of a child combined in a childish body is to encounter certain difficulties." (Webb, 1994, p. 101) Students who are gifted are, by nature, asynchronous in their development. A student may have the chronological age of 10, and the mental age of 15. This can cause a great deal of difficulty when processing information and overcoming emotional situations. Hallmarks of the emotional lives of students who are gifted include: asynchronous development, perfectionism which can lead to a lack of risk taking, the imposter syndrome, extreme frustration when work is incorrect or not perfect, and extremes in emotions and reactions to events and situations. These students may also have difficulty winding down for the day and/or sleeping at night.

Many students who are gifted experience intense perfectionism along with the "imposter syndrome" on a daily basis, and the possibility of failure can lead to some unusual and distracting emotional situations. Students who are gifted have often been told from a very young age that they are smart or a genius. These laudatory comments can become a heavy mantle for students who are gifted as they may begin to define their self-worth through their successes and the amount of intellectual feats they accomplish.

For some students who are gifted, the music classroom may pose the first real challenge they have experienced. Music performance requires a unique set of skills and a student who is intellectually gifted may be very challenged by these new skills and expectations. Playing a musical instrument can be difficult, and the mastery of an instrument does not occur in a short amount of time. For students unaccustomed to this process, extreme frustration, inordinate feelings of inadequacy, and a palpable fear of being discovered as not being as gifted as the school community had assumed are very real concerns.

Being aware of the students who are intellectually gifted in the music classroom and adjusting vocabulary and the way students are positively reinforced for demonstration of musical skills can lead to an increased sense of well-being and acceptance for all students. Students who are gifted may need to be reminded frequently that musical performance skills take years to master and that everyone improves at their own rate. They may not understand that while technical skill may be difficult now, it does not mean they do not have potential for success in music. Because of the possibilities of real challenge, the music classroom can be a powerful and affirming experience for students who are gifted. Being introduced to a process that is new, and possibly may require a new set of strategies for success, can truly change the way a student who is gifted views others around him and the challenges they face.

General Intellectual Ability

Students who are globally gifted often display the following characteristics at a young age: excellent attention and recognition memory, preference for novelty, precocious physical development, complex oral language, hypersensitivity and possible overreaction to stimuli and events, an ability to learn with minimal instruction, extreme curiosity, persistence and concentration, an abundance of energy, metacognitive awareness, and obsessive interests (Winner, 1996).

When most teachers think of students who are gifted, it is those students who are globally gifted that come to mind. Students who are globally gifted are gifted in almost every area of intellectual pursuit. They will have relative strengths and areas of challenge but also consistently demonstrate their inherent characteristics in all academic areas. These students are not necessarily gifted in the area of music yet their skills from other intellectual pursuits often provide an excellent level of basic preparation for the academic skills required for success in the music classroom.

The ability of students who are globally gifted to comprehend complicated and multistep processes in music is very high. They learn quickly and completely. They are insatiably curious about everything and using this curiosity and ability to become hyper-focused in an area of interest can allow a music educator the opportunity to create a meaningful and enduring set of experiences for a student who is gifted. Finding the access point for a student who is gifted (an area of interest that intersects with music) is an excellent starting place for these experiential pursuits.

Specific Academic Aptitude

Students who demonstrate precociousness in a single area (verbal, mathematic, etc.) are not always globally gifted. This sometimes leads to frustration on behalf of both teachers and students because the gifts a student displays in one area may not generalize to a holistically gifted student (Winner, 1996). It can be difficult for a student who is extraordinarily gifted in one academic area to understand that she is not necessarily as gifted in all areas.

Strategies for students who are gifted in one academic area are similar to those discussed above regarding students who are globally gifted. It is helpful to introduce an expanded or augmented project or curriculum using the area of giftedness possessed by the student. These experiences, again, can be very meaningful for students who are often not challenged by general curricula in place in the public schools.

INSTRUCTIONAL DELIVERY/PACING/PROCESS/MODIFICATIONS

Students who are gifted may need changes in the way their instruction is presented and paced. It is possible that some students who are gifted may be able to learn without intense modifications in the general education classroom. For students who are highly or profoundly gifted, a change in placement (least restrictive environment) may be necessary. These placement options are discussed below. There are also several options in the general classroom for enhancing the teaching and learning environment for students who are gifted.

Grouping Options

There are several options for grouping students who are gifted. They include: within class grouping, gifted pull-out (once or twice a week), enrichment classes, resource room, and mentoring (Winner, 1996). Other options include separate classes (self-contained gifted class, AP Classes), separate programs within schools (I.B., gifted programs), separate schools (magnet), acceleration (by subject or by grade) "testing out," concurrent high school/college enrollment, independent study, and compacting (by subject or by grade). In the music classroom and ensemble setting, students who are gifted can benefit from occasional homogenous grouping strategies. These strategies can include grouping for chamber music, centers, whole-class grouping (sometimes already in place in center-based elementary schools for students who are gifted), and by music theory achievement levels.

Some research has shown that students who perform at an average to below-average level in the inclusion classroom benefit more from a heterogenous classroom. For gifted students, however, the opposite is true. They benefit more from homogenous grouping with other students who are gifted (Winebrenner, 2001). A few guidelines for working with students who are gifted include an emphasis on less drill and repetition in the classroom. Furthermore, students who are gifted respond to increased opportunities to demonstrate mastery and to differentiation strategies that include adaptations to: content, process, product, environment, and assessment

(Winebrenner, 2001). Using grouping strategies in the music classroom will benefit the academic enrichment of students who are gifted.

TEACHER CHARACTERISTICS THAT ARE SUCCESSFUL WHEN TEACHING STUDENTS WHO ARE GIFTED

Music educators who work with students who are gifted will be more successful if they possess a specific set of behaviors and dispositions. Some of these characteristics are inherent and some are learned and strengthened through experience and purposeful planning. These characteristics are delineated below and, while they are specified for teachers who work with students who are gifted, many are also beneficial for all teachers.

Walker (1991) recommends the following characteristics:

- Understand and respect gifted
- Encourage while challenging students to achieve
- Provide depth in assignments
- Include specific comments on student work to note level of achievement
- Be a responsible, efficient, gifted, loving, and caring teacher

Webb (1994) makes the following suggestions to the teachers of students who are gifted:

- Communicate that the student's beliefs, feelings and behaviors are important
- Facilitate identification, expression and acceptance of feelings
- Convey understanding and acceptance of their own feelings
- Make it clear they value the whole student rather than just abilities and achievements
- Express that you value the uniqueness of the student
- Encourage pursuit of the special interests of the student
- Create time to share with the student
- Encourage students for attempts rather than merely successes
- Emphasize the value of productive cooperation and model these traits for students

Winebrenner (2001) shares these suggestions for teachers:

- Have enthusiasm for teaching and the subject being taught
- Be a lifelong learner
- Be flexible in your teaching style
- Hone your listening and inquiry strengths

- Increase your knowledge of the characteristics of students who are gifted
- Possess an interest in adapting and accommodating students who are gifted
- Have a strong sense of humor
- Demonstrate excellent organization and time management skills
- Be an effective advocate for students

VanTassel-Baska (1998) found the following characteristics to be beneficial for teachers when working with students who are gifted:

- Maturity and experience; self-confidence
- High intelligence
- Non academic [0]interests that are intellectual in nature
- High achievement needs; desire for intellectual growth
- Favorable attitude toward gifted students
- Systemic, imaginative, flexible, and creative in attitudes and responses
- Sense of humor
- Willingness to be a "facilitator" rather than a "director" of learning
- Capacity for hard work; willingness to devote extra time and effort to teaching
- Wide background of general knowledge; specific areas of expertise (particularly secondary teachers)
- Belief in understanding of individual differences

TWICE EXCEPTIONAL

Students who are designated as "twice exceptional" are intellectually gifted and also possess a special need that requires an IEP or 504 Plan for appropriate inclusion in public school classrooms. These "unevenly gifted" (Winner, 1996) students are sometimes misdiagnosed or undiagnosed as

---

Vignette 8.2 David

David was excited to have auditioned well enough to play in District Band as a ninth-grade student. Being second chair trombone in ninth grade was quite an achievement. He was also happy to be able to miss a day of school to rehearse as part of the weekend band event. He was definitely eager to be away from the teachers at school who were constantly telling him to pay attention and that he was not performing up to his potential.

How boring! Well, those teachers would just have to find someone else to pick on today.

On the way to the event, David had a great time talking to the other students. They were polite to him, however, it was clear to everyone but David that he was talking too much and that his impulsiveness was intruding on the personal space and conversations of others. The band director had told the other students to be nice to David and that the bus ride was only 45-minutes long.

Once David arrived at the site of the rehearsals, he ran through the auditorium to see his friends from other schools. He tripped over some backpacks, spilled a set of folders onto the ground, and ended up rolling down the aisle toward the stage. The conductor learned his name very early in the rehearsals and knew his band director and school name within the first hour.

David's excitement was soon lessened as he settled into the long (excruciatingly long to him) two days of rehearsals. He then realized that this event was going to be the same as many others he had experienced. His intellectual abilities and talents often earned him honors and experiences that his brain and body were not able to handle. How embarrassing to have both the band director and District Band conductor talk to his mom about his behavior (hyperactive and impulsive were the words they used) at the end of the day. Suddenly, David hated band and was ready to quit. He knew he wouldn't be allowed to quit because he had already quit soccer, baseball, violin, and the chess team. Maybe he could fake sick tomorrow morning to get out of his second day of District Band.

Questions for Consideration:

1. How can a director or music teacher prepare a student who is "twice exceptional" for an experience that may be difficult? What strategies can be put in place to increase the possibility that this will be a positive experience?
2. How can the five areas highlighted in this book (cognition, communication, sensory, behavioral/emotional, and physical) be addressed in these situations?
3. When is it appropriate for a music educator to intervene in a situation like this to protect a student from embarrassment, a negative experience, or his own impulsiveness?
4. What are the signs that a student is frustrated or struggling in an honor ensemble situation?

their strengths and areas of challenge sometimes mask each other. Until recently, the "global giftedness" premise was the accepted norm and many students who had disabilities and were gifted were only recognized for their giftedness. This sometimes led to uneven learning needs that were labeled underachievement, laziness, or a behavior disorder. Students who are twice exceptional also are often adept at hiding their disabilities by utilizing their giftedness and strengths as often as possible (Winner, 1996).

It is also possible that students can be identified as having a disability that is masking their giftedness. In these cases, some students are never appropriately identified as "twice exceptional" because their disability becomes the focus of instructional interventions and amelioration efforts (Winebrenner, 2001). If a student is undiagnosed or misdiagnosed (e.g., ADHD rather than gifted), they can be labeled as having behavior issues and may feel increasingly isolated and different from their peers. These feelings can lead to depression and thoughts of suicide (Webb, 1994). Moreover, the asynchronous development often seen in students who are gifted is multiplied in students who are twice exceptional (Kay, 2000).

PUTTING IT ALL TOGETHER

Teaching students who are gifted can be a truly enriching experience for music educators. The task assigned to music educators is to channel their cognitive abilities into an artistic endeavor. If music educators are aware of their strengths and areas of challenge, and are mindful of their responsibilities as educators, they have the opportunity to make a real difference in the lives of these learners as well as those with other cognitive challenges.

Attention to the needs of students who are gifted and who do not possess a high aptitude for music is also important as the awareness that many students are not "globally gifted" may be received by the student with great appreciation. Because of the many areas of potential giftedness, the task for the music educator may be to adapt instruction to the asynchronicity that can occur between intellect and musical ability in a student who is gifted in one area, yet, more like his classmates in others. An ability to modify teaching practices according to the areas of giftedness and recognizing the possibilities that exist for students who are gifted are important first steps in serving as an effective teacher for all students in the music classroom.

CONCLUSION

While we have termed students with superior abilities in the area of cognition as gifted, we also know they are students with special needs who can be effectively included in music classrooms and ensembles provided appropriate consideration and strategies are applied to meet their specific needs. The difference in approach involves differentiation, course and concept compacting, acceleration of educational experiences, and a vertical (delving deeply into topics) rather than horizontal (linear) approach to curriculum and instruction. When these general principles are introduced, students with special needs, and all students, will benefit from the enhanced teaching and learning environment.

DISCUSSION QUESTIONS

1. How can a music educator prepare for the inclusion of a student with enhanced cognition in the music classroom or ensemble?
2. What specific strategies would be employed for a third-grade student in a general music classroom who has already mastered the curriculum for elementary general music?
3. How can secondary music ensemble conductors differentiate instruction in a small or large ensemble setting to meet the needs of students at various levels of cognitive ability?
4. Which strategies outlined in chapter 4 would be effective when working with students who have enhanced cognition abilities and also have challenges in the area of communication?

REFERENCES

Binet, A. (1894). *Psychologie des grandes calucateurs (et de jouers d'echecs)*. Paris: Hachette.

Hollingsworth, L. S. (1931). *Gifted children: Their nature and nurture*. New York: Macmillan.

Hollingsworth, L. S. (1975). *Children above 180 IQ*. New York: Arno Press.

Kay, K. (2000). *Uniquely gifted: Identifying and meeting the needs of the twice-exceptional student*. Gilsum, NH: Avocus Publishing Inc.

Kerr, B. A. (1994). *Smart girls: A new psychology of girls, women and giftedness*. Scottsdale, AZ: Gifted Psychology Press.

Renzulli, J. S. (1977). *The enrichment triad model*. Mansfield Center, CT: Creative Learning Press.

Renzulli, J. S. (1986). The three-ring conception of giftedness: A developmental model for creative productivity. In R. J. Sternberg & J. Davidson (Eds.), *Conceptions of giftedness* (pp. 53–92). New York: Cambridge University Press.

Silverman, L. K. (1993). *Counseling the gifted and talented.* Denver, CO: Love Publishing Company.

Sousa, D. A. (2003). *How the gifted brain learns.* Thousand Oaks, CA: Sage Publications.

Terman, L. M. (1925). *Genetic studies of genius: Vol. 1. Mental and physical traits of a thousand gifted children.* Stanford, CA: Stanford University Press.

Terman, L.M., & Oden, M. H. (1947). *Genetic studies of genius: Vol. 4. The gifted child grows up.* Stanford, CA: Stanford University Press.

Terman, L. M., & Oden, M. H. (1959). *Genetic studies of genius: Vol. 5. The gifted group at mid-life: Thirty-five years' follow-up of the superior child.* Stanford, CA: Stanford University Press.

VanTassel-Baska, J. (1998). *Excellence in educating gifted and talented learners.* Denver, CO: Love Publishing Company.

Walker, S.Y. (1991) *The survival guide for parents of gifted kids.* Minneapolis, MN: Free Spirit Publishing.

Webb, J. T., Meckstroth, E. A., & Tolan, S. S. (1994). *Guiding the gifted child.* Scottsdale, AZ: Gifted Psychology Press.

Winebrenner, S. (2001). *Teaching gifted kids in the regular classroom.* Minneapolis, MN: Free Spirit Publishing.

Winner, E. (1996). *Gifted children: Myths and realities.* New York, NY: Perseus Books Group.

PART IV

RESOURCES FOR MUSIC EDUCATORS

Chapter 9

Resources for Music Teachers and Music Teacher Educators Regarding Teaching Students with Special Needs

The majority of this text has been built around the concept of teaching students with special needs in an inclusive, label-free, environment built around the five areas of music teaching and learning. As mentioned in chapter 1, music teachers must also learn about the challenges a student might be facing in their general or self-contained classroom. This is equally important in learning to teach a student who might be faced with the challenge of a disability. This chapter will consist of three sections. Section 1 is a comprehensive list (as of the publication date) of the standard Internet-based resources for students with a variety of special needs. Section 2 is an up-to-date resource list of practitioner articles, books, and research in the field of teaching students with special needs.

SECTION 1: INTERNET RESOURCES

The following web-based resources follow the IDEA (2004) categorization of disabilities. Each URL has been tested and reviewed by the authors and editors.

Internet Resources Pertaining to Persons with Autism

The Ability Project: Autism

http://www.ability.org.uk/autism.html
 This site has over 150 links to other autism-related resources. The Internet resources are wide in scope and include sites from countries all over the world. This site is a great resource for learning more about autism.

Autism One International

http://www.autismone.org/
 This site contains many media images and links regarding various aspects of autism. You will also find current articles on related topics including

research, treatments, awareness, and social networking for parents and teachers. Links to several notable autism sites are included as part of the A+ *Autism Collaboration*.

Autism Research Institute

http://www.autism.com/ari/

Although this site cites current autism research as the main topic, it also includes concise information about autism, treatment options, and frequently asked questions. Triggers for autism and dietary treatment as well as several links to articles on many topics related to autism treatment and recovery are embedded in this interactive site.

Autism Society of America

http://www.autism-society.org/

This site offers basic information about autism and signs for early identification. Treatment options, education laws, family issues, and links to the autism community are also provided. This site offers access to current research on autism, resources for parents, and a link to a very large database called *Autismsource*, which contains sources for autism-related services and support.

Autism Speaks

http://www.autismspeaks.org/

This site contains a wide variety of information regarding autism and is available in Spanish. Several treatment options are presented including additional links to related websites. The rights of children with autism and families of children with autism are presented in a direct manner, as are the expectations for living with autism. The site also includes resources for family services and links for current research and conferences.

Fighting Autism

http://www.fightingautism.org/

This site provides a wealth of statistics about autism rates, treatment effectiveness, and national demographics. Other IDEA 2004 disabilities are also included in the statistical graphs. The statistical information is interactive and easy to understand.

The National Autism Association

http://www.nationalautismassociation.org/

This site offers abundant information regarding nearly every aspect of autism. Details about autism terminology, diagnosis, research, numerous autism resources, and family support services are easily accessed from this website. The resource list includes links to many valuable sites related to autism and treatment.

The National Autistic Society

http://www.nas.org/uk/

This site represents England's National Autism Society. Many facts about autism, known causes, treatments, and current research are presented. The process of diagnosis is presented in clear detail. This site promotes early intervention and the importance of specialized education as the ideal treatment. The site also provides a list of resources and support services provided by the organization.

Internet Resources Pertaining to Students with Sensory Challenges

A–Z of Deaf-blindness

http://www.deafblind.com/

This site contains the most complete listing of links to websites supporting those who are deaf-blind on the Internet. Almost every kind of service from education and devices to international organizations and research groups has links posted on this database.

American Association of Deaf-Blind (AADB)

http://www.aadb.org/

This site is the national consumer website for AADB. Information regarding publications, conferences, emergency preparations, FAQs, communication technology, and articles related to the people in the deaf-blind community are available.

Deaf-blind International (DbI)

http://www.deafblindinternational.org/

This is the homepage for Deaf-blind International, a worldwide organization that promotes services for people who are both deaf and blind. Links to conferences, publications, news, and membership are helpful. Another highlight of the site is a list of known conditions and syndromes that can result in deaf-blindess.

Deafblind Resources

http://www.deafblindresources.org/

This website is a project to promote the exchange of information and intervention strategies for persons with deaf-blindness. The site includes articles, communication devices, a chat room, and a listserv for daily interaction.

Helen Keller National Center (HKNC)

http://www.hknc.org/

This site provides information about the only national rehabilitation program exclusively for children and adults who are deaf-blind. Links to sources for devices, camps, related agencies and services, and HKNC publications are provided.

National Coalition on Deaf-blindess

http://www.dbcoalition.org/

This website is designed to provide feedback to legislators and policy makers about the needs of children who are deaf-blind. Important statistics, research results, stories, and links to contact legislators in every state are easily accessed from this resource.

National Consortium on Deaf-Blindness (NCDB)

http://www.nationaldb.org/

The home page of the NCDB provides information in three areas. Technical services provide ongoing assistance to children and families. DB-LINK is a collection of information related to deaf-blindness worldwide that is supported by NCDB. Links to a system for training personnel to provide professional support to children with deaf-blindness completes the mission of this group.

National Family Association for Deaf-Blind (NFADB)

http://nfadb.org/

This site exists to support people who are deaf-blind and their families through training and support, collaboration with organizations, and advice regarding research. Links to other resources, conferences, and a listserv are useful.

New York Institute Special Education

http://www.nyise.org/deaf.htm

The site displays an annotated resource guide of deaf-blind related websites with links worldwide. The links are excellent and include; books, conferences, braille history, low-vision resources, organizations, and research information.

SENSE

http://www.sense.org.uk/

The site is supported by the National Deaf-blind and Rubella Association: the world's largest organization of support for persons who are deaf-blind, their families, and professionals. A wide variety of valuable resources are available through this comprehensive website.

Specific Visual Impairment Internet Resources

American Council of the Blind

http://www.acb.org/

The American Council of the Blind is one of the leading organizations for persons who are blind or visually impaired. They strive to improve the well-being of persons who are blind by promoting education, building morale, coordinating services, and fostering greater understanding of blindness. They support the *Braille Forum*, a monthly magazine, and the website contains links to state organizations, audio recordings, and other helpful resources.

American Foundation for the Blind

http://www.afb.org/

The American Foundation for the Blind is focused on the expansion of possibilities for persons with vision loss. In addition to helpful Internet links for education, braille sites, technology, employment, and a section that shares strategies for living with vision loss, there is a Family Connect page to assist parents who are raising children with visual impairments and a Career Connect page to help locate jobs.

American Printing House for the Blind

http://www.aph.org/

American Printing House for the Blind has been the the largest provider of educational and daily living products for more than 150 years. Software, large-type books, and many types of learning products are available online. The LOUIS database contains information in various media formats for over 200,000 publications related to visual impairment.

Association for the Blind and Visually Impaired

http://www.abvi-goodwill.org/

The Association for the Blind and Visually Impaired works in conjunction with Goodwill Stores to support persons who are blind. Their website outlines their vision services, publications, resources, and ways to volunteer or donate.

The Blindness Resource Center

http://www.nyise.org/blind.htm

The New York Institute for Special Education is a private educational facility for persons who are blind or visually impaired. The Blindness Resource Center in an online index of links to websites that cover visual impairment topics such as: braille history, literacy, disabilities, eye conditions, low-vision resources, organizations, research, and vendors of vision products.

National Association for the Visually Handicapped

http://www.navh.org/

The National Association for the Visually Handicapped works to provide services and strategies for success for persons who are "hard of seeing." Links to information regarding vision differences, large print publishers, and visual aid products make this a worthwhile site to visit.

National Braille Press

http://www.nbp.org/

The National Braille Press is a nonprofit braille printer and publisher of resources for persons who are blind. Links to the NBP bookstore, books for children, a special reading program, and a visual tour of the printing plant highlight their home page. Newly printed materials can be viewed through their Highlights link.

National Federation of the Blind

http://www.nfb.org

The National Federation of the Blind attempts to address issues that arise from a misunderstanding and lack of information available to persons who are visually impaired. Viable details regarding vision loss for parents, teachers, students, and professionals are included. Additional resources, products, technology, and publications are aimed toward bridging the knowledge gap online.

Royal National Institute of Blind People

http://www.rnib.org.uk/

The Royal National Institute of Blind People is England's leading charity that offers information and support to persons with sight loss. Some of the best links focus on general eye information, daily life with vision loss, jobs, reading rehabilitation, social services, technology, and citizen's rights.

The Seeing Eye

http://www.seeingeye.org/

The Seeing Eye Organization seeks to enhance the independence and self-confidence of persons with vision loss through the use of seeing-eye dogs. This site guides the reader through the detailed process of applying for a seeing-eye dog and even the possibility of raising a puppy.

Specific Hearing Impairment Internet Resources

American Society for Deaf Children (ASDC)

http://www.deafchildren.org/

This site is dedicated to helping families raise children who are deaf by providing valuable links to services, camps, conferences, educational sources, and organizations connected to persons in the deaf community.

Another Path

http://www.deafhomeschool.com/

This site includes a comprehensive guide to homeschooling children who are deaf or hard of hearing. Many links to essential instructional materials, laws, family support, and education are embellished by links to major subject area resources that serve to create an expansive network of educational support.

Central Institute for the Deaf (CID)

http://cid.edu/

This website focuses on education and services for people who are deaf or hard of hearing. Although the actual school is located in St. Louis, Missouri, the resources online offer excellent strategies for parents and school personnel.

Deaf Culture Online

http://www.deaf-culture-online.com/

This site offers many perspectives on the experience of being deaf. Resources for parents, sign language links, communication awareness, and overall wellness links help readers understand the challenges of being deaf and gain an understanding of deaf culture.

Deaf Library

http://www.deaflibrary.org/

This site is a virtual library of reference materials and links pertaining to persons who are deaf or hard of hearing. A quick search of concepts related to deafness yields a variety of useful information.

Deaf Resources

http://www.deafresources.com/

This website offers products for persons who are hearing impaired and those involved within the deaf community. Information about teacher resources, books, technology, and communication devices are helpful and easy to navigate on this site.

Journal of Deaf Studies and Deaf Education

http://jdsde.oxfordjournals.org/

This website is sponsored by Oxford University Press. The *Journal of Deaf Studies and Deaf Education* seeks to integrate and coordinate research related to individuals who are deaf. Links for educators include cultural, developmental, and linguistic topics.

National Association of the Deaf (NAD)

http://www.nad.org/

This website represents the National Association of the Deaf which serves as a civil rights organization to support individuals who are deaf or hard of hearing in the United States of America. Links to resources on education, civil rights, sign language, and health services are excellent.

Internet Resources Pertaining to Persons with Developmental Delays

American Academy of Pediatrics

http://www.aap.org/

This website is dedicated to the health of all children and includes many resources for parents and professionals on nearly every health issue facing children today. Specific details on education, publications, advocacy, and a quick topic search for related links are also included.

Centers for Disease Control and Prevention

http://www.cdc.gov/ncbddd/actearly/index.html

This site is packed full of health information related to early development and includes an alphabetical index to numerous links. This page is also linked to the National Center for Birth Defects and Developmental Disabilities home page, which provides a wealth of childhood developmental information. *Act Early* promotes knowledge and early detection as optimal treatment tools.

Developmental Delay Resources (DDR)

http://www.devdelay.org/

This site is dedicated to providing conventional and holistic resources to meet the needs of children with developmental delays. A directory of service providers includes over 20 links to related areas. A calendar of disability-related events and a detailed list of books complete the site.

My Child Without Limits

http://www.mychildwithoutlimits.org/

This site compares normal developmental milestones with five large categories of potential delay: gross motor, fine motor, language, cognitive, and social. Extensive resources and references are given as well as inclusive links to 10 common serious health issues that are associated with developmental delays.

First Signs

http://www.firstsigns.org/

The mission of this organization is to provide information about early warning signs for developmental delays. Research and resources are useful and appropriate. The links to diagnosis and treatment are combined with screening options to show the viewer multiple early intervention options.

Zero to Three

http://www.zerotothree.org/

This site is sponsored by the National Center for Infants, Toddlers, and Families. Several key topics are thoroughly covered, including child development, with many links to comprehensive resources. Extensive information is also focused toward professionals and parents.

Internet Resources Pertaining to Persons with Emotional Disturbances

American Academy of Child and Adolescent Psychiatry (AACAP)

http://www.aacap.org/

The American Academy of Child and Adolescent Psychiatry is an important children's medical health organization that seeks to improve the quality of life for persons affected by mental, behavioral, and developmental disorders. This site includes links to quality information for both professionals and families by supporting education, medication, legislation, culture, and policy.

Council for Exceptional Children

http://www.cec.org/

The Council for Exceptional Children is an organization dedicated to being the voice and vision of special education. The resources available at the site are expansive and far-reaching in scope. Links to articles on many topics such as inclusion, teaching and learning, news, policy, and professional development are included to be helpful to both parents and educators who work with children with special needs. A quick search yields a multitude of materials that relate to students with emotional disturbance.

Internet Mental Health

http://www.mentalhealth.com/

This site contains extensive descriptions, possible diagnoses, treatment options, related research, and additional resources for the 52 most common mental disorders. Facts about mental health in America and links to depression, schizophrenia, phobias, conduct disorders, and obsessive-compulsive disorder are most directly related to the IDEA 2004 definition of emotional disturbances.

Mental Health Matters

http://www.mental-health-matters.com/

The site is a clearinghouse for articles related to mental health. A pulldown menu allows the reader to choose any disorder and then access all of the articles related to that topic. In addition to disorders, links to treatments, medications, community, and other resources can be found at this informative website.

National Alliance on Mental Illness (NAMI)

http://www.nami.org/

This site is supported by the National Alliance of Mental Illness: a nonprofit organization that strives to share information and offer possibilities to the persons and families who suffer from mental illness. Major illnesses are linked to the home page, as well as medications, support, and programs intended to improve the quality of life for everyone.

National Mental Health Information Center

http://www.mentalhealth.samhsa.gov/

This website is the informational component of the Substance Abuse and Mental Health Services Administration (SAMHSA), which is an arm of the United States Department of Health and Human Services. Mental health programs, special topics, news, publications, and resources are explained in detail at this government-supported website.

Special Education Resources on the Internet (SERI)

http://www.seriweb.com/

This site is the main Internet resource index for the Special Education Resources of the Internet. Web-accessible information is linked by a large database of articles to a variety of special education topics. A tab for behavioral disorders provides the viewer with links to websites regarding emotional disturbance.

Internet Resources Pertaining to Persons with Cognitive Disabilities

American Association for Mental Retardation (AAMR)

http://www.aamr.org/

This website is the home page of the national organization for professionals and others interested in learning more about mental retardation. Links to research, support, basic facts, and national resources can be accessed from this website.

The Arc

http://www.thearc.org/

The Arc is a volunteer nonprofit organization that exists to support persons with mental retardation and their families. Links to disability resources, public policy, and federal laws guide the reader to informed understanding and mental health related articles.

Family Village

http://www.familyvillage.wisc.edu/

The Family Village is a global community of disability-related resources that are supported by the University of Wisconsin. Informational links to resources on specific diagnoses, communication, adaptive products, education, health issues, and medications appear on this website.

The National Down Syndrome Society

http://www.ndss.org/

This national organization home page serves as an advocate for persons with Down syndrome. Acceptance and inclusion are treatments supported by articles that also include education, policy, research, and self-advocacy.

Special Olympics

http://www.specialolympics.org/

The Special Olympics is a nonprofit international program of sports training and competition for individuals with mental retardation. Personal stories are combined with a vast wealth of worldwide resources to make this website a powerful tool for awareness and advocacy of persons with mental retardation.

Multiple Impairment Internet Resources

National Dissemination Center for Children with Disabilities

http://www.nichcy.org/

The National Dissemination Center for Children with Disabilities is an organization that provides the nation with information about disabilities, support services, IDEA specifics, No Child Left Behind, and current research into each of the disability categories. Major headings include families and community, early intervention providers, schools and administrators, state agencies, laws, and resources.

PAMIS

http://www.dundee.ac.uk/pamis/

The Profound and Multiple Impairment Service is an organization in Scotland working with persons who have learning disabilities. PAMIS supports families by providing information, activities, and consultation. Publications related to multiple disabilities and a virtual online library offer additional support.

Teaching Students with Visual and Multiple Impairments

http://www.tsbvi.edu/

This website is an excellent resource for educators. Links to curriculum, instruction, technology, publications, and life with multiple impairments are features of this site. This website is supported by the Texas School for the Blind and Visually Impaired.

Internet Resources for Children with Physical Disabilities

American Academy of Special Education Professionals (AASEP)

http://www.aasep.org/

This site has a large listing of professional resources that include many support therapists in nearly every possible venue. Links to very specific data on each of the IDEA 2004 disabilities are available, as well as intervention resources for parents and teachers. Links to legal issues, transition services, conferences, reading materials, and career opportunities complete the website of this professional organization.

The Hydrocephalus Association

http://www.hydroassoc.org/

This site seeks to aid persons who are challenged with hydrocephalus through research, support, education, and advocacy campaigns. Extensive links to publications, physicians, scholarships, events, research, medical articles, and advocacy help broaden the understanding of hydrocephalus.

iScoliosis

http://www.iscoliosis.com/

This is a user-friendly website that provides salient information regarding scoliosis. Symptoms, causes, treatments, and personal stories are geared toward teenagers and their parents. Suggested exercises, a section of FAQs, and links to finding qualified doctors are part of the support from this site that is sponsored by Medtronic.

Muscular Dystrophy Association (MDA)

http://www.mda.org/

One of the nation's largest and most visible organizations for persons with disabilities, the MDA is associated with the annual Labor Day Muscular Dystrophy Telethon hosted by Jerry Lewis. Many valuable links to family services, research, clinics, and the telethon guide viewers to a better understanding of Muscular Dystrophy and where to find help.

National Association of Parents with Children in Special Education (NAPCSE) *http://www.napcse.org/*

This site is loaded with detailed information for parents and teachers about nearly all of the IDEA 2004 disabilities. For best results the viewer should join NAPCSE to see all of the information. The major topics include: bone diseases, cerebral palsy, hydrocephalus, muscular dystrophy, polio, scoliosis, and spina bifida.

The Spina Bifida Association (SBA)

http://www.spinabifidaassociation.org/

This site is dedicated to the most common disabling birth defect in the United States. The Spina Bifida Association promotes prevention and life improvement for all people affected. Links to research, fact sheets, clinics, a national resource center, publications, news, and events help educate the viewer about SB. Pregnant women who take folic acid can reduce the risk of having a baby with spina bifida according to SBA research.

United Cerebral Palsy (UCP)

http://www.ucp.org/

This site is one of the leading places for information and advocacy for people with cerebral palsy. The home page offers links to education, employment, health and wellness, housing, parents and families, products and services, sports and leisure, transportation, and travel. Additional links to grants, news and a one-stop guide for services in every state provide resources at the local level.

Internet Resources for Persons or Students with Chronic Medical Conditions

American Diabetes Association (ADA)

http://www.diabetes.org/

This national organization is committed to helping persons with diabetes manage their lives healthily. Both Type I and Type II diabetes are explained. Extensive information about nutrition management, fitness, lifestyle, research, local advocacy, professionals, parenting tips, and support are linked to this well-designed and helpful website. All facts provide valuable insight into a health condition that nearly 8% of Americans live with every day.

American Heart Association

http://http:americanheart.org/

This national group promotes healthy lifestyle and knowledge as keys to a better heart. Warning signs for stroke and heart attack are given along with information on CPR, heart diseases, children's heart health, research, and advocacy.

American Lung Association

http://www.lungusa.org/

This site contains a wealth of information about asthma and other lung diseases. Asthma can affect persons of all ages differently as this site explains. Links to asthma management, asthma research, how asthma changes as persons grow older, publications, and locations for Asthma Clinical Research Centers nationwide are important assets of this website.

Attention Deficit Disorder Association

http://www.add.org/

Although this website is in the midst of a redesign phase, the links for attention deficit hyperactivity disorder are working and are very applicable. Links to numerous articles related to relationships, career, research, school, treatment, and legal issues are excellent.

Epilepsy Foundation

http://www.epilepsyfoundation.org/

The Epilepsy Foundation of America is dedicated to helping people with seizures participate in all aspects of life, be valued in society, and promote research for a cure. Information about seizures, diagnosis, treatments, current research, and advocacy are well presented and helpful.

Leukemia and Lymphoma Society

http://www.leukemia.org/

The Leukemia and Lymphoma Society is the world's largest voluntary health organization dedicated to funding blood cancer research, education, and support. Links to blood disease information, patient services, advocacy, and research are very detailed.

National Heart, Lung, and Blood Institute

http://nhlbi.nih.gov/

The National Heart, Lung, and Blood Institute is part of the U.S. Department of Health and Human Services. This website includes links to major blood diseases and disorders. Clicking on a specific disorder reveals additional links to detailed explanations, causes, symptoms, diagnoses, treatments, preventions, and additional resources.

National Tourette Syndrome Association (TSA)

http://www.tsa-usa.org/

The National Tourette Syndrome Association works to promote awareness and offer help in overcoming life's challenges for persons affected by

Tourette Syndrome. Explanations about how Tourette affects the body and lives of persons with Tourette, research, professional help, support, education, and newsletters are all part of the information found at this site.

One ADD Place

http://www.oneaddplace.com/

This site has a multitude of links to every aspect of ADHD. The links include information on diagnosis, treatments, symptoms, diet, services, resources, products, news, and many special features that make this website a great resource for parents and teachers.

Internet Resources for Students with Specific Learning Disabilities

Dyslexia—The Gift

http://www.dyslexia.com/

The Davis Dyslexia Association International supports this website which offers books that contain teaching strategies designed to address dyslexia. In addition to learning resources, the site has links to research, a library of articles, free software, education, family support, and many other topics related to dyslexia.

The International Dyslexia Association (IDA)

http://www.interdys.org/

The International Dyslexia Association is a nonprofit organization dedicated to helping individuals with dyslexia. The website provides a variety of links for information including interventions, research, a grant program, online bookstore, discussion forum, publications, conferences, and membership.

Internet Special Education Resources

http://www.iser.com/

This learning disabilities directory of professionals, organizations, and schools serves those with learning disabilities and assists parents in locating area special education services, professional therapists, and advocacy strategies. Links to government agencies, teacher training and certification programs, and special needs software are located at this interesting site.

Learning Disabilities Association of America

http://www.ldanatl.org/

This organization seeks to provide cutting-edge information regarding learning disabilities to parents, students, educators, and professionals. Overviews of several types of learning disabilities, assessment information, early childhood detection, navigation of the special education process, and guidelines to better mental health are just a few of the resources provided through this website.

LD Online

http://www.ldonline.org/

This website contains a wide variety of excellent information for parents, teachers, and students on learning disabilities. A section on Learning Disabilities and ADHD basics is a good overview of each topic that includes links to questions, answers, and a glossary of terms. A link to LD Topics brings up hundreds of articles and resources concerning LD. A special section for teachers and a link to the learning store are unique.

LD Resources

http://www.ldresources.com/

This site has provided information for persons with learning disabilities and those who work with them since 1995. The collection of resources includes a topic search, a blog, an archive, and hundreds of links to many issues related to learning disabilities.

The National Aphasia Association (NAA)

http://www.aphasia.org/

The National Aphasia Association promotes public education, research, rehabilitation, and support services to assist persons with aphasia. Aphasia, which impairs the ability to speak and understand others and often causes difficulty in reading and writing, is usually the result of a stroke or other brain injury. This site includes links to the law, books, articles, support materials, health professionals, research, and rehabilitation.

The National Center for Learning Disabilities

http://www.nld.org/

This website is the informational connection for the National Center for Learning Disabilities. It exists to ensure that people with learning disabilities have every opportunity to succeed in school, work, and life. The section on LD basics has a clear explanation of learning disabilities, how LD can affect learning, social issues, keys for success, and research. Links for home, work, school, and college provide the reader with strategies to address challenges.

Speech and Language Impairment Internet Resources

American Speech-Language-Hearing Association

http://www.asha.org/

The American Speech-Language-Hearing Association is a scientific and professional organization comprised of speech-language pathologists and scientists worldwide who strive to improve effective communication for all people. Access to online journals and other information related to speech and language challenges are available.

The Children's Hospital of Philadelphia

http://www.chop.edu

A quick search of the Children's Hospital of Philadelphia website includes a Center for Childhood Communication. At this site various speech disorders are explained as well as medical conditions that can increase speech differences. Related services, additional online sources, physicians, and research findings are also linked to this medical website.

Children's Speech Care Center

http://www.childspeech.net/

This site provides an overview of speech impairments and then delineates various diagnoses, treatment options, and the 15 most common speech impairments. Resources for finding a clinic, early intervention, and links to many support agencies offer the viewer a variety of services and information related to speech impairments.

Language Disorders Arena

http://www.langiagedisordersarena.com/

The Language Disorders Arena provides researchers, teachers, and students with information regarding a range of journals, books, and other resources pertaining to language disorders.

National Stuttering Association

http://nsastutter.org/

The National Stuttering Association states they are the largest self-help organization for persons who stutter. Information on stuttering, its causes and treatments, local chapters, research projects, PDF files of publications, and links to other stuttering websites are found at this site.

The Stuttering Homepage

http://www.stutteringhomepage.com

This site provides several links to a variety of topics related to stuttering. A complete listing of websites that support those who stutter can be found at this site. The site is supported by Minnesota State University.

Internet Resources Pertaining to Persons with Traumatic Brain Injury

Brain Injury Association of America

http://biausa.org/

The Brain Injury Association of America serves persons whose lives are affected by Traumatic Brain Injury. Fact sheets and links to A–Z Topics of brain injury provide detailed information. Brain Injury Association office locations in each state are listed, as well as links to research, recovery, education, and a national directory of support services.

Café Plus

http://www.dreamscape.com/cafeplus/

The Café Plus is a special coffee shop in East Syracuse, New York, for persons who have experienced a head injury. The coffee shop is designed to be a place for meeting new friends, watching movies, playing games, enjoying meaningful activities, and sharing a good time with others. The purpose of Café Plus is to help persons overcome feelings of isolation as they recover after a brain injury. This site also has information on Internet resources related to Traumatic Brain Injury (TBI).

TBI Resource Guide

http://www.neuroskills.com/

The Traumatic Brain Injury Resource Guide is the educational Internet resource for services and products related to TBI. The site is supported by the Centre for Neuro Skills in California and Texas. This site has some outstanding links to information about brain injuries and exactly how they can affect almost every aspect of life. Treatment options, resources, a TBI shop, and a list of publications can be found at this comprehensive website.

Traumatic Brain Injury.com

http://www.traumaticbraininjury.com/

The Pennsylvania Brain Injury Hospitals support this wonderful Internet resource. Information explaining the basic facts about TBI, the symptoms, diagnoses, treatment options, legal resources, and an extensive video library all provide information regarding this complex disability.

Traumatic Brain Injury Survival Guide

http://www.tbiguide.com/

This site is supported by Dr. Glen Johnson, a clinical neuropsychologist. His guide to head injuries offers specific information regarding ways traumatic brain injuries occur, what to do about them, the stages of recovery, common challenges, returning to school, and communicating with medical professionals.

SECTION 2: PRINT RESOURCES FOR MUSIC TEACHERS AND MUSIC TEACHER EDUCATORS

The next section of this text is a comprehensive compilation of research, practitioner articles, and books for music teachers and music teacher educators to utilize in their planning and approach to this subject in music education.

RESEARCH WITHIN MUSIC EDUCATION PERTAINING TO STUDENTS WITH SPECIAL NEEDS

Abad, V. (2007). Early intervention music therapy: Reporting on a 3-year project to address needs with at-risk families. *Music Therapy Perspectives, 25*(1), 52–58.

Allgood, N. (2005). Parents' perceptions of family-based group music therapy for children with autism spectrum disorders. *Music Therapy Perspectives, 23*(2), 92–99.

Brunk, B. K. (2000). Special feature: Development of a special education music therapy assessment process. *Music Therapy Perspectives, 18*(1), 59–68.

Burnard, P. (2008). Inclusive pedagogies in music education: A comparative study of music teachers' perspectives from four countries. *International Journal of Music Education, 26*(2), 109–126.

Chase, K. M. (2004). Music therapy assessment for children with developmental disabilities: A survey study. *Journal of Music Therapy, 41*(1), 28.

Colwell, C. M. (2000). "Inclusion" Of information on mainstreaming in undergraduate music education curricula. *Journal of Music Therapy, 37*(3), 205–221.

Colwell, C. M. (2003). Integrating disability simulations into a course for student music therapists. *Music Therapy Perspectives, 21*(1), 14–20.

Crowe, B. J. (2004). Implications of technology in music therapy practice and research for music therapy education: A review of literature. *Journal of Music Therapy, 41*(4), 282–320.

Darrow, A.-A. (1993). The role of music in deaf culture: Implications for music educators. *Journal of Research in Music Education, 41*(2), 93–110.

Darrow, A.-A. (1999). Music and deaf culture: Images from the media and their interpretation by deaf and hearing students. *Journal of Music Therapy, 36*(2), 88–109.

Darrow, A.-A. (2003). Attitudes of junior high school music students' from Italy and the USA toward individuals with a disability. *Bulletin of the Council for Research in Music Education, 155*, 33–43.

Darrow, A.-A. (2006). The role of music in deaf culture: Deaf students' perception of emotion in music. *Journal of Music Therapy, 43*(1), 2–15.

Darrow, A.-A. (2007a). Looking to the past: Thirty years of history worth remembering. *Music Therapy Perspectives, 25*(2), 94–99.

Darrow, A.-A. (2007b). The effect of vision and hearing loss on listeners' perception of referential meaning in music. *Journal of Music Therapy, 44*(1), 57–73.

DeBedout, J. K. (2006). Motivators for children with severe intellectual disabilities in the self-contained classroom: A movement analysis. *Journal of Music Therapy, 43*(2), 123–135.

Douglass, E. T. (2006). The development of a music therapy assessment tool for hospitalized children. *Music Therapy Perspectives, 24*(2), 73–79.

Farnan, L. A. (2007). Music therapy and developmental disabilities: A glance back and a look forward. *Music Therapy Perspectives, 25*(2), 80–85.

Forgeard, M. (2008). The relation between music and phonological processing in normal-reading children and children with dyslexia. *Music Perception, 25*(4), 383–390.

Frisque, J., Niebur, L., & Humphreys, T. (1994). Music mainstreaming practices in Arizona. *Journal of Research in Music Education, 42*, 94–104.

Gfeller, K. (2007). Music therapy and hearing loss: A 30-year retrospective. *Music Therapy Perspectives, 25*(2), 100–107.

Gfeller, K., Darrow, A.-A., & Hedden, S. (1990). Perceived effectiveness of mainstreaming in Iowa and Kansas schools. *Journal of Research in Music Education, 38*(2), 90–101.

Gilbert, J. P., & Asmus, E. P. (1981). Mainstreaming music educators' participation and professional needs. *Journal of Research in Music Education, 29*(1), 31–37.

Goldstein, D. (2000). Music pedagogy for the blind. *International Journal of Music Education, 35*(1), 35–39.

Gregoire, M. A. (2006). Book reviews: "Music in special education," By Mary S. Adamek and Alice-Ann Darrow. *Music Therapy Perspectives, 24*(1), 52–53.

Gregory, D. (2002). Music listening for maintaining attention of older adults with cognitive impairments. *Journal of Music Therapy, 39*(4), 244–264.

Hammel, A. M. (2001). Preparation for teaching special learners: Twenty years of practice. *Journal of Music Teacher Education, 11*(1), 5–11.

Hébert, S. (2008). A case study of music and text dyslexia. *Music Perception, 25*(4), 369–381.

Hooper, J. (2008a). A review of the music and intellectual disability literature (1943–2006) part one—descriptive and philosophical writing. *Music Therapy Perspectives, 26*(2), 66–79.

Hooper, J. (2008b). A review of the music and intellectual disability literature (1943–2006) part two - experimental writing. *Music Therapy Perspectives, 26*(2), 80–96.

Hourigan, R. M. (2007) Teaching Music to Students with Special Needs: A Phenomenological Examination of Participants in a Fieldwork Experience. Doctoral Dissertation, The University of Michigan (ISBN#: 9780549174868/VDM Verlag (2008) ISBN#: 978-3-8364-7663-8).

Hourigan, R. M. (2007b). A special needs field experience for preservice instrumental music educators. *Contributions to Music Education, 34*, 19–33.

Ingber, J. (2003). Information sharing: Using MIDI with adults who have developmental disabilities. *Music Therapy Perspectives, 21*(1), 46–50.

Jackson, N. A. (2003). A survey of music therapy methods and their role in the treatment of early elementary school children with ADHD. *Journal of Music Therapy, 40*(4), 302–323.

Jellison, J. A. (2002). On-task participation of typical students close to and away from classmates with disabilities in an elementary music classroom. *Journal of Research in Music Education, 50*(4), 343–355.

Kaiser, K. A. (2000). The effect of an interactive experience on music majors' perceptions of music for deaf students. *Journal of Music Therapy, 37*(3), 222–234.

Kaplan, R. (2004). Music therapy, sensory integration and the autistic child. *Music Therapy Perspectives, 22*(1), 56–58.

Kaplan, R. (2008). Book review: "Music therapy groupwork with special needs children: The evolving process," By K. D. Goodman. *Journal of Music Therapy, 45*(4), 507–511.

Kaplan, R. S. (2005). An analysis of music therapy program goals and outcomes for clients with diagnoses on the autism spectrum. *Journal of Music Therapy, 42*(1), 2–19.

Katagiri, J. (2009). The effect of background music and song texts on the emotional understanding of children with autism. *Journal of Music Therapy, 46*(1), 15–31.

Kennedy, R. (2006). Movement, singing, and instrument playing strategies for a child with myotonic dystrophy. *Music Therapy Perspectives, 24*(1), 39–51.

Kern, P. (2006). Using embedded music therapy interventions to support outdoor play of young children with autism in an inclusive community-based child care program. *Journal of Music Therapy, 43*(4), 270–294.

Kern, P. (2007). Improving the performance of a young child with autism during self-care tasks using embedded song interventions: A case study. *Music Therapy Perspectives, 25*(1), 43–51.

Kwak, E. E. (2007). Effect of rhythmic auditory stimulation on gait performance in children with spastic cerebral palsy. *Journal of Music Therapy, 44*(3), 198–216.

Langan, D. (2009). A music therapy assessment tool for special education: Incorporating education outcomes. *The Australian Journal of Music Therapy 20,* 78–98.

MacDonald, R. A. R. (2003). An empirical investigation of the anxiolytic and pain reducing effects of music. *Psychology of Music, 31*(2), 187–203.

Martínez-Castilla, P. (2008). Singing abilities in Williams Syndrome. *Music Perception, 25*(5), 449–469.

McCarthy, J. (2008). A survey of music therapists' work with speech-language pathologists and experiences with augmentative and alternative communication. *Journal of Music Therapy, 45*(4), 405–426.

McFerran, K. (2008). Book reviews: "Music therapy groupwork with special needs children: The evolving process," By Karen D. Goodman. *The Australian Journal of Music Therapy 19,* 95–97.

Miceli, J. S. (2006). A four-way perspective on the development and importance of music learning theory-based prek-16 music education partnerships involving music for special learners. *Journal of Music Teacher Education, 16*(1), 65–78.

Ockelford, A. (2000). Music in the education of children with severe or profound learning difficulties: Issues in current U.K. Provision, a new conceptual framework, and proposals for research. *Psychology of Music, 28*(2), 197–217.

Overy, K. (2000). Dyslexia, temporal processing and music: The potential of music as an early learning aid for dyslexic children. *Psychology of Music, 28*(2), 218–229.

Overy, K. (2003). "Music and dyslexia: Opening new doors," Edited by Tim Miles and John Westcombe. *Psychology of Music, 31*(1), 116–118.

Paciello, M. (2003). "Music therapy, sensory integration and the autistic child," By Dorita S. Berger. *British Journal of Music Education, 20*(1), 112–115.

Parsons, K. (2006). Preserved singing in aphasia: A case study of the efficacy of melodic intonation therapy. *Music Perception, 24*(1), 23–35.

Pasiali, V. (2004). The use of prescriptive therapeutic songs in a home-based environment to promote social skills acquisition by children with autism: Three case studies. *Music Therapy Perspectives, 22*(1), 11–20.

Perry, M. M. R. (2003). Relating improvisational music therapy with severely and multiply disabled children to communication development. *Journal of Music Therapy, 40*(3), 227–246.

Register, D. (2002). Collaboration and consultation: A survey of board certified music therapists. *Journal of Music Therapy, 39*(4), 305–321.

Register, D. (2007). The use of music to enhance reading skills of second grade students and students with reading disabilities. *Journal of Music Therapy, 44*(1), 23–37.

Rickson, D. J. (2006). Instructional and improvisational models of music therapy with adolescents who have attention deficit hyperactivity disorder (ADHD): A comparison of the effects on motor impulsivity. *Journal of Music Therapy, 43*(1), 39–62.

Robb, S. L. (2003). Music interventions and group participation skills of preschoolers with visual impairments: Raising questions about music, arousal, and attention. *Journal of Music Therapy, 40*(4), 266–282.

Robey, K. L. (2000). The use of identity structure modeling to examine the central role of musical experience within the self-concept of a young woman with physical disabilities. *Music Therapy Perspectives, 18*(2), 115–121.

Ropp, C. R. (2006). Special education administrators' perceptions of music therapy in special education programs. *Music Therapy Perspectives, 24*(2), 87–93.

Scheib, J. W. (2003). Role stress in the professional life of the school music teacher: A collective case study. *Journal of Research in Music Education, 51*(2), 124–136.

Schmid, W. (2004). Active music therapy in the treatment of multiple sclerosis patients: A matched control study. *Journal of Music Therapy, 41*(3), 225.

Scott, L. P. (2007). Talking with music teachers about inclusion: Perceptions, opinions and experiences. *Journal of Music Therapy, 44*(1), 38–56.

Shields, C. (2001). Music education and mentoring as intervention for at-risk urban adolescents: Their self-perceptions, opinions, and attitudes. *Journal of Research in Music Education, 49*(3), 273–286.

Silverman, M. J. (2006). Forty years of case studies: A history of clinical case studies in the "Journal of music therapy," "Music therapy," And "Music therapy perspectives". *Music Therapy Perspectives, 24*(1), 4–12.

Smith, D. S. (1999). Effects of field experience on graduate music educators' attitude toward teaching students with disabilities. *Contributions to Music Education, 26*(1), 33–49.

Surow, J. B. (2000). "Alternative medical therapy" Use among singers: Prevalence and implications for the medical care of the singer. *Journal of Voice–Official Journal of the Voice Foundation, 14*(3), 398–409.

Sussman, J. E. (2009). The effect of music on peer awareness in preschool age children with developmental disabilities. *Journal of Music Therapy, 46*(1), 53–68.

Taylor, D. M. (2007). Attitudes toward inclusion and students with disabilities: A review of three decades of music research. *Bulletin of the Council for Research in Music Education 172*, 9–23.

Thaut, M. H. (2008). Musical structure facilitates verbal learning in multiple sclerosis. *Music Perception, 25*(4), 325–330.

Thompson, L. K. (2001). Disability simulations and information: Techniques for modifying the attitudes of elementary school music students. *Journal of Music Therapy, 38*(4), 321–341.

Trehub, S. E. (2006). Pitch and timing in the songs of deaf children with cochlear implants. *Music Perception, 24*(2), 147–154.

VanWeelden, K. (2004). Effect of field experiences on music therapy students' perceptions of choral music for geriatric wellness programs. *Journal of Music Therapy, 41*(4), 340–352.

VanWeelden, K. (2005). Preservice teachers' predictions, perceptions, and actual assessment of students with special needs in secondary general music. *Journal of Music Therapy, 42*(3), 200–215.

VanWeelden, K. (2007a). An exploratory study of the impact of field experiences on music education majors' attitudes and perceptions of music for secondary students with special needs. *Journal of Music Teacher Education, 16*(2), 34–44.

VanWeelden, K. (2007b). Preservice music teachers' predictions, perceptions, and assessment of students with special needs: The need for training in student assessment. *Journal of Music Therapy, 44*(1), 74–84.

Walworth, D. D. (2007). The use of music therapy within the scerts model for children with autism spectrum disorder. *Journal of Music Therapy, 44*(1), 2–22.

Watkins, W. G. (2003). Music therapy to promote prosocial behaviors in aggressive adolescent boys—a pilot study. *Journal of Music Therapy, 40*(4), 283–301.

Whipple, J. (2004). Music in intervention for children and adolescents with autism: A meta-analysis. *Journal of Music Therapy, 41*(2), 90.

Whipple, J. (2005). The effects of field experience on music education majors' perceptions of music instruction for secondary students with special needs. *Journal of Music Teacher Education, 14*(2), 62–69.

Wolfe, D. E. (2009). The use of music with young children to improve sustained attention during a vigilance task in the presence of auditory distractions. *Journal of Music Therapy, 46*(1), 69–82.

Yokota-Adachi, H. (2003). Musical attention training program and alternating attention in brain injury: An initial report. *Music Therapy Perspectives, 21*(2), 99–104.

DISSERTATIONS WITHIN MUSIC EDUCATION

Bailey, R. M. (2000). *Visiting the music classroom through the use of case method in the preparation of senior-level music teacher education students: A study of reflective judgement.* Unpublished Doctoral Dissertation, College Conservatory of Music, University of Cincinnati.

Bauer, E. A. (2003). *What is an appropriate approach to piano instruction for students with Down syndrome?* Unpublished Doctoral Dissertation, Indiana University.

Behan, D. J. (2004). *Effects of setting events—music, visual imagery, and deep breathing—on task engagement and math performance of middle school students with behavior disorders in a residential treatment program.* Unpublished Doctoral Dissertation, The University of Iowa.

Boumpani, N. M. (2005). *An investigation of instrumental music educators' awareness, understanding, attitudes and approaches associated with teaching reading disabled students in inclusive instrumental music classes in the public middle schools of North Carolina.* Unpublished Doctoral Dissertation, The University of North Carolina at Greensboro.

Chen, Y. (2007). *A research procedure and study of elementary music curriculum for children with special needs in inclusive music programs.* Unpublished Doctoral Dissertation, University of Idaho.

Culton, C. L. (1999). *The extent to which elementary music education textbooks reflect teachers' needs regarding instruction of students with special needs: A content analysis.* Unpublished Doctoral Dissertation, University of Iowa.

Dansereau, D. R. (2005). *The musicality of 3-year-old children within the context of research-based musical engagement.* Unpublished Doctoral Dissertation, Georgia State University.

DeVito, D. (2006). *The communicative function of behavioral responses to music by public school students with autism spectrum disorder.* Unpublished Doctoral Dissertation, University of Florida.

Fredstrom, T. C. (1999). *Musically gifted students and promoted vigor: A grounded theory guiding instructional practices for teachers of musically gifted students in school music.* Unpublished Doctoral Dissertation, The University of Nebraska—Lincoln.

Frick, J. W. (2000). *A qualitative study of music and communication in a musically rich early childhood special education classroom.* Unpublished Doctoral Dissertation, George Mason University.

Hammel, A. M. (1999). *A study of teacher competencies necessary when including special learners in elementary music classrooms: The development of a unit of study for use with undergraduate music education students.* Unpublished Doctoral Dissertation, Shenandoah University.

Haywood, J. S. (2005). *Including individuals with special needs in choirs: Implications for creating inclusive environments.* Unpublished Doctoral Dissertation, University of Toronto.

Higdon, J. R. (1999). *A comparison of the effects of rock and roll and easy listening music on the incidence of aberrant behaviors in an intermediate care facility for the mentally retarded.* Unpublished Doctoral Dissertation, The University of Mississippi.

Hines, S. W. (2000). *The effects of motoric and non-motoric music instruction on reading and mathematics achievements of learning disabled students in kindergarten through ninth grade.* Unpublished Doctoral Dissertation, The University of North Carolina at Greensboro.

Hourigan, R. (2007). *Teaching music to students with special needs: A phenomenological examination of participants in a fieldwork experience.* Unpublished Doctoral Dissertation, University of Michigan.

Junkins, E. T. (2003). *An exploratory study of the relationship of music intervention techniques to reading performance among selected students.* Unpublished Doctoral Dissertation, Loyola University of Chicago.

Kim, S. W. (2002). *Effects of age, IQ, and three types of song instruction on singing accuracy among children with mental retardation.* Unpublished Doctoral Dissertation, Temple University.

Lapka, C. M. (2005). *A case study of the integration of students with disabilities in a secondary music ensemble.* Unpublished Doctoral Dissertation, University of Illinois at Urbana-Champaign.

Linsenmeier, C. V. (2004). *The impact of music teacher training on the rate and level of involvement of special education students in high school band and choir.* Unpublished Doctoral Dissertation, Kent State University.

McCord, K. A. (1999). *Music composition using music technology by elementary children with learning disabilities: An exploratory case study.* Unpublished Doctoral Dissertation, University of Northern Colorado.

Milne, H. J. O. (2001). *A comparative case study of persons with Williams Syndrome and musical interests.* Unpublished Doctoral Dissertation, The University of Connecticut.

Moss, F., Jr. (2009). *Quality of experience in mainstreaming and full inclusion of blind and visually impaired high school instrumental music students.* Unpublished Doctoral Dissertation, University of Michigan.

O'Loughlin, R. A. (2000). *Facilitating prelinguistic communication skills of attention by integrating a music stimulus within typical language intervention with autistic children*. Unpublished Doctoral Dissertation, The University of Toledo.

Ojeda, S. L. (2005). *The impact of culturally relevant music on the classroom behaviors of special education Latino students*. Unpublished Doctoral Dissertation, Widener University, Institute for Graduate Clinical Psychology.

Rowley, T. (2006). *The effect of music therapy as a behavior intervention for preschoolers in a head start program*. Unpublished Doctoral Dissertation, Ball State University.

Sharrock, B. (2007). *A comparison of the attitudes of South Carolina special education and chorus teachers toward mainstreaming students with mild and moderate mental disabilities*. Unpublished Doctoral Dissertation, University of South Carolina.

Shirk, C. (2008). *The preparedness of elementary music teachers to include students with challenging behavior in their classrooms*. Unpublished Doctoral Dissertation, University of Central Florida.

Stringer, L. S. (2004). *The effects of "Music play" Instruction on language behaviors of children with developmental disabilities, ages three to six*. Unpublished Doctoral Dissertation, The University of Southern Mississippi.

Summa-Chadwick, M. (2008). *Music—a gateway to reaching developmental processes of children with special needs*. Unpublished Doctoral Dissertation, University of Kansas.

Volpitta, D. M. (2005). *Socialization of students labeled learning disabled: Rewriting the text of self*. Unpublished Doctoral Dissertation, Columbia University Teachers College.

Walter, J. L. (2004). *Designed music for multimedia instruction: A study of music as a complementary aspect of instructional design*. Unpublished Doctoral Dissertation, Capella University.

Yune, J. (2008). *The effect of a solfege-related tactile indicator on pitch accuracy in the retention of a vocal song in visually impaired elementary and secondary students*. Unpublished Doctoral Dissertation, University of Southern California.

SELECTED RESEARCH WITHIN GENERAL EDUCATION

Adams, P. (2008). Positioning behaviour: Attention deficit/hyperactivity disorder (ADHD) in the post-welfare educational era. *International Journal of Inclusive Education, 12*(2), 113–125.

Andrews, J. F., & Covell, J. A. (2006). Preparing future teachers and doctoral-level leaders in deaf education: Meeting the challenge. *American Annals of the Deaf, 151*(5), 464–475.

Antle, B. J. (2004). Factors associated with self-worth in young people with physical disabilities. *Health and Social Work, 29*(3), 167.

Banda, D. R., Grimmett, E., & Hart, S. L. (2009). Activity schedules: Helping students with autism spectrum disorders in general education classrooms manage transition issues. *TEACHING Exceptional Children, 41*(4), 16–21.

Bennett, K. S., & Hay, D. A. (2007). The role of family in the development of social skills in children with physical disabilities. *International Journal of Disability, Development and Education, 54*(4), 381–397.

Bowerman, M. (2005). Technology for all: Successful strategies for meeting the needs of diverse learners. *T.H.E. Journal, 32*(10), 20.

Brodesky, A. R., Gross, F. E., McTigue, A. S., & Tierney, C. C. (2004). Planning strategies for students with special needs: A professional development activity. *Teaching Children Mathematics, 11*(3), 146–154.

Brown, D. W. (2006). Micro-level teaching strategies for linguistically diverse learners. *Linguistics and Education: An International Research Journal, 17*(2), 175–195.

Bruce, S., DiNatale, P., & Ford, J. (2008). Meeting the needs of deaf and hard of hearing students with additional disabilities through professional teacher development. *American Annals of the Deaf, 153*(4), 368–375.

Carnahan, C. R., Hume, K., Clarke, L., & Borders, C. (2009). Using structured work systems to promote independence and engagement for students with autism spectrum disorders. *TEACHING Exceptional Children, 41*(4), 6–14.

Carroll, K. L. (2008). In their own voices: Helping artistically gifted and talented students succeed academically. *Gifted Child Today, 31*(4), 36–43.

Chval, K. B., & Davis, J. A. (2008). The gifted student. *Mathematics Teaching in the Middle School, 14*(5), 267–274.

Cobb, S. V. G. (2007). Virtual environments supporting learning and communication in special needs education. *Topics in Language Disorders, 27*(3), 211.

Coencas, J. (2007). How movies work for secondary school students with special needs. *English Journal, 96*(4), 67–72.

Coster, W. J., & Haltiwanger, J. T. (2004). Social-behavioral skills of elementary students with physical disabilities included in general education classrooms. *Remedial and Special Education, 25*(2), 95–103.

Curtin, M., & Clarke, G. (2005). Listening to young people with physical disabilities' experiences of education. *International Journal of Disability Development and Education, 52*(3), 195–214.

Daniels, H. (2006). The dangers of corruption in special needs education. *British Journal of Special Education, 33*(1), 4–9.

Dantas, M. L. (2007). Building teacher competency to work with diverse learners in the context of international education. *Teacher Education Quarterly, 34*(1), 75–94.

Donegan, M., Hong, S. B., Trepanier-Street, M., & Finkelstein, C. (2005). Exploring how project work enhances student teachers' understanding of children with special needs. *Journal of Early Childhood Teacher Education, 26*(1), 37–46.

DuPaul, G. J., & Weyandt, L. L. (2006). School-based intervention for children with attention deficit hyperactivity disorder: Effects on academic, social, and behavioural functioning. *International Journal of Disability, Development & Education, 53*(2), 161–176.

Eckstein, M. (2009). Enrichment 2.0 gifted and talented education for the 21st century. *Gifted Child Today, 32*(1), 59–63.

Edwards, C. J., Carr, S., & Siegel, W. (2006). Influences of experiences and training on effective teaching practices to meet the needs of diverse learners in schools. *Education, 126*(3), 580–592.

Egilson, S. T., & Traustadottir, R. (2009). Assistance to pupils with physical disabilities in regular schools: Promoting inclusion or creating dependency? *European Journal of Special Needs Education, 24*(1), 21–36.

Guskey, T. R., & Jung, L. A. (2009). Grading and reporting in a standards-based environment: Implications for students with special needs. *Theory Into Practice, 48*(1), 53–62.

Hale, A., Snow-Gerono, J., & Morales, F. (2008). Transformative education for cultur-ally diverse learners through narrative and ethnography. *Teaching and Teacher Education: An International Journal of Research and Studies, 24*(6), 1413–1425.

Hart, J. E. (2009). Strategies for culturally and linguistically diverse students with special needs. *Preventing School Failure, 53*(3), 197–208.

Heflin, L. J., & Bullock, L. M. (1999). Inclusion of students with emotional/behavioral disorders: A survey of teachers in general and special education. *Preventing School Failure, 43*, 103–111.

Hoover, J. J., & Patton, J. R. (2005). Differentiating curriculum and instruction for English-language learners with special needs. *Intervention in School and Clinic, 40*(4), 231–235.

Howard, R., & Ford, J. (2007). The roles and responsibilities of teacher aides support-ing students with special needs in secondary school settings. *Australasian Journal of Special Education, 31*(1), 25–43.

Hudson, R. F., High, L., & Al Otaiba, S. (2007). Dyslexia and the brain: What does cur-rent research tell us? *Reading Teacher, 60*(6), 506–515.

Humphries, T., & Allen, B. M. (2008). Reorganizing teacher preparation in deaf edu-cation. *Sign Language Studies, 8*(2), 160–180.

Jamieson, S. (2004). Creating an educational program for young children who are blind and who have autism. *RE:view: Rehabilitation Education for Blindness and Visual Impairment, 35*(4), 165.

Jobling, A., & Moni, K. B. (2004). "I never imagined i'd have to teach these children": Providing authentic learning experiences for secondary pre-service teachers in teaching students with special needs. *Asia Pacific Journal of Teacher Education, 32*(1), 5–22.

Karp, K., & Howell, P. (2004). Building responsibility for learning in students with special needs. *Teaching Children Mathematics, 11*(3), 118–126.

Kim, O., & Hupp, S. C. (2005). Teacher interaction styles and task engagement of elementary students with cognitive disabilities. *Education and Training in Devel-opmental Disabilities, 40*(3), 293–308.

Kim, O., & Hupp, S. C. (2007). Instructional interactions of students with cognitive dis-abilities: Sequential analysis. *American Journal on Mental Retardation, 112*(2), 94–106.

Kos, J. M., Richdale, A. L., & Hay, D. A. (2006). Children with attention deficit hyper-activity disorder and their teachers: A review of the literature. *International Jour-nal of Disability, Development & Education, 53*(2), 147–160.

Leaf, J. B., Taubman, M., Bloomfield, S., Palos-Rafuse, L., Leaf, R., McEachin, J., & Misty, L. O. (2009). Increasing social skills and pro-social behavior for three chil-dren diagnosed with autism through the use of a teaching package. *Research in Autism Spectrum Disorders, 3*(1), 275–289.

Li, A. (2009). Identification and intervention for students who are visually impaired and who have autism spectrum disorders. *TEACHING Exceptional Children, 41*(4), 22–32.

Lindsay, G. (2007). Annual review: Educational psychology and the effectiveness of inclusive education/mainstreaming. *British Journal of Educational Psychology, 77*(1), 1–24.

Long, L., MacBlain, S., & MacBlain, M. (2007). Supporting students with dyslexia at the secondary level: An emotional model of literacy. *Journal of Adolescent & Adult Literacy, 51*(2), 124–134.

Lovin, L. A., Kyger, M., & Allsopp, D. (2004). Differentiation for special needs learners. *Teaching Children Mathematics, 11*(3), 158–167.

Luckner, J. L. (2006). Evidence-based practices with students who are deaf. *Communication Disorders Quarterly, 28*(1), 49–52.

Lytle, R., & Todd, T. (2009). Stress and the student with autism spectrum disorders:
Strategies for stress reduction and enhanced learning. *TEACHING Exceptional
Children, 41*(4), 36–42.

Madrazo, G. M., Jr., & Motz, L. L. (2005). Brain research: Implications to diverse
learners. *Science Educator, 14*(1), 56–60.

Mortimore, T. (2005). Dyslexia and learning style—a note of caution. *British Journal
of Special Education, 32*(3), 145–148.

Murray, D. S., Ruble, L. A., Willis, H., & Molloy, C. A. (2009). Parent and teacher report
of social skills in children with autism spectrum disorders. *Language, Speech, and
Hearing Services in Schools, 40*(2), 109–115.

Pelham, J. W. E., Fabiano, G. A., & Massetti, G. M. (2005). Evidence-based assessment
of attention deficit hyperactivity disorder in children and adolescents. *Journal of
Clinical Child and Adolescent Psychology, 34*(3), 449–476.

Schrandt, J. A., Townsend, D. B., & Poulson, C. L. (2009). Teaching empathy skills to
children with autism. *Journal of Applied Behavior Analysis, 42*(1), 17–32.

Schroth, S. T., & Helfer, J. A. (2008). Identifying gifted students: Educator beliefs
regarding various policies, processes, and procedures. *Journal for the Education of
the Gifted, 32*(2), 155–179.

Sheehan, J. J., & Sibit, S. A. (2005). Adapting lessons for the special needs student.
Social Studies and the Young Learner, 18(1), 4–6.

Skarbrevik, K. J. (2005). The quality of special education for students with special needs
in ordinary classes. *European Journal of Special Needs Education, 20*(4), 387–401.

Stichter, J. P., Randolph, J. K., Kay, D., & Gage, N. (2009). The use of structural analysis
to develop antecedent-based interventions for students with autism. *Journal of
Autism and Developmental Disorders, 39*(6), 883–896.

Supalo, C. A., Mallouk, T. E., Amorosi, C., Lanouette, J., Wohlers, H. D., & McEnnis, K.
(2009). Using adaptive tools and techniques to teach a class of students who are
blind or low-vision. *Journal of Chemical Education, 86*(5), 587–591.

Zonnevylle-Bender, M. J. S., Matthys, W., van de Wiel, N. M. H., & Lochman, J. E.
(2007). Preventive effects of treatment of disruptive behavior disorder in middle
childhood on substance use and delinquent behavior. *Journal of the American
Academy of Child and Adolescent Psychiatry, 46*(1), 33–39.

BOOKS WITHIN MUSIC THERAPY AND MUSIC EDUCATION

Adamek, M. S., & Darrow, A.-A. (2005). *Music in special education.* Silver Spring, MD:
American Music Therapy Association.

Atterbury, B. W. (1990). *Mainstreaming exceptional learners in music.* Englewood
Cliffs, NJ: Prentice Hall.

Berger, D. S. (2002). *Music therapy, sensory integration, and the autistic child.* London:
Jessica Kingsley Publishers.

Brunk, B. K. (2004). *Music therapy: Another path to learning and communication for
children on the autism spectrum.* Arlington, TX: Future Horizons.

Fraser, D. L. (2000). *Childdance: The healing art of movement, music, and play with young special needs children: Six portraits.* Lincoln, NE: Writer's Club Press.

Froehlich, M. A. (2004). *101 ideas for piano group class: Building an inclusive music community for students of all ages and abilities.* Miami, FL: Summy-Birchard Music.

Goodman, K. D. (2007). *Music therapy groupwork with special needs children: The evolving process.* Springfield, IL: Charles C. Thomas.

Kirk, J. (2004). *Dyslexia and music.* London: British Dyslexia Association.

Lerner, N. W., & Straus, J. N. (2006). *Sounding off: Theorizing disability in music.* New York: Routledge.

Lewis, C. (2008). *Rex: A mother, her autistic child, and the music that transformed their lives.* Nashville, TN: Thomas Nelson.

Lloyd, P. (2008). *Let's all listen: Songs for group work in settings that include students with learning difficulties and autism.* London: Jessica Kingsley.

MENC (2004). *Spotlight on making music with special learners.* Reston, VA: MENC.

MENC (2007). *Spotlight on making music with special learners: Selected articles from state MEA journals.* Lanham, MD: Rowman & Littlefield Education.

Miles, T. R., Westcombe, J., & Snowling, M. J. (2001). *Music and dyslexia: Opening new doors.* London.Whurr Publishers.

Miles, T. R., & Westcombe, J. D. D. (2008). *Music and dyslexia: A positive approach.* Chichester, West Sussex, England. John Wiley & Sons, LTD.

Nordoff, P. R. C. (2006). *Music therapy in special education.* Gilsum, NH: Barcelona Publishers.

Rief, S. F. (2005). *How to reach and teach children with ADD/ADHD: Practical techniques, strategies, and interventions.* San Francisco: Jossey-Bass.

Ruben, S. (2004). *Awakening ashley: Mozart knocks autism on its ear.* New York: IUniverse.

Standley, J. M., & Jones, J. D. (2007). *Music techniques in therapy, counseling, and special education.* Silver Springs, MD: American Music Therapy Association.

Streeter, E. (2001). *Making music with the young child with special needs: A guide for parents.* London. Jessica Kingsley Publishers.

Tubbs, J. (2008). *Creative therapy for children with autism, ADD, and asperger's: Using artistic creativity to reach, teach, and touch our children.* Garden City Park, NY: Square One Publishers.

Webb, P. G., Judith, M., & Grant, J. (2000). *Music for all kids: Using interactive songs to increase learning and participation.* Canning Vale, WA: Klik Enterprises.

Welch, G., Ockelford, A., & Zimmermann, S.-A. (2001). *Provision of music in special education "Promise".* London: University of London Institute of Education: RNIB.

Wills, P., & Peter, M. (1996). *Music for all: Developing music in the curriculum with pupils with special educational needs.* London: David Fulton Publishers.

Zimmerman, E. (2004). *Artistically and musically talented students.* Thousand Oaks, CA: Corwin Press.

BOOKS WITHIN GENERAL EDUCATION

Algozzine, R., & Ysseldyke, J. E. (2006a). *Effective instruction for students with special needs: A practical guide for every teacher.* Thousand Oaks, CA: Corwin Press.

Algozzine, R., & Ysseldyke, J. E. (2006b). *Teaching students with medical, physical, and multiple disabilities: A practical guide for every teacher.* Thousand Oaks, CA: Corwin Press.

Anderson, S. R. (2007). *Self-help skills for people with autism: A systematic teaching approach.* Bethesda, MD: Woodbine House.

Banks, J., Cochran-Smith, M., Moll, L., Richert, A., Zeichner, K., & LePage, P. (2005). Teaching diverse learners. In L. Darling Hammond & J. Bransford (Eds.), *Preparing teachers for a changing world.*Jessica Kingsley Publishers San Francisco: Jossey-Bass.

Batshaw, M. L., Pellegrino, L., & Roizen, N. J. (2007). *Children with disabilities.* Baltimore: Paul H. Brookes Pub.

Bender, W. N. (2002). *Differentiating instruction for students with learning disabilities: Best teaching practices for general and special educators.* Thousand Oaks, CA: Corwin Press.

Bursztyn, A. (2007). *The praeger handbook of special education.* Westport, CT: Praeger Publishers.

Chivers, M. (2001). *Practical strategies for living with dyslexia.* London. Sage Publication.

Choate, J. S. (2000). *Successful inclusive teaching: Proven ways to detect and correct special needs* (3rd ed.). Boston: Allyn and Bacon.

Cimera, R. E. (2002). *Making ADHD a gift: Teaching superman how to fly.* Lanham, MD: Scarecrow Press.

Cimera, R. E. (2007). *Making autism a gift: Inspiring children to believe in themselves and lead happy, fulfilling lives.* Lanham, MD: Rowman & Littlefield.

Clark, B. (2002). *Growing up gifted: Developing the potential of children at home and at school* (6th ed.). Upper Saddle River, N.J.: Merrill/Prentice Hall.

Clough, P. (2005). *Handbook of emotional & behavioural difficulties.* London.

Darling-Hammond, L., & Bransford, J. (2005). *Preparing teachers for a changing world.* San Francisco: Jossey-Bass.

Davis, G. A. (2006). *Gifted children gifted education.* Scottsdale, AZ: Great Potential Press.

Dennis, K., & Azpiri, T. (2005). *Sign to learn: American sign language in the early childhood classroom.* St. Paul, MN: Redleaf Press.

Dettmer, P., Thurston, L. P., & Dyck, N. (2002). *Consultation, collaboration, and teamwork for students with special needs* (4th ed.). Boston: Allyn and Bacon.

Donnelly, K. J. (2000). *Coping with dyslexia.* New York: Rosen Pub. Group.

Fletcher-Janzen, E., & Reynolds, C. R. (2006). *The special education almanac.* Hoboken, NJ: J. Wiley & Sons.

Gore, M. C. (2004). *Successful inclusion strategies for secondary and middle school teachers: Keys to help struggling learners access the curriculum.* Thousand Oaks, CA: Corwin Press.

Grandin, T. (2008). *The way i see it: A personal look at autism and asperger's.* Arlington, TX: Future Horizons, Inc.

Guyer, B. P. (2000). *ADHD: Achieving success in school and in life.* Boston: Allyn & Bacon.

Harris, S. L., & Weiss, M. J. (2007). *Right from the start: Behavioral intervention for young children with autism* (2nd ed.). Bethesda, MD: Woodbine House.

Henderson, K. (2008). *Teaching children with attention deficit hyperactivity disorder: Instructional strategies and practices*. Washington, DC: U.S. Dept. of Education, Office of Special Education and Rehabilitative Services, Office of Special Education Programs.

Kluth, P. (2003). *"You're going to love this kid": Teaching students with autism in the inclusive classroom*. Baltimore, MD: P.H. Brookes Pub. Co.

Koegel, L. K., & LaZebnik, C. S. (2004). *Overcoming autism*. New York: Viking.

Kostelnik, M. J. (2002). *Children with special needs: Lessons for early childhood professionals*. New York: Teachers College Press.

Lerner, J. W. (2003). *Learning disabilities: Theories, diagnosis, and teaching strategies* (9th ed.). Boston: Houghton Mifflin.

Lerner, J. W., Lowenthal, B., & Egan, R. (2003). *Preschool children with special needs: Children at risk and children with disabilities* (2nd ed.). Boston: Allyn and Bacon.

Lewis, R. B., & Doorlag, D. H. (2006). *Teaching special students in general education classrooms* (7th ed.). Upper Saddle River, NJ: Pearson/Merrill/Prentice Hall.

Lougy, R. A., DeRuvo, S. L., & Rosenthal, D. K. (2007). *Teaching young children with adhd: Successful strategies and practical interventions for prek-3*. Thousand Oaks, CA: Corwin Press.

Marschark, M., Lang, H. G., & Albertini, J. A. (2002). *Educating deaf students: From research to practice*. London: Oxford.

Marschark, M., & Spencer, P. E. (2003). *Oxford handbook of deaf studies, language, and education*. London: Oxford.

Mayberry, S. C., & Lazarus, B. B. (2002). *Teaching students with special needs in the 21st century classroom*. Lanham, MD: Scarecrow Press.

Moores, D. F., & Martin, D. S. (2006). *Deaf learners: Developments in curriculum and instruction*. Washington, DC: Gallaudet University Press.

Nekola, J. (2001). *Helping kids with special needs: Resources for parenting and teaching children with emotional and neurological disorders*. Wayzata, MN: Nekola Books.

Nelson, D. (2008). Personal excellence: A new paradigm for gifted education. In Y. S. Freeman, D. E. Freeman & R. Ramirez (Eds.), *Diverse learners in the mainstream classroom: Strategies for supporting all students across content areas* (pp. 101-117). Portsmouth, NH: Heinemann.

Notbohm, E., & Zysk, V. (2004). *1001 great ideas for teaching and raising children with autism spectrum disorders*. Arlington, TX: Future Horizons.

Obiakor, F. E., Utley, C., Anita, R., & Rotatori, A. F. (2003). *Effective education for learners with exceptionalities*. Amsterdam. Elsevier Science Ltd.

Odom, S. L. (2007). *Handbook of developmental disabilities*. New York: Guilford Press.

Pierson, J. (2002). *Exceptional teaching: A comprehensive guide for including students with disabilities*. Cincinnati, OH: Standard Pub.

Polloway, E. A., Patton, J. R., & Serna, L. (2001). *Strategies for teaching learners with special needs* (7th ed.). Upper Saddle River, NJ: Merrill/Prentice Hall.

Reid, G. (2003). *Dyslexia: A practitioner's handbook*. Chichester, West Sussex, England. John Wiley & Sons, Ltd.

Ruf, D. L. (2005). *Losing our minds: Gifted children left behind*. Scottsdale, AZ: Great Potential Press.

Rutherford, R. B., Quinn, M. M., & Mathur, S. R. (2004). *Handbook of research in emotional and behavioral disorders*. New York: Guilford Press.

Sanders, M. (2001). *Understanding dyslexia and the reading process: A guide for educators and parents*. Boston: Allyn and Bacon.

Schwartz, D. (2005). *Including children with special needs: A handbook for educators and parents*. Westport, CT: Greenwood Press.

Shore, K. (2003). *Elementary teacher's discipline problem solver: A practical a-z guide for managing classroom behavior problems*. San Francisco: Jossey-Bass.

Siegel, B. (2003). *Helping children with autism learn: Treatment approaches for parents and professionals*. London: Oxford.

Siperstein, G. N., & Rickards, E. P. (2004). *Promoting social success: A curriculum for children with special needs*. Baltimore, MD: Paul H. Brookes Pub. Co.

Smith, T. E. C. (2001). *Teaching students with special needs in inclusive settings* (3rd ed.). Boston: Allyn and Bacon.

Smutny, J. F. (2003). *Gifted education: Promising practices*. Bloomington, IN: Phi Delta Kappa.

Strichart, S. S., Mangrum, C. T., & Strichart, S. S. (2002). *Teaching learning strategies and study skills to students with learning disabilities, attention deficit disorders, or special needs* (3rd ed.). Boston: Allyn and Bacon.

Swanson, H. L., Harris, K. R., & Graham, S. (2003). *Handbook of learning disabilities*. New York: Guilford Press.

Vaughn, S., Bos, C. S., Schumm, J. S., & Vaughn, S. (2007). *Teaching students who are exceptional, diverse, and at risk in the general education classroom* (4th ed.). Boston: Pearson Allyn & Bacon.

Wehmeyer, M. L. (2007). *Promoting self-determination in students with developmental disabilities*. New York: Guilford Press.

Westwood, P. S. (2007). *Commonsense methods for children with special educational needs*. London RoutledgeFarmer.

Widerstrom, A. H. (2005). *Achieving learning goals through play: Teaching young children with special needs* (2nd ed.). Baltimore: P.H. Brookes Pub.

Wilkins, J. (2001). *Group activities to include students with special needs: Developing social interactive skills*. Thousand Oaks, CA: Corwin Press.

Willis, C. (2006). *Teaching young children with autism spectrum disorder*. Beltsville, MD: Gryphon House.

Winebrenner, S. (1992). *Teaching gifted kids in the regular classroom: Strategies and techniques every teacher can use to meet the academic needs of the gifted and talented*. Minneapolis, MN: Free Spirit Publishing.

Zeigler Dendy, & Chris, A. (2000). *Teaching teens with ADD and ADHD: A quick reference guide for teachers and parents*. Bethesda, MD: Woodbine House.

PRACTITIONER ARTICLES WITHIN MUSIC EDUCATION

Abril, C. R. (2003). No hablo ingles: Breaking the language barrier in music instruction. *Music Educators Journal, 89*(5), 38–43.

Adamek, M. S. (2001). Meeting special needs in music class. *Music Educators Journal, 87*(4), 23–26.

Armstrong, T. (1999). Research on music and autism: Implications for music educators. *Update—Applications of Research in Music Education, 18*(1), 15–20.

Atterbury, B. W. (1986). Success in the mainstream of general music. *Music Educators Journal, 72*(7), 34–36.

Au, S. (2003). Principal themes: Musical interaction with autistic and multiple-handicapped children. *Canadian Music Educator, 45*(1), 19-21.

Bacon, R. (2007). Adapting drumming for individuals with special needs. *Percussive Notes, 45*(6), 30-32.

Bennett, A. (2003). Inspiration: Of starfish and strings. *American String Teacher, 53*(2), 39.

Bernstorf, E. D. (2001). Paraprofessionals in music settings. *Music Educators Journal, 87*(4), 36-40.

Butler, M. (2004). Special learners: How students with hearing impairments can learn and flourish in your music classroom. *Teaching Music, 12*(1), 30-34.

Cannon, M. C. (2008). Teaching & learning: Working with the autistic student. *American Suzuki Journal, 36*(3), 32-33.

Crouch, S. (2005). Keeping the beat: Movement activities for learning-disabled piano students. *American Music Teacher, 55*(3), 22-25.

Damer, L. K. (2001a). Inclusion and the law. *Music Educators Journal, 87*(4), 19-22.

Damer, L. K. (2001b). Students with special needs. *Music Educators Journal, 87*(4), 17.

Darrow, A.-A. (2005). Use of classwide peer tutoring in the general music classroom. *Update—Applications of Research in Music Education, 24*(1), 15-26.

Darrow, A.-A. (2006a). Sounds in the silence: Research on music and deafness. *Update—Applications of Research in Music Education, 25*(1), 5-14.

Darrow, A.-A. (2006b). Teaching students with behavior problems. *General Music Today (Online), 20*(1), 35-37.

Darrow, A.-A. (2007a). Adaptations in the classroom: Accommodations and modifications: Part I. *General Music Today (Online), 20*(3), 32-34.

Darrow, A.-A. (2007b). Teaching students with hearing loss. *General Music Today, 20*(2), 27-30.

Darrow, A.-A. (2008). Special learners—adaptations in the classroom: Accommodations and modifications, part 2. *General Music Today (Online), 21*(3), 32-34.

Darrow, A.-A., & Armstrong, T. (1999). Research on music and autism. *Update—Applications of Research in Music Education, 18*(1), 15-20.

de l'Etoile, S. K. (2005). Teaching music to special learners: Children with disruptive behavior disorders. *Music Educators Journal, 91*(5), 37-43.

Emmerson, G. (2003). Principal themes: Special education in music: Helping students experience success. *Canadian Music Educator, 45*(1), 16-18.

Fitzgerald, M. (2006). "I send my best matthew to school every day": Music educators collaborating with parents. *Music Educators Journal, 92*(4), 40-45.

Gfeller, K. (1989). Behavioral disorders: Strategies for the music teacher. *Music Educators Journal, 75*(8), 27-30.

Gowers, C. (2008). Teaching & learning—working with children with special needs: Nicola beattie. *American Suzuki Journal, 37*(1), 58.

Hagedorn, V. S. (2001a). A planning tool for use with special learners. *General Music Today, 15*(1), 21-24.

Hagedorn, V. S. (2001b). Resources, reviews, and research: Revisiting some "Oldies but goodies". *General Music Today, 15*(2), 27-29.

Hagedorn, V. S. (2002a). Accomodations for special needs students: What we "Can" Do. *General Music Today, 15*(3), 20-22.

Hagedorn, V. S. (2002b). Communicating with inclusion students. *General Music Today (Online), 16*(2), 37-41.

Hagedorn, V. S. (2003a). Musical activities using visual strategies for special-needs preschool students. *General Music Today (Online), 16*(3), 25-29.

Hagedorn, V. S. (2003b). Special learners: Music basal series texts and inclusion students. *General Music Today (Online), 17*(1), 38-44.

Hagedorn, V. S. (2003c). Special learners: Using picture books in music class to encourage participation of students with autistic spectrum disorder. *General Music Today (Online), 17*(2), 46-51.

Hagedorn, V. S. (2004). Including special learners: Providing meaningful participation in the music class. *General Music Today (Online), 17*(3), 44-50.

Hammel, A. M. (2001). Special learners in elementary music classrooms: A study of essential teacher competencies. *Update—Applications of Research in Music Education, 20*(1), 9-13.

Hammel, A. M. (2004). Inclusion strategies that work. *Music Educators Journal, 90*(5), 33-37.

Hockett, C. B. (2008). Teaching & learning—working with children with special needs: Nick shaw. *American Suzuki Journal, 37*(1), 59.

Holmes, M. (2005). One child, one special need, one solution. *Kodaly Envoy, 32*(1), 22.

Hourigan, R. (2007). Preparing music teachers to teach students with special needs. *Update—Applications of Research in Music Education, 26*(1), 5-14.

Hourigan, R. M. (2008). Teaching strategies for performers with special needs. *Teaching Music, 15*(6), 26-29.

Hourigan, R. M. (2009). The invisible student: Understanding social identity construction within performing ensembles. *Music Educators Journal, 95*(4), 34-38,35.

Iseminger, S. H. (2009). Keys to success with autistic children. *Teaching Music, 16*(6), 28-31.

Jahns, E. (2001). Introducing music to the hearing-impaired. *Teaching Music, 8*(6), 36-40.

Jellison, J. A. (1999). Life beyond the jingle stick: Real music in a real world. *Update—Applications of Research in Music Education, 17*(2), 13-19.

Karma, K. (2003). Technology for musicianship: Audilex—the missing link? *General Music Today (Online), 16*(3), 32-34.

Kassner, K. (2003). Technology for musicianship: Introduction to "Audilex—the missing link?" *General Music Today (Online), 16*(3), 30-31.

Kernohan, L. (2001). Music students with visual impairments: Issues, challenges, and solutions. *Canadian Music Educator, 42*(4), 7-10.

Knapp, M. A. (2007). Teaching dyslexic students. *Flute Talk, 26*(6), 20-25.

Kostka, M. J. (1999). Secondary music students' attitudes toward atypical peers. *Update—Applications of Research in Music Education, 17*(2), 8-12.

Lam, R., & Wang, C. (1982). Integrating blind and sighted through music. *Music Educators Journal, 68*, 44-45.

Lapka, C. (2006). Students with disabilities in a high school band: "We can do it!" *Music Educators Journal, 92*(4), 54-59.

Lehrman, P. D. (2007). Insider audio: The healing power of music—autism research explores response to specific frequencies. *Mix, 31*(5), 20, 22, 24, 26.

Lind, V. R. (2001). Adapting choral rehearsals for students with learning disabilities. *Choral Journal, 41*(7), 27-30.

Mahlmann, J. (2008). There's room for everyone. *Teaching Music, 16*(2), 7.

Mann, J. (2003). The outcome starts here—motivating the gifted student: Realistic challenges—pedagogy saturday VII lunchtime discussion. *American Music Teacher, 53*(2), 37–38.

Mazur, K. (2004). An introduction to inclusion in the music classroom. *General Music Today (Online), 18*(1), 6–11.

McCord, K. (2001). Music software for special needs. *Music Educators Journal, 87*(4), 30–35, 64.

McCord, K. (2006a). Children with disabilities playing musical instruments. *Music Educators Journal, 92*(4), 46–52.

McCord, K. (2006b). Collaboration and access for our children: Music educators and special educators together. *Music Educators Journal, 92*(4), 26–33.

McCord, K. (2006c). For your library: "Music in special education," By Mary S. Adamek and Alice-Ann Darrow. *Music Educators Journal, 93*(2), 20.

McGrane, B. (2006). Someone special in the choir. *Pastoral Music, 30*(5), 27–29.

Mixon, K. (2005). Special learners: Including exceptional students in your instrumental music program. *Teaching Music, 13*(3), 30–34.

Montgomery, A. (2008). "Playing it their way: An innovative approach to teaching piano to individuals with physical or mental disabilities," By Karen Z. Kowalski. *American Music Teacher, 58*(1), 63–64.

Montgomery, J. (2006). Partnering with music therapists: A model for addressing students' musical and extramusical goals. *Music Educators Journal, 92*(4), 34–39.

Moore, M. (2001). Attention deficit disorder. *Music Connection, 25*(16), 50.

Nevolo, J. (2002). Teaching special-needs students. *Modern Drummer, 26*(5), 140–141.

Nordlund, M. (2006). Finding a systemized approach to music inclusion. *General Music Today (Online), 19*(3), 13–16.

Patterson, A. (2003). Music teachers and music therapists: Helping children together. *Music Educators Journal, 89*(4), 35–38.

Pontiff, E. (2004). Special learners: Teaching special learners—ideas from veteran teachers in the music classroom. *Teaching Music, 12*(3), 52–58.

Rose, L. (2004a). Inclusion with integrity. *General Music Today (Online), 18*(2), 37.

Rose, L. (2004b). Tapping into the spirit of the sensitive child: A foundation for understanding and bringing the joy of music to children who have sensory integration challenges. *General Music Today (Online), 18*(1), 45–48.

Rose, L. (2005). A proactive strategy for working with children who have special needs. *General Music Today (Online), 19*(1), 35.

Rose, L. (2006). Book review: "Music in special education," By Mary Adamek and Alice-Ann Darrow. *General Music Today (Online), 19*(3), 44.

Scheib, J. W. (2004). Why band directors leave: From the mouths of maestros. *Music Educators Journal, 91*(1), 53–57.

Siligo, W. (2001). Adaptive techniques for teaching music to visually impaired students. *American Music Teacher, 50*(5), 20–23.

Siligo, W. R. (2005). Enriching the ensemble experience for students with visual impairments. *Music Educators Journal, 91*(5), 31–36.

Smaligo, M. A. (1998). Resources for helping blind music students. *Music Educators Journal, 85*, 23–26.

Surow, J. B. (2000). "Alternative medical therapy" Use among singers: Prevalence and implications for the medical care of the singer. *Journal of Voice–Official Journal of the Voice Foundation, 14*(3), 398–409.

Swanson, C. (2007). The private studio: Students with ADHD. *Journal of Singing–The Official Journal of the National Association of Teachers of Singing, 64*(2), 217–221.

Vance, K. O. B. (2004). Adapting music instruction for students with dyslexia. *Music Educators Journal, 90*(5), 27–31.

VanWeelden, K. (2001). Choral mainstreaming: Tips for success. *Music Educators Journal, 88*(3), 55–60.

VanWeelden, K. (2007). Music for the forgotten: Creating a secondary general music experience for students with special needs. *General Music Today (Online), 21*(1), 26–29.

Walczyk, E. B. (1993). Music instruction and the hearing impaired. *Music Educators Journal, 80*(1), 42–44.

Walter, J. S. (2006). The basic idea: The individuals with disabilities act in your classroom. *Teaching Music, 14*(3), 23–26.

Wicklund, K. (2003). Learning disabilities in singers: The teacher's role in recognition, diagnosis, and rehabilitation. *Journal of Singing–The Official Journal of the National Association of Teachers of Singing, 59*(4), 311–315.

Wikeley, J. (2008). New organ will aid physically impaired students. *Music Teacher, 87*(5), 8.

Zdzinski, S. F. (2001). Instrumental music for special learners. *Music Educators Journal, 87*(4), 27–29, 63.

About the Authors

Dr. Alice M. Hammel, a leader in the field of teaching music to students with special needs, currently teaches for James Madison University, Christopher Newport University, and St. Andrew's School. Her background in the field of music education is extensive and includes teaching and research with students in pre-school through post-graduate school. Her degrees are from the Florida State University (MME) and Shenandoah University (DMA and BME—Magna Cum Laude). Dr. Hammel also holds Level III Kodály Certification from James Madison University.

Pursuing a lifelong interest in the needs of students with special needs, Dr. Hammel has presented her research at more than 50 state and national conferences and maintains an active speaking engagement schedule at universities and conferences throughout the United States. Her research areas include the adaptation of methods and materials for students with special needs, learning styles, differentiation, universal design, urban education, early-childhood education, and teacher education and preparation. She has published more than 20 articles and was a member of the editorial board of the *Journal for Music Teacher Education*. Articles based on her research have been published by the *Music Educators Journal, UPDATE: The Applications of Research in Music Education, The Journal for Music Teacher Education, University Affiliated Programs in Developmental Disabilities, The American Music Teacher, The Keyboard Companion, Massachusetts Music News,* and *Virginia Music Educators Association—Notes*. She is a contributing author to two resources available through MENC—*Spotlight on Teaching Special Learners* and *Readings in Diversity, Inclusion, and Music for All*. An online supported course co-authored by Dr. Hammel, *On Music Education and Teaching Special Learners,* is available through Connect for Education. Dr. Hammel is the Students with Special Needs Chair for the Virginia Music Educators Association.

Dr. Hammel is also active as a professional flutist and maintains an independent flute studio. She has participated in numerous national panel presentations regarding woodwind pedagogy and learning styles. She is a nationally known adjudicator and clinician for solo wind, band, orchestra, and choral competitions, and frequently conducts master classes and presents lectures throughout the United States. Dr. Hammel was the Wind

Representative to the Pedagogy Board of the Music Teachers National Association for four years and was the Chair of Single-Line Sight Reading for the Virginia Music Teachers Association for many years. She can be heard as a flutist on two compact discs of music composed by Allan Blank (published by Arizona State Recordings and Centaur Recordings).

Dr. Hammel is a multiple recipient of awards honoring her commitment to music education and the inclusion of all students in music classrooms, including the 2000 Young Career Achievement Award by Shenandoah University, and is a frequent keynote speaker for events in the areas of education and students with special needs. She has been named to at least one Who's Who publication every year since 2000, has served as an MENC Online Networking Mentor and is a national spokesperson for MENC. Dr. Hammel is a member of the Music Educators National Conference (MENC), Society for Music Teacher Education (SMTE), Music Teachers National Association (MTNA), the Association for Supervision and Curriculum Development (ASCD), Sigma Alpha Iota (SAI), the Organization of American Kodály Educators (OAKE), the College Music Society (CMS), and the Council for Exceptional Children (CEC). She is married to Dr. Bruce Hammel. They have two daughters, Hannah and Hollie.

Dr. Ryan Hourigan (2010 Indiana Music Educators Association University Music Educator of the Year) joined the faculty at Ball State University in the fall of 2006 after nine years teaching instrumental and vocal music at the secondary and university level. A native of Illinois, Dr. Hourigan holds degrees from Eastern Illinois University (BM), Michigan State University (MM Wind Conducting) and a PhD in Music Education from the University of Michigan.

Dr. Hourigan teaches instrumental music education at Ball State University. His research interests include the preparation of pre-service music teachers, music students with special needs, professional development for music teachers, and pre-service music teacher identity development. Dr. Hourigan has been published or is in press in *The Journal of Research in Music Education, Update: Applications of Research in Music Education, Arts Education Policy Review, The Journal of Music Teacher Education, The Music Educators Journal,* and *The Bulletin for the Council of Research in Music Education.* In 2007, his dissertation, entitled *Teaching Music to Students with Special Needs: A Phenomenological Examination of Participants in a Fieldwork Experience,* won the national dissertation award from Council for Research in Music Education.

In 2007, Dr. Hourigan founded the Prism Project. This program provides an opportunity for Ball State students to gain skills in the area of teaching students with special needs. In April of 2009, the members of the Prism

Project presented a capstone performance at Pruis Hall highlighting scenes and music that were created through a collaborative effort between the Ball State volunteers and the 20 performers with special needs. There is a detailed documentary of the project including student and instructor interviews at http://prismproject.iweb.bsu.edu.

Dr. Hourigan has presented on teaching music to students with special needs at state and national conferences including the American Educational Research Association (AERA) and the Music Educators National Conference. Dr. Hourigan is a member of the American Educational Research Association (AERA), College Music Society (CMS), Music Educators National Conference (MENC), the Society for Music Teacher Education (SMTE), and Phi Mu Alpha Sinfonia. Dr. Hourigan lives in Muncie, Indiana, with his wife Amy and his two sons, Joshua and Andrew.

Index

Note: Page numbers followed by f or v indicate figures and vignettes, respectively.